PORTFOLIO / PENGUIN

NETFLIXED

Gina Keating is a freelance business journalist. She previously covered media companies, law, and government as a staff writer for Reuters and United Press International for more than a decade. Her articles have been reprinted in newspapers around the world, and her freelance work has appeared in *Variety, Colloquy, Du Jour, Southern Living,* and *Forbes.* She lives in Texas. This is her first book.

NETFLIXED

The Epic Battle for America's Eyeballs

Gina Keating

PORTFOLIO / PENGUIN

PORTFOLIO / PENGUIN
Published by the Penguin Group
Penguin Group (USA) LLC
375 Hudson Street
New York, New York 10014

USA | Canada | UK | Ireland | Australia | New Zealand | India | South Africa | China
penguin.com
A Penguin Random House Company

First published in the United States of America by Portfolio/Penguin, a member of
Penguin Group (USA) Inc., 2012
This paperback edition with a new afterword published 2013

THE LIBRARY OF CONGRESS HAS CATALOGED THE HARDCOVER EDITION AS FOLLOWS:
Keating, Gina.
Netflixed : the epic battle for America's eyeballs / Gina Keating.
p.cm.
Includes bibliographical references and index.
ISBN 978-1-59184-478-5 (hc.)
ISBN 978-1-59184-659-8 (pbk.)
1. Netflix (Firm) 2. Video rental services—United States. 3. Video recordings industry—United
States. 4. Internet videos—United States. I. Title.
HD9697.V544N484 2012
384'.84—dc23
2012027444

Printed in the United States of America
1 3 5 7 9 10 8 6 4 2

Set in Minion Pro
Designed by Pauline Neuwirth

While the author has made every effort to provide accurate telephone numbers, Internet addresses, and
other contact information at the time of publication, neither the publisher nor the author assumes any
responsibility for errors or for changes that occur after publication. Further, publisher does not have any
control over and does not assume any responsibility for author or third-party Web sites or their content.

To the people of Netflix and Blockbuster for letting me into their story

and

To John A. Sopuch III and Margaret Romero for holding me up

CONTENTS

CAST OF CHARACTERS

NETFLIX (ALPHABETICAL)

Lisa Battaglia-Reiss	Human Resources manager
Jessie Becker	Marketing, vice president
James Bennett	Recommendation System, vice president
Corey Bridges	Marketing, Customer Acquisition
Jim Cook	Finance/Operations, director
Deborah Crawford	Investor Relations, vice president
Chris Darner	Product Management, director
Shernaz Daver	Corporate communications consultant
Tom Dillon	Chief operating officer
Boris Droutman	Web Engineering, manager
Vita Droutman	Senior Systems, architect
Jonathan Friedland	Corporate Communications, vice president
Reed Hastings	Cofounder/chairman and chief executive
Jay Hoag	Board member/investor
Neil Hunt	Chief technology officer
Leslie Kilgore	Chief marketing officer
Paul Kirincich	Financial Planning and Analysis, vice president

Christina Kish	Merchandising, director
Kirby Kish	Business Development, director
Stan Lanning	Cinematch, developer
Mitch Lowe	Business Development and Strategic Alliances, vice president; Redbox, president
Barry McCarthy	Chief financial officer
Patty McCord	Chief talent officer
Eric Meyer	Chief information officer
Joel Mier	Research and Analysis, director
Marc Randolph	Cofounder/chief executive
Andy Rendich	Chief service and operations officer
Ken Ross	Corporate Communications, vice president
Ted Sarandos	Chief content officer
Therese "Te" Smith	Corporate Communications, director
Steve Swasey	Corporate Communications, director
David Wells	Chief financial officer
Erich Ziegler	Marketing, director

BLOCKBUSTER (ALPHABETICAL)

John Antioco	Chairman/chief executive
Bryan Bevin	U.S. Store Operations, senior vice president
Edward Bleier	Board member
Sam Bloom	Business Development, vice president
Aaron Coleman	Blockbuster Online, chief technology officer
Ben Cooper	Blockbuster Online, director of marketing acquisition and business development

J. W. Craft	Blockbuster Online, vice president of strategic planning
Rick Ellis	Blockbuster Online, operations consultant
Shane Evangelist	Blockbuster Online, senior vice president and general manager
Gary Fernandes	Board member
Bill Fields	Chairman/chief executive before Antioco
Sarah Gustafson	Blockbuster Online, senior director, customer analytics
Jules Haimovitz	Board member
Lillian Hessel	Blockbuster Online, vice president, customer marketing
Jim Keyes	Chairman/chief executive
Karen Raskopf	Corporate Communications, senior vice president,
Nick Shepherd	Chief operating officer
Michael Siftar	Blockbuster Online, director, applications development
Nigel Travis	President
Strauss Zelnick	Board member
Larry Zine	Chief financial officer

COSTARS (ALPHABETICAL)

Robert Bell	AT&T Laboratory, Statistics Division, researcher
Jeff Bezos	Amazon.com founder/chief executive
Martin Chabbert	Netflix Prize winner, French-Canadian programmer
Tom Dooley	Viacom, senior vice president

Roger Enrico	PepsiCo, chairman
John Fleming	Walmart, chief executive
Brett Icahn	Carl Icahn's son
Carl Icahn	Blockbuster investor/board member
Michael Jahrer	Netflix Prize winner, Big Chaos team, machine learning researcher
Mike Kaltschnee	HackingNetflix, founder/blogger
Gregg Kaplan	Redbox, chief executive
Mel Karmazin	Viacom, chief operating officer
Yehuda Koren	Netflix Prize winner, AT&T Laboratory, scientist
Warren Lieberfarb	Warner Home Video, president
Joe Malugen	Movie Gallery, chairman/chief executive
Dave Novak	Yum! Brands, chairman/chief executive
Michael Pachter	Wedbush Morgan, analyst
Martin Piotte	Netflix Prize winner, French-Canadian programmer
Sumner Redstone	Viacom, chairman
Stuart Skorman	Reel.com, founder/chief executive
Andreas Toscher	Netflix Prize winner, Big Chaos team, machine learning researcher
Chris Volinsky	Netflix Prize winner, AT&T Laboratory, Statistics Division, executive director
Mark Wattles	Hollywood Video, founder/chief executive

PROLOGUE

IT IS EARLY MORNING ON a workday in the spring of 1997. A dusty maroon Volvo station wagon pulls into a commuter parking lot in Scotts Valley, California, in the foothills of the Santa Cruz Mountains.

The dot-com bubble is on the rise and the parking lot is lousy with twenty-something computer geeks, male and female, gathering in carpools to take them "over the hill" to Silicon Valley.

They carry canvas cases with logos: Apple Computer, Sun Microsystems, Oracle Corp., and other hot technology companies. Most wear the Valley uniform of board shorts or Levis with a wrinkled T-shirt, a fleece jacket, and some form of Teva footwear. Several have "bed head" from not showering and a dazed look from long-term lack of sleep.

The Volvo pulls toward a space on the deserted far side of the lot, where a shining steel blue Toyota Avalon is the lone occupant. The Toyota driver sits in the driver's seat, door wide open. At the sight of the Volvo, the Toyota driver jumps out of his car.

He is Reed Hastings, a tall lean man in his midthirties, wearing pressed Levis, a white T-shirt under a worn corduroy button-down shirt, brilliant-white running shoes, and black socks. He has close-cropped brown hair, a neat goatee, intense blue eyes, and a perpetually guarded expression. His normal posture, slightly forward and a bit hunched in the shoulders, reflects years of staring at computer monitors in pursuit of "beautiful" mathematical algorithms to define all manner of natural and man-made phenomena.

Hastings paces impatiently, his hands jammed into the pockets of his jeans, as he watches the Volvo approach, park off-kilter, then vaguely repark.

Finally satisfied, the driver of the Volvo, Marc Randolph, gets out, stands up, and greets Hastings over the roof of the Volvo.

Randolph, in his late thirties, is as happy-go-lucky as Hastings— who is his boss at a soaring software company—is intense. Loose-limbed and lanky, with thinning dark hair, Randolph has engaging brown eyes, a bemused, wide mouth, and an easy laugh. Randolph is Hastings's mirror opposite, a "people person," exactly the guy you want to be your marketing manager when you are not.

Despite their differences, there is an obvious ease, trust, and camaraderie between them: They share that confidence conferred by privileged upbringings and a passion for spinning ideas into businesses.

Randolph, clad in a fleece jacket, T-shirt, torn jeans, and flip-flops, circles the car and stands next to Hastings.

"It came," Hastings tells him.

Hastings reaches into the Avalon, digs an oversized rose-colored greeting card envelope out of a Pure Atria briefcase on the passenger's seat, and holds it up. Randolph swallows hard, and nods for Hastings to go ahead and open it.

Hastings takes an antique monogrammed silver penknife from his shirt pocket and slits open the envelope. He pulls a silver compact disk out of the envelope and turns the disk in his hand, minutely inspecting it. It is in perfect condition.

"It's fine," Hastings says flatly.

A huge smile spreads across Randolph's face.

"Huh. This online movie rental thing might actually work," Randolph says.

LIKE ALL GOOD stories, the one about the founding of Netflix Inc., the world's largest online movie rental company, mixes a little bit of fact with some entertaining fiction. But the version above is closer to reality than the company's official story—the one about how tech millionaire Reed Hastings had an epiphany for his next company after returning an overdue movie to his local video store, and later dreamed up its signature subscription model on a treadmill at his gym.

"The genesis of Netflix came in 1997, when I got this late fee, about $40, for *Apollo 13*. I remember the fee, because I was embarrassed about it. That was back in the VHS days, and it got me thinking that there's a big market out there," Hastings, Netflix's chairman and chief executive, told *Fortune* in 2009, one year before the magazine named him its Business Person of the Year.

"I didn't know about DVDs, and then a friend of mine told me they were coming. I ran out to Tower Records in Santa Cruz, California, and mailed CDs to myself, just a disk in an envelope. It was a long twenty-four hours until the mail arrived back at my house, and I ripped them open and they were all in great shape. That was the big excitement point."

As a financial journalist, I heard that story a lot in the seven years I covered Netflix along with a handful of other U.S. entertainment companies and their executives. I never gave Hastings's story much thought back then. It was simple and straightforward and conveyed perfectly what Netflix was all about: DVD rentals by mail that you can keep as long as you want without paying late fees.

The odds against Netflix surviving were long when I took over the Los Angeles entertainment industry beat at Reuters in spring 2004. Blockbuster, the world's largest movie rental chain, was preparing to launch its own online rental service, and online bookseller Amazon was lurking on the sidelines, posting employment ads for software developers for a yet to be announced movie rental service. Retail behemoth Walmart Stores was making a halfhearted stab at protecting its enormous DVD store sales by offering online DVD rental, and Hollywood movie studios were belatedly forming joint ventures to test movie downloading. Netflix had just hit 1.9 million subscribers and was still showing losses as often as it booked profits.

In the ensuing years I watched Hastings and his underdog company claim an ever-larger share of the growing online rental market with gutsy moves that defied Wall Street predictions about the size of the market and the strength of his larger rivals.

I saw a gifted and disciplined team change the way people rent movies, not for the money, but for the challenge of disrupting a "real world" industry and taking it online. In the pursuit of elegant software and intuitive user interfaces, they created a tastemaker to rival Apple, an innovator on the order of Google, and a brand power equal to Starbucks. Netflix also became a story about how powerful algorithms perfected in a Netflix-sponsored science contest spawned technological breakthroughs that influence how anyone with a product or idea to sell rounds up likely buyers. By 2010, with a long-delayed international expansion underway, Netflix had changed how half the world watches movies.

I thought I had the story down cold when in 2010 I began to research and write a book about Netflix's rise from a start-up with no clear path to profitability to a $4 billion movie rental titan with a stake in everything from postage rates to Hollywood movie deals to federal rules on privacy, broadband use, and Web traffic.

I knew I would need good outside sources to solve a few mysteries about the company's early days, because Netflix's communications and marketing teams were excellent at staying on message with reporters and investors—and especially with consumers—on issues the company wished either to control or to avoid talking about.

Some of the questions for which I could not get answers from Netflix included: What happened to Netflix's other founder, Marc Randolph, and why is he never mentioned? Why was the *Apollo 13* founding story initially set at a Blockbuster store in Santa Cruz, then changed in 2006 to a now defunct mom-and-pop video store in La Honda? Why did founding team member Mitch Lowe leave to start his DVD rental kiosk company Redbox, now one of Netflix's main competitors, instead of launching it at Netflix?

At first these seemed like minor details that had little bearing on the story that I knew so well and had watched unfold from a front-row seat in the financial press. But answering one question only led to another, and soon I was down a rabbit hole that changed everything I thought I knew about Netflix.

What I found was much richer and more nuanced than the official story. The complete history of Netflix comprises a long and untidy striving for greatness with multiple disasters, lucky breaks, betrayal, and heartbreak.

The company does not gratuitously mislead the public. The official story is simply more elegant and useful, and everything at Netflix, from its 2,180 corporate employees (who turn over at an annual rate of 20 percent) to the scripts followed by its executives on quarterly conference calls, must serve the company's goals or be eliminated.

After all, discipline and focus account for how a tiny, broke Silicon Valley company slew three giants of the $8 billion movie rental world (the Blockbuster, Movie Gallery, and Hollywood Video chains), warded off Amazon, and forced movie studios into the digital age. Netflix is now employing the same tactics to undermine cable and satellite providers, but in an outwardly nonthreatening way, the better to sneak into these new markets and disrupt the competition.

"We're small enough that we don't want to incite World War II or World War III with the incumbents," Hastings said in early 2011, shortly before Netflix announced that its subscriber base had surpassed that of number one U.S. cable provider Comcast.

Hastings seemed to guide his company by stars invisible to others, often abandoning solid revenue sources or related businesses to pursue the one thing he was determined to do better than anyone—rent movies online.

Where Hastings pursued that goal, Wall Street analysts and the financial press saw only a seemingly simple business model (a software program, a bunch of warehouses, and some DVDs) and bigger companies with the means to buy what Netflix had invented. Their bleak forecasts resulted in frequent meltdowns for Netflix's stock price, which appeared not to bother Hastings. That his judgment proved correct, even visionary, in the face of market pressures was an added attraction to a story I believed showed the best of entrepreneurial culture in America.

It was in the wake of the terrible stock market crash of 2008 that I began to contemplate writing what I believed was a Wall Street fairy tale, in which the best ideas, a clean balance sheet, and the flawless execution of an inspired business plan allowed a company like Netflix to vanquish a bloated corporate giant or two and come out on top.

I got that and a lot more, starting with a conversation I had with Netflix's other founder on a bright, windy day in Santa Cruz, California.

I WASN'T SURE what to expect when we met for the first time at a breakfast joint in Los Gatos in August 2010—no one else had been able to tell me the circumstances that had led to Marc Randolph's departure from the company he helped found.

The fit, animated man who walked up to my outdoor table dressed in a fleece pullover and jeans showed every sign of enjoying a rather footloose life since leaving Netflix. He sat down, ordered eggs Benedict, and plunged into a tale that upended a lot of what I thought I knew—starting with the story of how Hastings's late fee for *Apollo 13* resulted in the founding of the company.

"That's a lot of crap," Randolph told me. "It never happened."

He explained that the *Apollo 13* story started as "a convenient fiction" to describe how Netflix's rental model works and became confused with its origins, because people wanted "a rage against the machine–type story."

Six months and several conversations later I persuaded Randolph to show me where the true Netflix founding took place, which was on a quiet stretch of downtown Santa Cruz.

At Randolph's suggestion I took a commuter bus from Silicon Valley "over the hill," on winding Highway 17 to simulate the drive he and Hastings made each day from their homes to and from the Sunnyvale offices of Hastings's software company, Pure Atria. On that commute in early 1997, they tossed around ideas for a new business that Randolph planned to start when he left Pure Atria, then in the process of merging with its largest rival, Rational Software.

Randolph, then head of corporate marketing, had long been particularly fascinated by how consumers respond to direct mail—catalogs, mail-in offers, coupons—or what most people, including Hastings, considered junk mail. Randolph saw in the Internet an instant way to monitor consumer response to such sales pitches, adjust the online "store" to make it more inviting, and theoretically boost sales. "Direct mail on steroids," he called it.

The drive on the two-lane mountain road through fog and forest was nerve-racking, and I felt as though I had arrived in a quaint Alpine ski town when the bus stopped to let off passengers.

Randolph picked me up in his immaculate Volvo station wagon at the tiny bus station in Scotts Valley, an affluent bedroom community in the foothills of the Santa Cruz Mountains where he had lived for about fifteen years. His Victorian farmhouse, tucked away on fifty acres of forest, is about three miles from Hastings's former home, a square yellow Victorian about a block from the ocean in Santa Cruz.

We drove to a nearly empty faux Mediterranean office park off Highway 17, where he and a team of about a dozen marketing specialists, programmers, and operations staff launched the Netflix Web site on April 14, 1998.

Hastings, who was studying for a master's degree in education at Stanford University and running a tech industry lobby group at the time, came that day to wish them luck. The one-room space of about a thousand square feet, where Randolph ran Netflix for nearly two years, was at the back of the complex.

Next we headed three miles south, toward Santa Cruz. Randolph followed the coastal road and pointed out a wide, neatly groomed path curving along cliffs overlooking Monterey Bay, where prosperous-looking adults strode along in pairs and threesomes, wearing baseball caps and fleece jackets bearing tech company logos.

What looked to me like groups of stay-at-home moms and dads taking exercise and sanity breaks actually could have been staff meetings of homeless tech start-ups. Randolph told me that many business plans and deals are hammered out along this stretch of road.

Santa Cruz, especially the section populated by well-to-do residents on the west side of the San Lorenzo River, is vehemently antigrowth and antimansion, and even fought a widening of Highway 17 that would have shortened the hour-long commute to Silicon Valley. The town's east siders share their wealthy neighbors' isolationism—not so much to keep out vulgarian McMansion builders as to preserve a surf-shack culture reminiscent of a 1960s beach party movie.

We turned north toward the center of town, near where the Pacific Coast Highway runs inland for a few blocks through a tony little business district, before it heads back toward the California coastline. Randolph parked the Volvo at a meter on Pacific Avenue, and we began to walk—past a vintage movie theater, a few upscale chain stores, and local boutiques.

He pointed out a café called Lulu Carpenter's, a hip coffee joint where people sat out front at sidewalk tables in the weak morning sunshine. He and Hastings often met at this café to discuss business—and formed the plan that brought Netflix to fruition.

One particular day their debate centered on how to distribute the movies they hoped customers would rent via a hypothetical e-commerce Web site, and they decided they had to test whether the new DVD format that Randolph had heard of could travel across the country on a first-class stamp and survive the hazards of bulk mailing.

They couldn't get their hands on a DVD, then available in only a half-dozen test markets, but a used book and music store called Logos Books & Records a couple of blocks down the street sold compact disks. When we drove up that day a giant Borders bookstore was liquidating its stock and preparing to shut down, another casualty of the inexorable move to online distribution of media that its parent company embraced too late. I wondered if Logos's staff had any idea of the role their iconic indie store played in helping Netflix bring down another huge bricks-and-mortar entertainment chain.

A few doors down from the record store was the gift shop where Randolph and Hastings bought a greeting card with an envelope large enough to accommodate the CD after they stripped off its packaging.

They threw away the card, stuffed the CD into the envelope, and addressed it to Hastings's home. They then walked to the central Santa Cruz post office, where they paid for first-class postage and sent the CD on its short but crucial journey.

They would later learn, through close collaboration with the U.S. Postal Service, that local mail was hand-canceled in Santa Cruz and not sent through postal service sorters—a fact that could have changed everything had they known it then, Randolph told me.

A day or two later, the two met up for their morning commute to Sunnyvale.

"It came," Hastings told Randolph, as he climbed into the car. "It's fine."

"And I thought, 'Huh, this might work after all,'" Randolph said, as he drove me back to the bus station. "If there was an 'aha moment' in the story of Netflix, that was it."

CHAPTER ONE

A SHOT IN THE DARK

(1997–1998)

THE DAY HE FOUND OUT he was about to lose his job, Marc Randolph thought, "I'm going to start a business."

He had no idea what sort of business, only that he wanted to sell something on the World Wide Web. His new company would be the Amazon.com of something besides books. He wasn't sure what, exactly.

It was early spring 1997, and a few months earlier Randolph had become the head of corporate marketing at a Sunnyvale, California, software company called Pure Atria.

In late 1996, Pure Atria had acquired the nine-person software start-up for which Randolph worked as chief of product marketing. He figured he would lose his job in the merger, but Pure Atria's thirty-six-year-old cofounder and chief executive, Reed Hastings, had asked him to stay and promote Hastings's rapidly expanding company.

Randolph spent the dawn of the Internet age at a series of short jobs at start-ups after devoting seven years to building a direct-to-consumer marketing operation at software giant Borland International. He found the intense bursts of highly creative work suited him, especially when the companies were acquired or went public, and he and the other managers exited with healthy severance packages, chunks of valuable equity, and time off.

It was a common dance in 1990s Silicon Valley, a verdant and sunny groove of flat land sandwiched between the southern reaches of the San Francisco Bay in the east and the Santa Cruz Mountains in the west. Start-ups bloomed for a year or so, watered by plentiful venture capital dollars, and were quickly swallowed up by private investors or large, rich companies fishing for the next big innovation in software, biomedical engineering, telecoms, or the ever-evolving Internet. It was the new gold rush, and venture capital investors would pour more than $70 billion into Silicon Valley start-ups before the decade was out.

Things moved so quickly and money was so plentiful that most entrepreneurs had no chance, or any need, to turn a profit, or even run to their companies for long.

The pace was grueling, and everyone was expected to bring his or her top game each day for months of sixteen-hour days, until it was clear whether a fledgling business would fly or crash. The money was easy, but in exchange the entrepreneurs had to return tens, if not hundreds of times the VCs' initial investment.

Extreme risk was part of the equation and a factor that everyone—down to landlords and office equipment rental companies—took for granted, because the payoffs, when they came, were mind-blowing. And when things didn't work out, it was no big deal to shrug your shoulders and hop onto the next great idea.

Thinking that he could use a few months off to travel with his wife, Lorraine, and hang out with their three small children, Randolph hesitated to accept Hastings's offer to stay at Pure Atria.

The company made software for detecting bugs that often cropped up in computer code when multiple developers worked on it. Its customers were other businesses that developed software programs. Pure Atria was founded in 1991 by Hastings and Mark Box and had grown rapidly through a series of acquisitions; it had new offices in Europe and Asia, whose marketing departments would report to Randolph.

He would have felt no fear or stigma at the prospect of being let go with a nice severance—jobs were plentiful in the Valley, and as a cofounder of a glittering roster of start-ups, Randolph knew he was a catch.

Staying at Pure Atria was a high-pressure job, but next to the hectic software development schedules, long days, and chaos of start-ups, the regular hours and steady if unexciting task of promoting Pure Atria seemed like leisure to Randolph. He met with Hastings a couple of times and decided his prospective boss was intense and extremely smart.

Despite having completely opposite personalities, Randolph and Hastings had a lot in common. Both were East Coast transplants from wealthy families who attended small private colleges and wandered about for a few years before settling into careers they were passionate about.

Both had tremendous enthusiasm for the high-tech industry that was blossoming in Silicon Valley, and each was a strong leader in his own way, inspiring protégés to throw around the word "genius" with conviction.

WILMOT REED HASTINGS, JR., came from America's patrician class, and it showed in an easy confidence in his own abilities and opinions. His mother's family were founding members of the *Social Register*; their births, marriages, and other life passages were chronicled in the *New York Times* society pages.

His maternal great-grandfather Alfred Lee Loomis applied a mathematical genius to investing and became one of the few on Wall Street to profit handsomely from the 1929 crash. Loomis was viewed as cold and odd by his wealthy and pedigreed peers, mainly because of his obsession with using physics to develop weapons technology. Loomis lavished his fortune on an experimental physics laboratory in a mansion in Tuxedo Park, New York, and invited the world's most brilliant scientists to work there on technology for military applications. Their scientific breakthroughs led to the development of radar, the atomic bomb, and global positioning systems. After World War II the federal government formed the Defense Advanced Research Projects Agency essentially to take over the Loomis lab's role as a pure defense research lab. Scientists at DARPA developed the precursor to the World Wide Web to allow computers at far-flung locations to share data about national security threats in real time.

Hastings's mother, Joan Amory Loomis, was presented to society at the Boston Cotillion and the Tuxedo Park ball in New York in 1956. She attended Wellesley College and married his father, Wil Hastings, a magna cum laude graduate of Harvard College, in 1958 after both spent a year studying at the Sorbonne in Paris.

Hastings, the first of their three children, was born in 1960. He grew up in the liberal and discreetly wealthy Belmont suburb of Boston, attended private schools, and bucked the family tradition of attending Harvard or Yale, instead choosing Bowdoin College, a liberal arts school in Maine.

Like his great-grandfather Loomis, Hastings was drawn to mathematics, a pursuit he found "beautiful and engaging." He won Bowdoin's top math honors in his sophomore and senior years and, after graduating, set out to see the world.

Hastings hoped to attend the Massachusetts Institute of Technology's graduate computer science program after completing a three-year stint as a Peace Corps math teacher in Swaziland, but he wasn't admitted. Instead, he earned a graduate degree from Stanford University and found himself swept up in Silicon Valley's technology boom. He started his first company, Pure Software, at age thirty. Pure went public in 1995 and two years later acquired the Boston software company Atria and Integrity QA, a start-up where Randolph was a founding team member.

RANDOLPH SAW IN Hastings an equal in entrepreneurial spirit and drive, and so he took the marketing post and moved to Pure Atria's headquarters shortly before the end of 1996. They began working together on speeches and product launches. On their first cross-country commercial flight together to Atria, Hastings sat down, buckled his seat belt, and turning to Randolph, proceeded to describe that company's inner workings and his plan for integrating it into Pure—for the entire six-hour trip.

Randolph was impressed with Hastings's command of the minutiae of his recently acquired subsidiary and his determination that it would not capsize Pure in the process of combining operations.

Warm and voluble, Randolph loved nothing more than to be argued into or out of an idea or point of view. Hastings, cool and analytical, could be stubbornly sure of himself. Somehow, the relationship worked. Hastings's supercomputer mind perfected the logic of a business plan or organizational structure or product, and Randolph sold it—to customers, employees, or the public.

In spring 1997, Randolph began assembling his marketing staff at Pure Atria. One of his first calls was to Christina Kish. The athletic and pretty thirty-two-year-old California native was a tightly wound product manager who had gained her direct-marketing chops at the software industry's biggest names, Software Publishing and Intuit. She had interviewed Randolph at the Mountain View–based desktop scanner manufacturer Visioneer; she had liked the mix of his laid-back style and sharp intellect and agreed he should be her boss.

Randolph had an appealing wit and a sensitivity about people that was uncommon in Silicon Valley's male-dominated culture. He also possessed unparalleled abilities as a public relations strategist, as Kish learned during their wild ride at Visioneer, which went from struggling unknown to industry leader shortly after shipping its first product, the PaperMax scanner, in 1994.

Cutthroat corporate politics annoyed both of them enough that they left Visioneer after short stays, but Kish had enjoyed working with Randolph, especially appreciating the work atmosphere he created—focused and intense yet collaborative, as if they were throwing a big party together. So when he called three years later to offer her a comparatively low-stress job building a customer database at an established software company, she jumped. She gave notice at the dial-up Internet service provider Best Internet and left for a two-week vacation in Italy with her husband, Kirby, intending to join Pure Atria when she returned.

Next, Randolph wheedled Therese "Te" Smith, another protégé, into leaving Starfish Software's marketing department. Smith, a baby-faced forty-year-old with long curly brown hair and the broad accent of Boston's blue-collar North Shore, had been doing consumer-facing marketing for the hot new Sidekick personal organizer developed by Starfish, a former division of Borland. But after Randolph's call, Smith quit her job and planned to land at Pure Atria in early April, after taking a few weeks off between gigs.

As Randolph negotiated salaries and perks for his new team, the Pure Atria and Rational Software boards hammered out the terms of the merger. The deal, announced on April 7, 1997, called for a stock swap worth about $850 million—the largest merger in Silicon Valley history.

Hastings and the Pure Atria board had decided rather abruptly to sell in late 1996, after sales unexpectedly fell short of Wall Street forecasts, potentially exposing the company to a stock price collapse. Pure Atria had rebuffed Rational's previous merger offers, but this time Hastings and his board of directors decided to accept.

Although the deal's final value dropped to $585 million, Hastings suddenly was an extremely wealthy man and a hero to the venture capitalists he had enriched in the deal.

CHRISTINA KISH GOT to enjoy her plush corporate office, with unaccustomed perks like espresso machines and dry cleaning pickup, for five days. Randolph called her at home the following Sunday. He told her they would both lose their jobs as soon as federal antitrust regulators approved the merger. He laid Smith off her first day on the job.

They all had a four-month grace period, during which Pure Atria paid them simply to show up at the Sunnyvale offices while the companies waited for regulatory approval. Smith worked on a couple of product rollouts. Randolph and Kish showed up each day and sat in their offices without much to do. But Randolph had a large whiteboard, a fast Internet connection, and the beginnings of an idea for a company.

After joining Pure Atria, Randolph started commuting over the mountains into Sunnyvale with Hastings and, occasionally, other company executives—a trip of an hour each way over winding, narrow, and often traffic-clogged Highway 17.

On these drives he and Hastings began talking about what they would do when the merger was completed and they were free. Hastings wanted to get his master's degree in education and put some of his new millions into educational philanthropy to try to revive California's moribund public school system.

Randolph revealed his plan to start a company and said he had gotten no further than deciding it would sell something over the Internet. He had watched e-commerce develop with growing excitement and knew that his entire life had led him to this opportunity.

Marc Bernays Randolph grew up privileged in the leafy New York suburb of Chappaqua, the eldest son of an Austrian-born nuclear engineer turned investment adviser, Stephen, and a realtor, Muriel, who was born in Brooklyn's Flatbush neighborhood. Stephen Randolph was proud to be the great-nephew of psychoanalysis pioneer Sigmund Freud but spoke less of another famous uncle, Edward Bernays, the father of modern public relations, who used Freud's theories, at times to devastating effect, in propaganda campaigns for powerful clients such as American Tobacco, United Fruit, and the U.S. government.

Bernays's signature accomplishment was unleashing people's unconscious desires—for love, respect, sex—and using them to mold modern American consumers. Like Bernays, Marc Randolph would obsess over how to use product messaging to entice consumers to behave in specific ways.

Two generations after Bernays and his contemporary, Alfred Lee Loomis, set in motion two of the modern era's most powerful forces—American consumerism and high technology—Randolph and Hastings would combine the two in a venture that showed the reach and profit in harnessing science purely to serve consumers.

Randolph spent his summers as a teenager at the National Outdoor Leadership School in Lander, Wyoming, and became one of its youngest wilderness guides. The experience of leading trekkers twice his age—making snap decisions based on incomplete information and keeping control of situations even when he had no clue where a trail led—proved to be ideal training for forming tech start-ups.

In a strange parallel to Bernays, an agriculture major who began experimenting with marketing and public relations as a Broadway show promoter, Randolph discovered his life's passion during a stint at Cherry Lane Music Company, in a clerical job his father helped him get after he graduated, with a geology degree, from Hamilton College in upstate New York.

Despite knowing nothing about marketing or direct mail, he was put in charge of Cherry Lane's mail-order operation. This consisted, in its entirety, of a small order form on the back of each sheet music booklet that customers could return for "a list of more great Cherry Lane songbooks." Randolph collected the orders from the incoming mail and mailed back the requested items, noting what song booklets prompted the most orders, whether new purchases followed, and the like.

He found this process fascinating and began tinkering with the order form—its arrangement, color, and size—to try to spur orders. He won permission to create a catalog and try a few mailings and soon realized he needed to learn more about direct marketing. He attended conferences and read whatever he could find about best practices, taking his newly acquired knowledge back to his "laboratory" at Cherry Lane.

When desktop computers and inventorying software came on the market, Cherry Lane tapped Randolph to help design the programs for a mail-order processing system. Later he designed the specifications for a program to manage Cherry Lane's customer service and the circulation data for the company's new music magazine.

The software added an exciting new dimension to direct marketing—the ability to quickly morph order and renewal form designs and track which approach worked best to attract and retain customers.

In 1984, he helped found the U.S. version of *MacUser* magazine, which was brought to the United States by British publisher Felix Dennis and pornography impresario Peter Godfrey to capitalize on the growing consumer interest in PCs. About a year later, Godfrey tapped Randolph to a start a new venture—the computer mail-order businesses MacWarehouse and MicroWarehouse. Randolph chose the product mix, published the mail-order catalogs, and set up the telemarketing sales force.

Here Randolph learned that overnight delivery coupled with superior customer service translated into increased sales and better retention. He partnered with up-and-coming overnight shipper Federal Express and targeted zero tolerance for shipping errors. At the end of each day his customer service workers called to apologize to people whose orders had not shipped. "Every customer you get, you're never going to lose them" was Randolph's mantra.

Direct mail was as beautiful and elegant to Randolph as mathematics was to Hastings. There's no middleman in the customer relationship, Randolph told Hastings one day during a drive over the hill. You control the relationship, and if you want it to be perfect, you can make it perfect.

Randolph knew he had to find a large category of products that were portable and related to an activity that consumers would someday prefer to do online, either because of convenience or better selection. He began bouncing ideas off Hastings each day on their commute.

Each morning, when they met at the Scotts Valley Medical Clinic parking lot, Randolph would start the ride in his Volvo, or in the backseat of Hastings's Toyota Avalon (chauffeured by a student who acted as Hastings's regular driver), by saying, "All right, I've got a new one." He would spend a good part of the drive laying out his plan to Hastings, who would shoot holes in it.

Early on they considered and rejected the $12.6 billion video rental and sell-through category as a natural equivalent to the $12 billion bookselling industry that was dominated online by Amazon. Neither Blockbuster nor Hollywood Entertainment's Hollywood Video chain, the two largest U.S. movie rental companies, seemed to have any interest in potentially cannibalizing their brick-and-mortar stores' revenues to sell or rent movies online. But others, with deeper pockets—maybe even Amazon—would surely decide to sell movies online soon, and shrinking profit margins would force out all but high-volume players. If it was going to work, Randolph knew, he had to do something to differentiate an online Video Business.

"Operationally, I bet we could do rental. You ship it there and then someone ships it back," he said. They ultimately rejected the idea because of VHS inventory costs of sixty-five dollars to eighty dollars per tape, and because the bulky tapes cost too much to mail back and forth.

In his research, Randolph learned about an optical media storage format called DVD that movie studios and electronics manufacturers were testing in a few markets and planning to launch later that year. The five-inch disks looked exactly like compact disks. Then they test-mailed one to Hastings's house and it arrived unscathed a day or two later.

By this time Randolph and Hastings had started sharing ideas with Kish. One day Randolph called her into his office, where she found Hastings waiting. Alarm bells went off in her head as she sat down and Randolph shut the door. *Now what?* she thought.

They told her that Hastings planned to put up $2 million to back Randolph's e-commerce start-up. They needed help researching which ideas were feasible, and in marketing the new online business. Hastings was giving them six months to get it going—was she in?

After they settled on renting DVDs by mail, Kish began studying the economics of home entertainment by pulling apart Blockbuster's and Hollywood Video's operations and finances. But it was not clear how Blockbuster made money, no matter how she modeled the numbers, after covering its store leases and massive inventory costs.

They used the whiteboard in Randolph's office and spent hours plotting how to convince Blockbuster customers to abandon convenient, familiar video stores for a store that existed only in cyberspace. Customers would also have to wait a week to receive their movies. It seemed ludicrous to imagine that they could challenge Blockbuster by manipulating its own model. By examining Amazon, however, they found their selling point: Their company would boast the largest selection of movies on DVD in the world.

They decided the customer interface had to meld the familiar layout of a video rental store with the pictorial and descriptive come-ons of a catalog to make the merchandise seem worth the wait.

The ordering process had to be easy; it could not take more steps to choose a DVD online than to pick up a movie from a store and return it.

Randolph was acutely aware of the importance of engaging consumers' emotions, and he wanted the site to be a personal experience, as if each customer opened the door to find an online video store created just for him or her.

In early summer 1997, Hastings urged Randolph and Kish to take the whiteboard musings and develop a business plan for the DVD rental company before someone beat them to it.

Now officially unemployed after the merger of Pure Atria and Rational, Hastings admitted to being a little depressed that the company he had identified with so closely was now closed to him. He had been accepted to Stanford for graduate education studies and was beginning to get involved in politics, but he wanted to keep his hand in a tech venture in Silicon Valley.

Hastings recommended a gifted French programmer named Eric Meyer to design and build the Web site, and Randolph brought Te Smith aboard to handle public relations and customer acquisition, as she had done with Lotus 1-2-3 software and for Sidekick.

The initial company meetings took place at Buck's Restaurant in Woodside or the Hobee's restaurant in Cupertino, and then in a dingy conference room in the Best Western in Scotts Valley. The new team first dealt with the nuts and bolts of setting up the company—finding office space and furniture, deciding on benefits, pay, and titles. To Kish, Randolph, Meyer, and Smith, it was thrilling and absurd all at once. Here was a company with which they could test their dreams and ideas, and that they were aiming squarely at the flank of one of the largest U.S. entertainment corporations.

ALTHOUGH THEY WERE long on marketing and software development smarts, they had no experience with movie rental or the entertainment industry. That summer Randolph went looking for some outside expertise at the annual Video Software Dealers Association convention in Las Vegas, an enormous trade show that showcased home entertainment products and VHS releases for movie studios and their natural enemies, home video retailers.

The studios had long resented the video retailers as interlopers that took no risks yet siphoned off profits from moviemaking through the burgeoning home entertainment category. Home video sales and rental started in 1977, when Magnetic Video founder Andre Blay convinced 20th Century Fox to license fifty titles to him to sell directly to consumers. Blay took out an ad in *TV Guide* offering the first theatrical motion pictures on home video through his Video Club of America. Even though Betamax and VHS copies of the movies cost fifty dollars apiece, and video players retailed for a thousand dollars, Blay got thirteen thousand responses.

The high prices put video purchases out of reach of most American consumers, and many merchants balked at the $7.50 licensing fee on each video sale, and at the advance payments required on bulk orders. As a result, mom-and-pop retailers bought copies of the pricey videos from Blay and started their own home video rental businesses. As the prices of players dropped, video clubs sprang up across the country, offering movie lovers their first chance to watch commercial-free movies at home for an annual membership fee plus up to ten dollars a day.

The studios threatened lawsuits to curtail the rental operations, leading the merchants to form the Video Software Dealers Association in 1981, to lobby against attempts to force them to pay a royalty on each video sale or rental. The U.S. Supreme Court ruled that a 1908 U.S. copyright law, known as the First Sale Doctrine, protected the merchants' rights to sell or rent videos they owned.

By 1988, annual video rental revenue had surpassed box office receipts for the first time—$5.15 billion to $4.46 billion. Home video rental was here to stay.

RANDOLPH WANDERED THROUGH aisles of booths of the enormous exhibition hall on the VSDA convention's final day, a backpack slung over his shoulder, stopping to hear product pitches and soaking in as much information as he could. He stopped at a booth selling software for retail stores to chat with an affable-looking guy with longish hair and a biker-style horseshoe mustache.

Mitch Lowe owned a ten-store rental chain called Video Droid in northern California's Marin County, and had just started a side business building Web sites to manage customer databases for video rental stores.

Over the years the forty-four-year-old Lowe had spent thirteen thousand hours behind the counters at his stores, watching customers surf the aisles and observing what got their attention, what titles they took home, which films were likely to be hits, and how many times he had to turn a VHS tape to make a profit.

Impressed with Lowe's deep knowledge of movie rental, Randolph took a card from the counter and asked, "Can I ever call you sometime to ask questions about this business?"

"Sure, sure," said Lowe. As Randolph turned to leave, Lowe, on impulse, grabbed his backpack and pulled him back.

"What exactly are you trying to do?" Lowe asked. They agreed to meet at Buck's in Woodside a week or so after the show to share ideas and information. Later that day, as Randolph leafed through the trade show program, he saw a photo of Lowe and realized he had been talking to the president of VSDA.

A placid and sweet-natured man, Lowe was liked and respected enough in the industry to help guide the conversion from VHS to DVD among the rival factions represented by merchants, studios, and video wholesalers.

The meetings at Buck's became an almost weekly event that produced the ideas for Netflix's FlixFinder, a search engine to locate movies by title, actor, or director, and the FilmFacts link to synopses and ratings, and to cast and crew lists and DVD features. Browse the Aisles let shoppers scan lists of movies grouped around a genre or theme or enter a favorite film and be shown similar titles—functions typically performed by a video store clerk.

Randolph often brought along Kish, and sometimes Hastings, too. He frequently pressed Lowe to join their start-up. Lowe resisted. First, his video stores were already taking a backseat to his fledgling Web site building project and VSDA business, and second, his wife, Zamora, and three kids thought the idea of renting movies by mail was a loser.

But the intersection of retail and technology fascinated Lowe. He had built his own video rental vending machine a decade earlier after becoming fed up with his flaky staff and high store overhead. Lowe installed the kiosk in a Japanese hospital and never made back his investment in it, but the experience had not stopped him from experimenting. In November Lowe realized his software enterprise was going nowhere, and he finally agreed to join Randolph's still-unnamed company as a video rental domain expert and movie acquisitions chief.

THE ANGEL FUNDS supplied by Hastings and augmented by Randolph's parents and Integrity QA cofounder Steve Kahn allowed the little company the rare luxuries of office space, regular salaries, benefits, and proper equipment from the beginning. The founding team now numbered eight, with the additions of programmers Vita and Boris Droutman, a young Ukrainian couple recruited by Meyer, and operations and financial director Jim Cook.

Randolph found a small space once used as a bank branch in an office park off Highway 17 in Scotts Valley. The office had luminous green carpet—they joked it was the color of the money they hoped to make—and a strange, narrow room on one end with an armored door, which Randolph supposed had been used as a vault. It made a perfect space for storing DVDs. He furnished the large central room with rows of long folding tables and cheap desk chairs so that Meyer could buy top-of-the-line computers and costly Oracle software. Randolph claimed one of the tiny offices on the room's perimeter, installed Smith and Kish in another, and designated a third as a conference room. The servers were installed in a closet. Cook also had a small office, but worked mainly in the vault. The Droutmans and Meyer and their desktop computers occupied the folding tables.

Everyone had a say in the two main tasks: building a Web site with an enticing and easy-to-use customer interface and a smoothly functioning back end; and getting DVDs into customers' hands quickly and in one piece.

Kish and Meyer set to work on the Web site. Kish sketched out crayon drawings to show Meyer and Boris Droutman in color the steps of the journey she wanted customers to take from their arrival in the virtual store until they paid and left the site with the promise of receiving their purchases quickly.

Meanwhile, Vita Droutman worked with Jim Cook to create programs to ring up sales and rental transactions, maintain inventory, move DVDs in and out of shopping carts, and charge customers' credit cards.

Boris and Vita met as teenagers and immigrated to the United States separately as college students—Vita as a political refugee. They were working as programmers at separate companies when Meyer, who had worked with Vita at auditor and professional advisory firm KPMG, asked them both to help with the new start-up. Vita, petite and spirited, joined first, and the tall and laid-back Boris came along a few months later, after working only at night to help set up the new company's content management system.

They had initially hesitated to leave two steady jobs to work at the same start-up, but the chance to work together, and with Meyer, was too tempting. Besides, they were still in their twenties—the youngest team members—and like most programmers in Silicon Valley in those days, they were always fielding calls from employment recruiters.

The push-pull of turning the marketing department's concepts for the user interface, inventory management, shipping, and even the credit card application into intuitive and consumer-friendly software was so satisfying that the grueling hours of coding seemed like play. Marketing and technology waltzed together in a harmony that the young technologists had never before experienced.

Meyer insisted on customizing Oracle programs to one day handle search and fulfillment operations for up to ten million users. Vita Droutman thought the number was a bit ridiculous—they all believed they'd be lucky to get one hundred orders in the first month. Meyer also instructed Vita and Boris to build the platforms that would accommodate later features that they didn't have time or money to build before launch.

The list included a recommendation engine to suggest movies based on customers' previous choices, a reminder function to retrieve titles that customers had flagged on earlier visits, and a subscription plan.

The initial business plan called for both selling and renting DVDs on an à la carte basis. The company would charge the video stores' going rate for VHS rental—four dollars plus two dollars shipping for a single disk, and three dollars for each additional one. Renters could keep movies for seven days and return them in a postage-paid mailer. If customers liked a particular title they could buy it for 30 percent below the retail price. Their hook would be something that retail stores could not offer—a selection that included almost every DVD ever released.

The title count in late 1997 was an underwhelming five hundred DVDs of mostly older movies. Only Warner Home Video had risked releasing new titles onto DVD, and strictly because its home video chief, Warren Lieberfarb, was pushing the format.

Before he took over finance and operations, Jim Cook had reviewed Randolph's business plan as a favor to Kish, a former colleague at Intuit. He had had serious doubts about its viability.

Based on his experiences as VP of finance and operations at the Internet Shopping Network, Cook saw problems with nearly every aspect of the proposed video rental operation: the labor costs for filling orders were too high and the costs of replacing broken and lost DVDs were unpredictable. DVD players were still too expensive and titles too few to interest mainstream consumers. The technology was iffy—even duplication houses were having trouble standardizing copies so that all DVDs worked in all players.

Randolph and Kish went away from their first meetings with Cook and worked out reasonable fixes for each of the obstacles he raised and returned with a modified plan.

The moment that Cook decided he wanted to join the venture came when Randolph asked him pointedly, "Jim, don't you agree that when we solve all these 'what ifs?' it will create such a high barrier to entry that there's no way anybody else could solve this stuff, because it's so hard to do?"

Cook spent the first three months as the new operations chief at the general mail facility on Meridien Road in San Jose, learning everything he could about the U.S. postal system. The ability to deliver product economically, promptly, and in one piece would make or break their new company, so mastering the post office was critical.

Smith took charge of designing the mailers, and she enlisted an outside design firm to work rapidly through dozens of possible layouts, sizes, inks, and paper stock, as they learned from their mistakes.

She pressed Cook, Kish, and Lowe to recruit friends and family members in cities across the country to help field-test each version. They mailed test shipments back and forth for weeks, asking their testers to report by e-mail about the condition of the envelopes and the DVDs. So few people had DVD players at the time that they often had to have their testers send the disks back so they could pop them into the office's players to see if the disks had been damaged in the mail.

The team argued over whether to leave the company's name off the packaging to discourage theft of the DVDs, and they fussed over minute details in the placement of the crucial bar code that let the mailer bypass the high-speed drum sorters that frequently ripped open envelopes and crushed disks. San Jose post office officials even allowed Cook to dump trays of DVDs into its sorters, day after day, to watch what happened.

Slowly, over dozens of iterations, the elements of a viable fulfillment operation took shape. Randolph discovered "skip shipping," a way to bypass all automation by sorting mail into twenty-seven bags by zone and delivering them straight to the post office freight docks. Once Netflix went live, Cook generally made the last post office run, stuffing mailbags into his Merkur Scorpio and dropping them at the freight bays before the 9:00 P.M. cutoff.

The result of their experiments was a three-part mailer constructed of stiff but light cardboard that could both fit up to three disks at a time and serve as a return mailer after the original address flap was torn off.

Cook also tested layouts for the tiny DVD storage vault and timed workers to see how fast they could find titles, pack and label them, and sort them into mailbags. The most efficient configuration turned out to be a miniature reproduction of a Blockbuster store. DVDs hung in glassine envelopes from pegboards that covered the walls and rows of shelves set up in the middle of the room. The aisles were so narrow that only one person could pass at a time. It probably did not meet Occupational Safety and Health Administration standards, but Cook figured they'd have plenty of time to perfect the fulfillment operation as orders slowly grew.

The process of naming the company dragged on for several weeks. Randolph incorporated it as Kibble Inc., in a nod to their contention that, above all, the "dog" had to want to eat the "kibble." Randolph, Kish, and her husband, Kirby, created a working list of possible names during a brainstorming session shortly after they moved to the Scotts Valley office.

They decided the name should consist of two syllables—something about the Internet and something about movies. One afternoon they scribbled side-by-side columns of movie terms and Internet slang on a whiteboard in Randolph's office and matched them up.

Randolph left the list on the whiteboard and encouraged team members to add to it. His personal favorite was Replay.com, but Directpix. com, NowShowing.com, Netflix.com, eFlix.com, and CinemaCenter. com were all contenders. The Droutmans and Meyer favored Luna, after the black Labrador retriever who accompanied Randolph to work each day, as well as for the lunatic nature of their venture.

With time running short to design and print a new logo for PR and promotions, Smith pushed them to decide. Most of the team already favored one choice, so one day, without fanfare, they decided: "We're Netflix." They paired the new name—with a capital F to emphasize the film connection—with a purple-and-white logo that depicted an unspooling reel of film.

In January 1998, Randolph and Smith began formulating a launch and customer acquisition strategy with the help of Corey Bridges, a bright and hyperkinetic twenty-nine-year-old product manager who had worked with them at Borland. Bridges was coming off a stressful stint at Netscape Communications, where he had helped launch the company's iconic Internet browser. His specialty was tapping Usenet newsgroups and discussion groups, a forerunner of blogs, to spread the word about new products among early technology adopters.

Randolph and Smith had had to work hard to persuade Bridges to delay his plan to become a Hollywood screenwriter and instead help market Netflix. With less than two months to go before the planned launch, Bridges gave in, mainly because he admired Randolph and had enjoyed working with the calmly capable Smith at Borland. "I'll only work fifty hours a week—sixty at the most," he warned them.

His engineer roommate at the University of California–Berkeley had turned Bridges on to Usenet, a university-based precursor to the Internet, and its tightly focused newsgroups that ran ongoing discussions of topics ranging from esoteric scientific theories to purebred puppies. Bridges watched as the Internet developed, how quirky online communities formed and acquired their own tastemakers, bullies, and sheep, just like in the real world. The dynamic of the virtual societies fascinated him, and he studied them carefully.

DVD player owners were the ideal test market; they were among the most discriminating early technology adopters, already talking about their newest toy online.

He set out to influence the influencers—he'd drop into discussion groups posing as a consumer to observe, and then he'd contact the main players secretly to say, "I'm working on something interesting that I think you'll like."

Once he had hooked a couple dozen influencers, he recruited them for a closed beta test of the site with the promise that if they gave Netflix feedback, they could be the first to post the news on launch day.

Every one of them said yes. "It's like shooting fish in a barrel," Bridges exulted to Smith and Randolph. "I can post something that literally every potential customer of Netflix will see."

By early spring, the Web site and back-end systems that enabled customers to search the inventory of films and order them were in place. By later standards it was rudimentary: tiny graphics and short blurbs about each film set on a vast white field. They had to cut a deal to use movie descriptions generated by allmovie.com, a cinephile Web site based in Ann Arbor, Michigan, after the studios refused to grant Netflix permission to use box art and copy on its Web site. The Netflix team decided to scan in photos and titles from the boxes anyway and wait for the cease-and-desist letters.

The staff had grown with new programmers crammed together at the folding tables and marketing hires sharing Kish's cramped office. The dress code was beyond relaxed. Randolph sometimes showed up in jeans and a T-shirt that he had dropped on the floor before crawling into bed for a few hours' sleep, only to put back on in the morning. Kish slept at the office on the increasingly frequent nights she worked too late to drive home to Redwood Shores.

A stultifying funk built up from too many bodies crammed into a small space with a balky ventilation system. Mountains of discarded DVD jewel cases piled up in one corner as the DVD inventory grew and the vault readied for action.

They all had a lot at stake, and it started to show in arguments that often escalated to shouting matches. They were not a typical start-up staff of kids just out of college—most had had seniority at big software names, and all had taken big pay cuts to work at Netflix. They had done so gladly to realize a shared dream of a consumer-oriented company that reflected their ideals and carried their intellectual DNA.

It felt more like a family than a company, because they were all so passionate about every decision, Vita Droutman reflected in March 1998, as launch day loomed. On April 14, 1998, six months after the first line of code was written, they were ready. Netflix went live.

Hastings, now in his second semester of Stanford's graduate education program, came to watch the launch but stayed on the fringes. He and Randolph had conferred frequently over the previous six months, but he was in the office so little that many of the newer employees barely knew him.

That morning, Randolph and Smith sat for two press conferences over the phone with a full roster of journalists calling in from mainstream newspapers such as the *San Jose Mercury News*, venture capital magazines such as *Red Herring* and *Upside*, and the tech Web site CNET.

Meyer pushed the site up, and Bridges unmuzzled his newsgroup influencers. Curious visitors filed into the virtual store. The site worked exactly as planned. As the visitor count ticked higher, Meyer began getting nervous.

The servers reached capacity about ninety minutes after launch—and crashed. Meyer sent Boris Droutman to a nearby Fry's Electronics, in company controller Greg Julian's battered Toyota pickup truck, to buy ten new computers to boost capacity while he worked on a fix to bring the site back up.

In the vault, the laser printer jammed, unable to handle the heavy flow of orders. The pegboards were in disarray; orders were half completed and lying in piles on benches as workers squeezed through the narrow aisles, trying to keep up.

Everyone who wasn't working on fixing the capacity problem pitched in to help with the orders that flooded in each time the site came back up. By nightfall they had received more than one hundred orders to ship more than five hundred disks, and Meyer was still struggling to keep the site online.

"We have to put a page up on the site saying something like 'The store is too crowded; come back later,'" Hastings told them.

That's funny, Smith thought. *It's the Internet. It can't get too crowded.* Nor had it occurred to her until that moment that on the Internet the store never closes.

CHAPTER TWO

THE GOOD, THE BAD, AND THE UGLY

(1998–1999)

IT HAD BEEN AN ABSTRACT thing; a concept they invented, converted into a business plan, and launched into existence in the space of a year. The Netflix team set out to challenge an established industry, and the reality of that wish came calling as soon as the launch was over.

The team had not expected the level of success or attention that they received from day one, and they quickly started to feel the responsibility of not screwing it up. *So this is what it's like to have a tiger by the tail*, Kish thought.

Lowe came home the night of the launch and told his wife he was unsure, after all the work that had gone into launching Netflix, what came next. "It's like having a baby," she told him. "Now that it's here, what do you do with it?"

Like a real infant, Netflix gave its caretakers many more sleepless nights, and suffered from growing pains associated with disrupting two business paradigms—the VHS format and the bricks-and-mortar rental—in its first year of life.

"We had difficulty using the Netflix site last week and apparently weren't alone—site carried message 'Sorry, due to extreme opening week demand, the Netflix Store may be slow,'" *Audio Week* wrote the week after the launch. "Spokeswoman said site has had 'overwhelming' number of visitors since April 14 launch but couldn't provide specifics on hits. However, she said company tripled site capacity to accommodate demand, and we saw improvement by week's end."

By launch day DVD players were selling far faster than videocassette recorders—four hundred thousand units in the first six months after the optical format's U.S. release in March 1997. It had taken VHS two years to get into half as many households. Prices of players were falling fast, to an average $580 in April 1998 from $1,100 a year earlier.

Initially wary, movie studios finally accepted the new format and were releasing DVD titles at a clip of one hundred per month. The number of titles in Netflix's vault climbed to fifteen hundred by August. Blockbuster and Hollywood Video, correctly viewing the new format as a threat, refused to stock it in stores, ceding the field to Netflix throughout the summer of 1998. Every factor that could have tripped Netflix up had instead fallen exactly the right way.

"Be sure to bookmark Netflix.com to revisit as their popular titles become available," CNN correspondent Dennis Michael urged viewers of *Showbiz Today* that summer.

Consumer adoption of the DVD format surged, and the Netflix team found itself swept along. In the first four months the vault mailed out and got back twenty thousand rented DVDs, and Netflix hit $100,000 in monthly revenue, becoming in theory a $1 million company.

The launch-day crash of the Netflix site was a harbinger of the work that still awaited Randolph and his team in the months that followed. He and Kish and Meyer had made trade-offs to get the site up and running within the time Hastings had specified when he funded them. In prelaunch brainstorming sessions they had outlined but not built a suite of features they felt were important to make the site compelling and easy to use.

Kish and Meyer wanted a function to remind customers about

movies they wanted to see, inspired by Kish's trips to bookstores to scope out new titles so that she could borrow them from the library.

In internal memos they called the feature The List, but it came to be known as the Queue when Meyer built it a year later. It would be difficult to build, because it included "intelligent" functions that allowed customers to sort through and prioritize inventory in individual accounts. Meyer had not wanted to spend time on it until more critical functions were added.

In its place, Meyer and Kish came up with a Remind Me icon—an extended index finger with a red bow tied around it—to give customers a way to designate films they were interested in. The programmers disliked the rudimentary graphic and ribbed Kish about it, nicknaming it "The Bloody Finger."

Lowe wanted to build in a digital shopping assistant, based on his observation of customers at his Video Droid stores; they often avoided asking his opinions about movies and went straight to clerks who shared their tastes.

Ideally, the digital shopping assistant would have a personality and a photo and could point customers to movies they would like in Netflix's (future) vast library. They weren't able to build the shopping assistant for the launch either, but the idea became the basis for a recommendation engine that also had been on an early drawing board.

Another of Lowe's dicta—never falsely raise customers' hopes by placing empty VHS boxes on shelves, as Blockbuster did—took shape as a search engine quirk that led customers deep into the catalog and away from newly released titles. Meyer programmed it to guide people to films that were in stock, as opposed to showing them everything that was available.

The decision to deemphasize new movies also sprang from problems Lowe encountered in negotiating a break on DVD prices to mitigate the soaring cost of building Netflix's inventory.

The typical reaction he got from the studios when he came to meetings representing Netflix was "Okay, kind of an interesting idea, but this will never work. We'll sell you some movies but don't expect any price break."

With the studios unwilling to drop the fifteen-dollar wholesale DVD price, Netflix learned to be judicious in how it drove interest and in which films it featured on the Web site. Instead of featuring the latest or most popular DVD releases, movie promotions centered on lists of older films inspired by holidays, popular actors, or news events.

To generate more rentals of the older and obscure movies that made up the bulk of their early inventory, they implemented a movie ratings system that grouped customers together in "mentor groups," which were designed to direct customers to films they might never have considered. It was known as collaborative filtering and worked on the premise that, if two customers rated ten films the same way, they would likely enjoy other films that each rated highly.

Netflix's focus on niche and foreign films sharpened with Lowe's discovery that many of the service's early customers were Indian students and immigrant technologists whose selection of Bollywood films was limited to what they could find at local Indian markets. At Lowe's request, the Web site began surveying customers, and it found a deep interest in Hindi films. It was a good lesson, and soon Netflix became known in other immigrant communities, as well as among cinephiles, as the best source for Japanese anime and Chinese martial arts movies. The inventory initially included soft-core pornography but nothing with an X rating—not because of any moral objection, but because Randolph wanted to wait until federal trade laws clarified the patchwork of the states' obscenity laws.

"The last thing we want is to be dragged into court on some obscenity charge just because some small-town DA is behind in the polls," he said.

By July, the operation had outgrown the Scotts Valley office, and Randolph was looking for a bigger space. Bridges's newsgroup influencers still drove most of the Web site traffic, but he and Smith had begun thinking about new ways to use their meager advertising budget to get mainstream customers in the door.

Smith initiated an affiliates program after the launch, copied from Amazon, to pay newsgroup tastemakers who sent followers to Netflix. She and Bridges persuaded Randolph to spend money on a few critical Web sites, such as Harry Knowles's aintitcool.com (which evolved from Knowles's newsgroup postings) and Bill Hunt's digitalbits.com, in exchange for regular mentions by Knowles and Hunt to their young, hard-core movie fans.

It was tough at first to find effective ways to reach people who both owned DVD players and shopped online. Randolph mused that out of a thousand banner ads, perhaps one would reach a target consumer. Besides, Hastings often disparaged start-ups that waged expensive advertising campaigns before they had anything to sell.

Online commerce still accounted for less than 1 percent of U.S. retail sales at the time, and Randolph knew he had to use conventional tactics to find more mainstream customers. Before the launch, Randolph, Smith, and Kish designed a plan to place coupons into DVD player boxes, and went out to sell it to the mainly Japan-based electronics manufacturers.

Randolph persuaded Kirby Kish, then working for a company that made microprocessors for DVD players, to tap his U.S.-based contacts at DVD manufacturers.

In January 1998, Kirby approached representatives for Sony, Toshiba, Pioneer, Panasonic, and Philips at the Consumer Electronics Show—the premiere U.S. hardware show—in Las Vegas, cornering them in corridors and speed talking through five-minute pitch meetings.

Without a Web site, or even screen shots, to illustrate Netflix's novel rental plan, Kish ran into a wall of skepticism. The manufacturers' representatives did not shut him down immediately, but their dismissal of Netflix's business model was disheartening. "Why do you think you can compete with Blockbuster?" one rep asked him. "I don't understand that concept—this is not how people get VHS tapes," another said, waving him away.

Finally, Kish persuaded his Toshiba contact to meet with Randolph at Toshiba's New Jersey offices. Randolph convinced the corporation's U.S. representatives that the proposition would offer Toshiba a leg up on market leader Sony, which would not even take his calls. The Toshiba deal later opened doors to Hewlett-Packard and Apple, whose new Internet-ready HP Pavilion and Apple PowerBook featured DVD-ROM drives. Months later, Sony agreed to a meeting when those deals became public.

Manufacturers quickly discovered that Netflix offered a way out of a dilemma that was holding down sales: Consumers did not want to buy DVD players because DVDs were not widely available at stores. Retailers did not want to stock DVDs because no one had DVD players.

By including a Netflix coupon in the box a DVD player manufacturer could promise consumers access to a library of more than one thousand titles.

It took most of their first year to get the coupons in the coveted bill of materials (BOM), but by the end of 1998 customers were beginning to claim the free rentals that came with their DVD players.

Lowe, who had taken over the negotiations with electronics manufacturers, now leveraged his entertainment industry contacts on Netflix's behalf. He persuaded David Bishop, president of a newly formed nonprofit home entertainment lobbying organization called the Digital Entertainment Group, to mention Netflix in a speech to the media and the industry in Las Vegas in June 1998.

The brief mention—about how Netflix was promoting DVDs—was enough to stir interest in the convention hall. A stream of industry executives stopped and talked to Lowe about his new start-up. Little by little, Lowe built Netflix up as a player in the new digital entertainment ecosystem.

Lowe extracted a joint promotion from Warner, whose home entertainment chief Warren Lieberfarb was later billed as the father of the DVD, for the release of Warner's *LA Confidential* and *Boogie Nights* titles, as well as twenty-five thousand dollars for a full-page ad in the *San Francisco Chronicle.*

Lieberfarb meant to undercut video rental and shift home entertainment revenue back to the studios by retailing movies in the new digital format for as little as twenty-five dollars. He had backed the DVD aggressively, making Warner the first to release new movies in the new format; and ending the studio's use of the VHS format in 2000.

Despite Lieberfarb's strong-arm tactics, to force the adoption of a universal DVD standard, he initially had difficulty getting industry players to endorse the format over a competing technology: DIVX was backed by Circuit City and an entertainment law firm representing rival movie studios. Ironically, Lieberfarb had to beat back DIVX by providing movie rental companies, including Netflix, with promotional kits that included DVD players and free rentals to acquaint consumers with DVD technology.

For four dollars, customers could watch DIVX disks for forty-eight hours after activating them in compatible players. The disks then became unplayable unless the buyer paid an additional fee for more time. The player had to be connected to a modem to verify that the heavily encrypted disks were playable.

Circuit City had backed the format with a $100 million investment that included "market development funds" paid to studios and retailers. DIVX was set for a mid-September 1998 launch.

Although Randolph considered Warner Home Video a major supporter, he was at first determined to be agnostic in the DVD versus DIVX format war.

Corey Bridges in particular argued strenuously against carrying DIVX, especially in light of Netflix's budget strains. He placed the format high on a list of offensive consumer products. "You pay for it, but it's not yours," he complained.

Bridges was convinced that Netflix could not survive a format war, and he conceived his own "dark ops" plan to kill DIVX.

He had created an extensive roster of aliases, or "sock puppets," that he used to make newsgroup postings, sometimes to prod discussions toward a certain topic or opinion. He now turned to these sock puppets, planted like spies inside a foreign government, to conduct highly choreographed arguments designed to discredit and vilify DIVX and to draw real consumers into the fray. To Bridges's delight, consumer sentiment soon turned against the closed system.

Randolph didn't exactly encourage him, but didn't stop him either, and even suggested with winks and sidelong looks that his "people" carry other messages to the online forums.

By late 1998, Randolph had changed course and bet Netflix's future on the success of DVD, mainly because the cost of stocking both formats was too great.

Since Hastings's initial investment, he and Randolph had tapped Hastings's contacts in the venture capital community to secure operating funds from a couple of angel investors. In August, Netflix scored a $6 million investment from Institutional Venture Partners, but those funds were barely enough to carry the company through the end of 1998.

Netflix was losing money on every transaction, mainly because of the high cost of both the free-rental coupon program and the labor-intensive mailing operation. And Randolph had picked up a troubling trend in the constant market research he and Kish conducted via the Web site: Most customers were not returning to rent at Netflix after exhausting their free rentals.

Their strongest revenue growth came from the sales of DVDs—a business that was doomed as soon as bigger retailers like Amazon or Walmart started carrying the format. He and Kish tested initiatives, one after another, aimed at customer retention—buy a punch card, buy ten rentals at once, two-week rentals, ninety-nine-cents-per-day rentals—but nothing worked.

One evening, as Randolph stood looking out a window at the Scotts Valley office into the parking lot, the responsibility of running a company upon which so many car payments and mortgages and lives were depending nearly overwhelmed him.

The Internet Recording Media Association forecast eight hundred thousand DVD player sales in North America in 1998, with first-adopters buying fifteen to twenty DVD titles, and an installed base of 8.6 million players by 2002. *Why couldn't Netflix find a viable business model?* he wondered.

Randolph later recalled in a letter to protégé Matt Mireles, who went on to found and become chief executive of SpeakerText, that Randolph "pissed blood for years keeping Netflix alive while we figured that shit out—as did every successful entrepreneur in the valley."

A few self-inflicted wounds that autumn added to a sense that they might be in over their heads in trying to ride an unproven technology into an unexplored world of online commerce.

In September, Lowe and Randolph decided to burn DVD copies of President Clinton's grand jury testimony in the Monica Lewinsky matter and sell them on Netflix. When the DVD duplication house got backed up with other orders, Lowe agreed to forgo DVD labels to speed up delivery of the already sold disks.

Netflix took more than a thousand orders for the Clinton DVD—spurred by news stories about the offer in the *Washington Post* and *New York Times*. Randolph and Lowe counted the promotion a big success until a few days later, when they learned that, due to a mix-up at the dub house, a few hundred customers received DVDs containing hard-core Chinese pornography instead of the Clinton testimony.

Another rookie mistake cost them more than a little embarrassment: Netflix had not assigned unique numbers for each DVD player coupon, to prevent fraud and duplication when setting up the fast-growing program, because the company's databases could not handle a matrix so large.

They expected a small amount of theft of free rentals, but a review of the shipping database—after vault workers realized that they were shipping dozens of free DVDs to one particular address—revealed that some customers had used the codes over and over. There was no telling how much the coupon fraud had cost in shipping fees, but there wasn't much they could do to stop it without penalizing honest customers.

Around the same time, Hastings began showing up at the Scotts Valley offices more often; he admitted that he had become disenchanted with classmates who seemed more interested in the pay bump that came with a graduate degree than in solving major problems in education.

Plus, Hastings's forays into political activism were becoming much more interesting. He helped organize the Palo Alto–based Technology Network lobby group, and became its first president. TechNet had a short agenda: to limit shareholder lawsuits against tech companies over stock volatility; to expand foreign visa quotas for high-tech workers; and to institute education reforms to improve students' math and science aptitude.

Hastings also helped write a California ballot initiative expanding the number of charter schools in the state, and threw the weight of TechNet behind it. The move infuriated the powerful California Teachers Association. However, the threat of an initiative backed by the money and political might of Silicon Valley broke a years-long deadlock over charter schools and spurred a compromise plan that passed the California legislature in late April, a couple of weeks after Netflix launched.

Under Hastings's leadership, TechNet endorsed and raised millions of dollars for high-profile Democrats, including the embattled President Bill Clinton. By late 1998 Hastings could claim concrete victories for TechNet's agenda, including congressional legislation addressing both the securities litigation and visa issues, but it had come at a price. Conservatives in the fledgling organization were furious at the overtly political agenda—tilted toward liberals—that Hastings had brought to the group.

As some at TechNet agitated for his ouster, Hastings took a renewed interest in Netflix, which by then was attracting almost as much press as he had received at TechNet. He announced his resignation from TechNet in January 1999, saying his new start-up was claiming too much of his attention,

The start-up Hastings joined in Scotts Valley had the atmosphere of a laboratory of mad scientists—a creative, unstructured workspace still furnished with worktables. There were no set hours or meetings with agendas—staff members showed up when they needed to be there and stayed as long as it took to finish a project. Meetings were called by consensus—usually an hour or two beforehand. Everyone had an opinion about every project underway, because they could all hear and see what everyone else was working on.

Randolph had worked with all his senior managers before and trusted them to find their own ways to reach a collective goal. Rather than acting as an overlord ordering around submissive subordinates, he preferred to set the company's direction and tone and occasionally step in to align the disparate departments.

It was an extremely creative time, he believed, because communication among the staff and management was so unhindered. Randolph thought his chemistry with Hastings was energizing—they represented the yin and yang of the cerebral and the intuitive. The freewheeling and sometimes volatile discussions that accompanied many staff meetings were invigorating and vital to proving the best ideas.

For Hastings, the strife was unnecessary and irritating. He was not one to lose control of his feelings but nevertheless clearly disliked being opposed. In the coming years, those who disagreed with him too often would find their personal capital dwindling and themselves marginalized at Netflix.

Shortly after Hastings arrived, he announced without preamble at an executive staff meeting that he wanted to run Netflix, and that he and Randolph would act as co–chief executives. From the wan look on Randolph's face it seemed clear to some in the room that Hastings either had not discussed the idea with him or had sprung it on Randolph shortly before the meeting.

Hastings then turned to Lisa Battaglia Reiss, the human resources manager that Randolph had recently hired from Borland, and laid her off in front of her shocked coworkers, saying he wanted to bring in Patty McCord, his longtime personnel manager from Pure Atria. McCord managed to smooth over his worst gaffes at Pure Atria, and people who knew Hastings well believed that she acted as an emotional sense organ to prevent him from alienating staff—mainly nonengineers—who did not respond well to his blunt observations and pointed criticism.

Hastings would often say in interviews years later that he had had the good fortune to remedy at Netflix the mistakes he made as a young CEO at Pure Atria. Those lessons included ruthlessly weeding out bureaucratic habits that slowed agility and focusing on one or two core competencies, but it apparently did not extend to treating his employees with more care.

And yet, Hasting was never mean-spirited. His constancy in demanding the best from his employees, and in acting in the company's interests, won him their admiration and loyalty. It was simply as if everything, including human relationships, broke down to a mathematical equation. Hastings kept an employee who challenged or irritated him only as long as the cost to the company of eliminating that person was too great.

In contrast to the amiable Randolph, who disliked having to take his managers to task for missing budget targets and project deadlines— let alone firing longtime colleagues—Hastings seemed to lack an empathy gene.

His new colleagues at Netflix observed that, along with his brilliance and much needed decisiveness, Hastings brought an uncomfortable level of process and formality that began to wither the little company's spontaneous creativity and cheerful disorder.

Chris Darner, a New York University film school graduate hired by Randolph as a product manager, was struck by the difference in tone and approach to customers once the "left brain" engineering mind-set began to dominate at Netflix.

"It went from being a futuristic utopia, where there were people who played flutes on the hill because the people had decided it was important to play flutes on the hill, and [we'd say], 'Reed, wouldn't it be great to have some flutes on the hill, and some unicorns?'" Darner later recalled. "And Reed would say, 'Let's just put a speaker up there and a cutout of a unicorn.' In his mind it's the same as having the real thing."

To the growing contingent of software engineers, however, Hastings was a rock star, a boss with the charisma to gather the smartest people he could find and set them into a productive competition with each other. Rather than the creative family Randolph had gathered around him, Hastings likened the company to a professional sports team, in which players won time on the field on merit alone. Some found the analogy inspiring—others, suffocating.

The "two in a box" co-CEO concept called for Hastings to take over the company's engineering work—the Web site and the back-end infrastructure and fulfillment mechanisms. Randolph would oversee the Web site design, customer service, and content acquisition.

Ceding control of Netflix was difficult for Randolph at first. While the founding team grumbled that Hastings had pushed out Netflix's rightful leader, Randolph tried to be philosophical about the arrangement. He had what it took to conceive and launch Netflix. What came next—ruthless optimization and relentless growth—were not his strong suits.

Netflix badly needed a large cash infusion and some hard decisions made about its direction, and Hastings could handle both tasks better.

Although the venture capital community poured a then record $5.4 billion into Silicon Valley start-ups in 1998, and interest in dot-coms was still climbing, investors were becoming wary of companies with no clear path to solvency and profit.

Nevertheless, when Hastings started making the rounds of the venture capital community he found checkbooks opening for him based on his success with Pure Atria. He also considered opportunities to sell

Netflix but found no offer large enough to return the capital that he and others had already invested.

They had to solve their retention problems fast and get out of DVD sales before high-volume retailers got in and crushed them. Hastings made it clear to Netflix's executive team that they were pulling out of DVD sales even though it was providing the company's only profit. They were on notice that they had to find a way to make rental work, or the company would go down.

Randolph and Hastings flew to Seattle and met with Amazon founder Jeff Bezos, who had indicated that he wanted to explore a partnership with Netflix. The two CEOs were willing to trade their DVD sell-through business for a crack at pitching online DVD rental to Amazon's customers. Hastings also wanted to discuss selling Netflix to Amazon, if the price was right.

While Randolph and Bezos hit it off immediately, trading launch-day stories, Hastings was less than impressed with Amazon's $12 million offer. Instead, they agreed to a cross promotion—Netflix would direct customers who wanted to buy DVDs to Amazon in exchange for placement of Netflix ads on Amazon's Web site and a royalty for each recommendation.

The arrangement went down hard at Netflix, where some team members felt Hastings had acted prematurely in ceding DVD sales to Bezos. Kish, charged with customer retention, objected vociferously to the plan. The idea of sending customers to a competitor's Web site undermined everything she was trying to accomplish, and violated every tenet of marketing.

After announcing the Amazon deal in November, Randolph made the same offer to Mark Wattles, founder and president of Hollywood Video. The two men met in a coffee shop during a trade show in Las Vegas to discuss a collaboration. When Wattles asked about buying Netflix, Randolph replied, "I'm not sure you want to spend what we think we're worth."

A few days later, Hollywood Video announced it had purchased

Reel.com, the online arm of a Berkeley, California–based video rental store owned by Stuart Skorman.

Reel.com had a library of eighty-five thousand VHS titles and Web traffic of about twenty thousand users per month when Hollywood Entertainment bought it for $100 million. Skorman considered online rental "a messy little business," and not a very profitable one, but it was essential for habituating consumers to ordering entertainment online. Skorman was not just thinking of VHS or DVD but video on demand, a movie rental option that cable companies were starting to offer. Like Hastings and Randolph, Skorman had an inkling that one day consumers would shop for entertainment primarily online, and the portal they chose now would have a big advantage.

As a result of the acquisition, Reel.com had access to Hollywood Video's twenty-five million customers, and also directed its own online visitors to its new parent's one thousand U.S. stores—making it a formidable rival to Netflix. Reel.com's traffic jumped to two hundred thousand per month after the deal became public on July 31, 1998.

Lowe and Hastings met with Wattles shortly after the merger to explore a cross promotion involving online DVD rental. They explained that a hookup with Netflix would allow Hollywood Video to avoid the costs and risks of converting its stores' inventory to the new DVD format. The stores could slowly build DVD inventory as the format caught on, focusing on the new releases that made up most of their business. In the meantime, Netflix would fulfill requests for titles from the back catalog by mail.

Wattles turned them down flat, insisting that he could build a DVD rental service using Reel.com. Meetings with Viacom-owned Blockbuster went nowhere—the giant renter's executives pointed out that VCRs were still selling at a clip of thirteen million a year.

To Lowe, who had arranged the meetings with Blockbuster and Hollywood Video, the rejections underscored a growing sense that there would be no easy way out—no white knight to ride to Netflix's rescue. They were truly on their own in solving the company's money and customer retention troubles.

The Christmas season held equal parts joy and anxiety; DVD player prices dropped below two hundred dollars a unit, as the year wound to a close, and became the fastest-selling electronic product in history. Tucked inside millions of DVD player boxes were coupons for free Netflix rentals that waited like tiny incendiary devices to burn through the company's dwindling cash and leave it in ashes—unless they could find a way to start making money.

CHAPTER THREE

THE GOLD RUSH

(1999–2000)

ALTHOUGH HE MAY HAVE HAD problems connecting with some of his new employees, Hastings had big fans among the investor community, and that is where he turned for help in early 1999. Netflix had posted an $11 million loss in 1998—not unexpected or particularly large for a start-up. But the rate at which the company was burning through funds was both impressive and alarming.

Netflix had exacerbated its cash-flow problems with the decision to punt DVD sales to Amazon. It needed money—and a lot of it—to make good on the free-rental coupons that started flowing in from Christmas DVD player sales. The most urgent needs were to build DVD inventory and to hire new programmers to keep up with the Web site's exponentially growing traffic.

By January 1999, 1.1 million DVD players had been sold, and sales stayed on track to reach 4 million by year's end. The costs of building Netflix's DVD library, now grown to three thousand titles, rose along with the adoption rate.

Randolph started designing and scheduling tests of new features and business models in hopes of showing would-be investors some progress in solving the retention issue.

Randolph and Meyer had designed the Web site to double as a market research platform that could display multiple versions of a page or feature to test groups of customers and gather detailed data on their reactions and preferences.

A typical A-B test involved measuring the effect of a red logo (choice A) versus a blue logo (choice B) on acquiring a customer, and their lifetime value, retention rate, and usage. Randolph particularly loved building market tests with the Web site engineers, and he insisted that the tests be conducted meticulously, with one variable at a time, to avoid confusing the results.

The constant testing, gathering of consumer input, and subsequent adjustments to the site formed an ongoing conversation between Netflix and its customers that would provide a crucial advantage in the coming battle with store-based renters. While Hastings pushed for metrics alongside Randolph and the marketing team, the answers were frustratingly slow in coming, and he became impatient.

Randolph and Kish knew from relentless focus groups and A-B testing on the Web site that customers enjoyed their visits to Netflix and understood how to use the site. But their main customers—the coupon-wielding buyers of DVD players—often would not plunk down their plastic and actually pay for rentals when their free disks ran out. There seemed to be no solution for failing to convert the free offers to sales, and it consumed them.

As Netflix's first birthday loomed, the marketing team tested new software that allowed them to personalize e-mails to consumers to prod them to return to the site, sending reviews for movies they had just rented or suggesting films they might like, based on past rentals.

The prevailing Internet industry belief was that content-rich sites attracted repeat business, so Randolph hired popular film critic and historian Leonard Maltin of NBC's *Entertainment Tonight* to write a monthly online column exclusively for Netflix about new DVD releases. The company signed deals to cross promote with Sam Goody/ Musicland stores and Best Buy.

HASTINGS AND RANDOLPH again made the rounds of venture capital funds that by early 1999, as the economy cooled, had started pulling back on their record-setting pace of investment in dot-com start-ups. In contrast to similar meetings a year earlier, in which Hastings made introductions and sat back as Randolph presented, Hastings now took over pitching Netflix.

Randolph noticed the eager interest with which the VCs received Hastings, no doubt recalling the spectacular return he generated for them two years earlier with Pure Atria's record-setting merger. Randolph knew he had less stature, as an unproven chief executive, in Silicon Valley's "bet the jockey, not the horse" culture, and he was grateful for Hastings's influence.

He was losing control of Netflix by inches, and sitting in the investors' offices that spring, he knew there was little he could do to stop it. The co-CEO experiment had ended with Randolph demoted to president in late 1998, and then to executive producer the following year, ostensibly to foster investor confidence that a proven CEO was at the helm.

Hastings became chairman, chief executive, and president, and after resigning as TechNet's president, took over as the public face of Netflix. They had argued about whether Randolph should sit on the newly formed board of directors. Hastings had wanted the seat for an investor, but Randolph had insisted on keeping it for himself.

The founding team Randolph had assembled was slowly drifting away, demoralized or picked off by Hastings and McCord to be replaced by staff members chosen by and loyal to Hastings. By mid-1999, the company's head count had been pushed past one hundred, and—with McCord having trouble convincing programmers to drive over the hill to work in Scotts Valley—Netflix went looking for bigger digs closer to the heart of Silicon Valley.

In a final capitulation, Randolph gave up his dream of working almost within walking distance of his home and moved the operation into a nondescript, low-slung building on University Avenue in Los Gatos, the southernmost town in Silicon Valley.

The other members of the founding team saw Randolph being pushed aside with mixed feelings. They had poured their energy and creativity into Netflix at a fraction of their usual salaries for two years to bring their dream company to life, and they wanted to see it succeed. Founders often had to step aside to let corporate "grown-ups" raise their babies—that was just how Silicon Valley worked. And Randolph seemed to take it with equanimity, plunging ahead with plans for a full roster of consumer tests and battling unreserved by Hastings, as he always had in staff meetings.

IN EARLY 1999, French luxury goods tycoon Bernard Arnault approached Technology Crossover Ventures cofounder Jay Hoag for advice about investing in dot-com companies. Hoag, a former fund manager whose earliest investments as a venture capitalist included Pure Software, pointed out Hastings's latest enterprise and scheduled a pitch meeting at his office for Arnault with Hastings and Randolph. Arnault's holding company committed $30 million to Netflix in July, becoming its largest investor just as the company was about to run out of money. Hastings raised more than $100 million from venture capital and angel investors over the following eighteen months, including Hoag's TCV, Foundation Capital, and Redpoint Ventures—a feat that Randolph, though a proven entrepreneur, admittedly could never have matched.

Hastings now held Netflix's reins firmly in hand, and the VC money gave him the power to begin shifting the company's culture away from Randolph's family of creators toward a top-down organization led by executives with proven corporate records and, preferably, strong engineering and mathematics backgrounds.

With McCord in place to recruit and purge, Hastings proceeded to transform Netflix's executive staff as soon as the Group Arnault deal closed. The founding team soon learned that those leadership positions were not open to them.

Jim Cook, who had asked for a shot at becoming Netflix's first chief financial officer, left after Hastings asked him to continue instead as VP of operations. Smith soon followed, and Bridges too wanted an escape from what he considered the "lather, rinse, repeat" routine that took hold. Kish, exhausted from two years of sixteen-to-twenty-hour days, and demoralized at the direction the company was taking, went on an extended sick leave to combat a chronic health problem and never came back full time.

Hastings hired forty-five-year-old W. Barry McCarthy, Jr., an ex–investment banker and chief financial officer for the cable and satellite music-programming service Music Choice, as Netflix's CFO, on April 19, 1999. McCarthy, who lived in Princeton, New Jersey, had first heard of Netflix and Hastings when he got a call during a ski vacation from a headhunter. He was impressed enough with Hastings's credentials and the freedom promised him that he accepted the offer a week later, for the relatively anemic annual salary of $170,000 and the prospect of a $20,000 bonus, if he did a good job.

McCarthy was smart and tough and made a practice of not tolerating stupid mistakes—his own or anyone else's. He had a volcanic temper that could erupt suddenly from his normally controlled resting state, making his profanity-laced outbursts doubly alarming when they came. He proved a perfect foil for the icy Hastings, who seemed to respect McCarthy's shrewdness in market matters and his ability to say no and mean it.

As ambitious as he was, McCarthy retained an old-style loyalty and sense of corporate hierarchy that dictated a respect for Hastings and Randolph, whom he addressed as "Mr. Founder," as well as strict ideas about running his company transparently and for the long term.

McCord unwittingly recruited Tom Dillon, a former colleague from Seagate Technologies, to run the fulfillment operations in Cook's place at around the same time. Dillon was chief information officer at flat-panel display maker Candescent Technologies when McCord called to ask him to recommend someone to remake Netflix's operations. He faxed in his own résumé that day.

Dillon connected with Hastings immediately. He was a self-taught programmer with a long career in warehouse management, and often hacked the operating systems of his warehouse machines to customize them. He liked that Hastings used a mathematician's approach to solving business problems in the most logical manner possible, and possessed an engineer's loathing of personal drama. Dillon was tall and burly and had snow-white hair, as well as a gruff demeanor that masked a mischievous sense of humor.

Randolph and Hastings initially hesitated in hiring him, worried about both the small salary and that Dillon, who had run international operations for Seagate, would not be hands-on enough in the Netflix vault warehouse, which lacked automation and had a tiny staff.

Dillon, then fifty-five, assured them he wanted to be around smart people who were doing something fun and interesting, and Netflix looked like the perfect opportunity. He signed a contract at a third of his normal pay rate as a show of good faith, and officially was hired the same day as McCarthy.

Before he started, Dillon called an old Seagate colleague who had been running Netflix's distribution on a contract basis. "It's not going to make it," the guy told Dillon. "They're shipping two thousand movies a day, and they have to ship one hundred thousand a day to break even. That's not going to happen."

Well, it may crash and burn, but you never know, Dillon thought.

One of the worst drags on Netflix's bottom line was the way the company assembled and shipped orders, a process that cost six dollars per order in labor, transportation, and postage costs. Dillon's first task was to cut that to below the two dollars they were actually charging for shipping.

Although most customers ordered three disks at a time, gathering and shipping each order in a single mailer proved so time-consuming that Dillon's analysis showed it was cheaper to ship each disk separately, as it became available, instead of waiting to accumulate complete orders.

Dillon improved on Cook and Meyer's software program, which assigned each order to a numbered mailbag based on its extended zip code in order to speed up the distribution of orders without costly automated postal sorters. The warehouse staff, then numbering about twenty, used a handheld supermarket scanner to read a bar code on the order form and then dropped the mailers into the correct bag. The system was rudimentary, but it soon cut total delivery costs below the two dollars per disk that Dillon had targeted.

Although Netflix continued collecting detailed information on customer behavior, a flawed analysis of that data nearly caused operations to miss a critical link between delivery times and customer acquisition rates. Randolph had assumed that overnight delivery would boost customer retention, but test after test showed no link between the two.

Since fast delivery seemed not to matter, Dillon designed a distribution system based on a single, giant, fully automated hub in San Jose. But before he locked down the lease on the extra-large space, the marketing team discovered an undeniable correlation between one-day delivery in the San Francisco Bay Area and the rate of new customers signing up. One-day delivery seemed like magic, and people started telling their friends about it. To test the one-day theory in a new market, they created a "hub" in Sacramento, in 2000 by driving the mailers there and back each day from the San Jose distribution center, and the sign-up rate bounced up dramatically.

The discovery fundamentally changed Netflix's distribution and marketing plans. The costs of attracting new customers came down as people in the overnight delivery zones recommended the service to their friends; Dillon had to rethink his distribution system.

Dillon used data he hacked from a post office compact disk that contained delivery data for all U.S. zip codes and designed a software program that pinpointed the best locations for Netflix distribution centers. The program plugged in customer addresses and arranged them all within the overnight delivery radius of the closest post office. Then Dillon sited the distribution center as close as possible to the post office's Area Distribution Centers, where each zip code's mail was sorted and sent out.

Dillon calculated that it took at least fifteen thousand Netflix customers to support a single distribution center. He developed a "satellite hub" system to achieve faster delivery outside the one-day delivery zones in which trucks delivered outbound DVDs from distribution centers to remote post offices that hand carried them to customers' homes the next day.

The beauty of Dillon's program was that it continually evaluated and adjusted the optimum locations for distribution centers as Netflix's customer base grew and changed. The program meticulously tracked postal carriers' daily rounds by asking customers to disclose when they mailed and received Netflix mailers, leading to a close collaboration between Netflix and the postal service. Dillon first shared his data with postal inspectors in hopes of improving delivery times and tracking occasional bubbles of DVD theft. The relationship later extended to helping postal inspectors nab mail thieves intent on skimming gift cards and checks. As efficient as the distribution system was, the intensive programming demands that attended its rapid growth led to the occasional glitch: Dillon once accidentally ordered the system to deliver every disk in customers' queues simultaneously. Some delighted subscribers received as many as three hundred disks in a space of a few days.

Dillon also engineered Netflix's abrupt exit from soft-core pornography after Hastings delivered the news at an executive staff meeting in early 2000 that he was about to be appointed to the California Board of Education. Hastings believed that distributing adult films could be a political liability. Either the porn had to go, Hastings told Dillon, or he could not take the board seat. Dillon and the engineers worked the rest of that day and through the night delisting each objectionable movie from customers' movie lists and from the inventory.

IN JULY 1999, Randolph's marketing team scheduled tests of new concepts designed to capture customers for several "rental turns," to try and instill in them the habit of online rental. These included a concept for a subscription program they dubbed the Home Rental Library and another they called Serialized Delivery, which allowed customers to have movies sent to them automatically, as soon as they returned a previous rental and the company billed their credit cards.

As originally conceived, Home Rental Library let customers rent up to six movies at a time for twenty dollars a month and keep them as long as they wanted without late fees. As soon as they returned all of the movies, they could get six more disks.

Serialized Delivery featured à la carte prices but gave each customer an account on the Netflix site, where they could store a list of desired DVDs. Rather than asking customers to simply designate a few extra titles at each rental turn, they decided to build the sortable, searchable list of desired films that Kish and Meyer had envisioned before launched. This third feature that Randolph tested that summer as part of Serialized Delivery became known as the Queue.

Although Randolph and Kish wanted to test the three features separately, Hastings insisted that they be evaluated at the same time. The serendipity of having these three particular concepts—Home Rental Library, Serialized Delivery, and the Queue—lined up together for testing literally saved Netflix.

Focus groups conducted that summer showed that consumers loved each program so much—all-you-can rent subscription with no due dates or late fees from Home Rental Library, the Queue, and the no-hassle exchange of DVDs from Serialized Delivery—that Randolph combined them as one offering.

One August evening, about a week before he officially joined Netflix as its new market research director, Joel Mier looked in on a focus group in progress at a market-testing facility on Sutter Street in San Francisco as Randolph, McCarthy, and Hastings intently watched consumer interviews from behind a two-way mirror.

Each time a test subject dismissed the combined plan Hastings passed a note into the room instructing the interviewers to lower the price or raise the number of monthly rentals allowed, and to ask again. McCarthy, watching this, dropped his head into his hands as he saw profitability recede farther into the distance.

On September 17, 1999, the combined plan debuted as a test on the Netflix Web site, offering customers the chance to choose and receive four movies for $15.95 per month. Only a fraction of the consumers who visited the Netflix page saw the offer, but the rate of sign-ups, or conversions to the new plan, told Randolph and Hastings they had a winner.

Netflix publicly rolled out the Marquee Plan, as they named the new program, to all customers as an alternative to à la carte rental about a week later. The company ran the two programs side by side, and watched with mounting excitement as Marquee subscribers pushed up the site's volume by 300 percent in just three months, to one hundred thousand disks shipped per week.

Hastings lauded the new program as a "near DVD-on-Demand service" in a news release, and made one of the company's first public knocks against Blockbuster. "Movie renters are fed up with due dates and late fees," Hastings said. "Netflix.com's Marquee program puts the joy back into movie rental. With no due dates, our customers can stock up on rental movies and always keep a few on top of their television, ready for impulse viewing."

BY LATE 1999, entertainment industry analysts were predicting big gains for DVDs, including sales of six million players and twenty-five million movies in the coming year. Movie rental stores still hesitated to carry movies on the eighteen-month-old format, so tiny Netflix, with its pledge to offer a comprehensive selection, seemed best positioned "to revolutionize the DVD rental market that we estimate will grow explosively to over $1 billion by 2002," media analyst Tom Adams told investors.

But the transition to the new digital format, with its tricky logistics and heavy inventory costs, was no sure thing, despite its soaring popularity, as some of Netflix's better-funded rivals soon learned.

Circuit City had pulled the plug on its DIVX format earlier that year, incurring a $200 million loss, and the Reel.com rental operation began foundering beneath heavy overhead costs in early 2000, forcing its parent company, Hollywood Video, to unload it and take a $48.5 million loss. It was a sobering lesson for Netflix, which closed out its 1999 fiscal year with a $29.8 million loss.

The end of the short-lived format war cleared the way for record DVD releases in 2000, as all six major studios finally embraced the surviving format and the wide profits margins it promised. Although the studios still had every intention of undermining the movie rental business with low DVD sales prices, they recognized that Netflix provided the best avenue for customers to test the new format.

The studios' home entertainment divisions had long detested the hard bargains Blockkbuster drove on inventory, especially its famously profane general counsel, Ed Stead, who seemed to make a sport of demanding ever-greater concessions for the huge and powerful chain. Helping Netflix spread awareness of the DVD format through joint promotions represented a small risk for the potentially great reward of shifting home entertainment toward lucrative DVD sales, and it offered the bonus of antagonizing Blockbuster.

Lowe also hoped to press the studios to accept revenue-sharing agreements patterned on deals Blockbuster's new chief executive, John Antioco, had cut to mitigate store inventory costs. Netflix suffered from inventory shortages as the subscription plan grew, caused and exacerbated by the fact that subscribers could keep disks as long as they wanted.

The costs of buying enough DVDs to satisfy the growing subscriber base would eventually crush the company unless Lowe could persuade studios to drop DVD prices drastically in exchange for a share of rental revenues.

In the meantime, Netflix engineers had been hard at work since shortly after launch on a recommendation engine—an in-house solution to DVD shortages that would theoretically drive up retention and get more of the company's catalog into circulation by directing customers away from the most popular films toward more obscure titles that they would like just as much.

As a result, the recommendation engine took over the editorial team's tasks of determining which movies to feature on certain themed Web pages, using machine logic rather than human intuition. The program ran through several criteria when considering which movies to show consumers: How many copies do we have in stock? Which titles have the most advantageous financial terms? Was it a new release?

Eventually they decided the algorithm should choose the films individual customers would like best and display them on personalized pages Randolph had envisioned. They quickly realized that the better Netflix could predict consumer demand, the better they could manage inventory.

Making accurate predictions proved terribly complicated, because the engineers could not at first find a mathematical means to determine why people liked a film by a certain director or actor, but disliked a seemingly similar film with the same cast and crew. Several in-house engineers, including Hastings, attacked the problem from different angles. Eventually Hastings brought in mathematicians to help formulate the underlying algorithms.

They named the recommendation system Cinematch, and launched it in January 2000 with a "Movies for Two" promotion that promised to help couples find common ground in their movie choices. Rather than using their initial approach of assigning traits to each movie and trying to match similar films, Cinematch created customer clusters— people who had rated movies similarly.

Cinematch noted the overlap in certain subscribers' tastes through a five-star ratings system, then presented films highly rated by cluster members to others in the same cluster who had not previously rented or rated them on Netflix.

The recommendation engine scoured Netflix's inventory hourly to take into consideration how many copies of each movie it had before issuing recommendations. A Not Interested rating quickly weeded out anomalies: for example, children's movies a customer rented occasionally for a grandchild, or an anime film requested once for a homework assignment.

Cinematch actually built on an electronic matchmaking concept originated by the ill-fated Reel.com, in which customers could type in a favorite actor or film and get a list of related movies. Reel.com's online catalog of eighty-five thousand VHS movies included, in addition to the movie comparisons: synopses; ratings of sex, violence, and cinematography; a summary of reviews; and links to star and director filmographies. Studio executives heralded it as "a complete electronic video store" that was bound to drive movie sales. Netflix wanted the same role in online DVD rental.

Netflix's board decided in 2000 that the time was ripe for an initial public offering. Hastings and McCarthy hit the road to convince investment banks of the company's viability as a movie-oriented portal for renting DVDs, marketing theatrical releases, and even selling movie tickets. They hoped that stating a broader business strategy for Netflix would persuade investors, now cooling to dot-coms, to overlook an unbroken string of losses and fund an $86 million marketing and subscriber growth plan.

By the time the company filed its prospectus with federal securities regulators in April, Netflix's subscriber base had grown to 120,000, and its San Jose warehouse was shipping eight hundred thousand DVDs per month. Its losses had ballooned from $11.1 million on revenue of $1.4 million in 1998 to $29.8 million on revenue of $5 million in 1999.

To improve Netflix's finances ahead of the IPO, Hastings homed in on the Marquee program as the best bet for a steady revenue stream and eventual profit. He insisted that supporting both subscription and à la carte rental wasted manpower and resources and needlessly confused consumers. He argued strongly for abandoning à la carte rental in a tense meeting in late 1999 or early 2000 with the company's executive and engineering teams. Several members of both teams had serious doubts about whether the sign-up rate for the subscription service could compensate for the loss of the à la carte business. Kish and Randolph feared the change would anger electronics manufacturers, who were still advertising Netflix coupons on their DVD player boxes. Instead of getting the ten free rentals they had advertised, the manufacturers' new customers would have to hand over their credit card numbers to receive a free one-month trial subscription. Randolph hoped consumers and manufacturers would not perceive the change as a bait-and-switch tactic.

"It feels like a big, risky step, and nobody knows if it's going to work," Boris Droutman said later, voicing the concern the dissenters felt.

Hastings brushed aside their objections. To survive, Netflix needed to focus its resources on the model that worked, even if that meant betting the company on incomplete data and a gut feeling.

On Valentine's Day 2000, Netflix dropped à la carte rental, renamed the Marquee program the Unlimited Movie Rental service, and raised the price to $19.95 per month. Customers got a free month of service to test the program, which now included all the movies they could watch in a month, four at a time. Hastings told the financial press he was confident that most would make the monthly financial commitment. "We're really only risking 3 percent of our customer base—so it's worth it," he said, adding, without elaboration, that Netflix expected to offer video downloading when the technology was ready.

THE LAST SENIOR executive team hire Hastings made, in spring 2000, was that of Leslie Kilgore, a former marketing executive for

Procter & Gamble and Amazon. Kilgore, then thirty-three, took over many of Randolph's marketing duties. She brought the same reliance on market research to the job, and in one of her first initiatives, reimagined Netflix's logo and image ahead of its first big advertising campaign.

Kilgore was an attractive and vigorous woman who seemed to pour every ounce of energy and focus into her work, in a manner very similar to Hastings's own. While they shared a social awkwardness and apparent lack of understanding of human emotions, some considered Kilgore to be more brilliant than Hastings.

The favor with which Hastings treated Kilgore set up a rivalry with McCarthy, who correctly saw Kilgore as the competition for the top job at Netflix. Hastings exacerbated the tension by baldly stating at a board meeting, in response to a director's question about succession, and in front of a surprised Randolph and McCarthy, that he considered Kilgore his successor.

Hastings invariably seemed to come down on Kilgore's side when she demanded more money from the company's tight budget for marketing and "business intelligence" programs. He also allowed her to consolidate marketing and public relations functions under her control, creating a fiefdom inside of Netflix that went unchallenged for more than a decade.

Her loyal number two was Jessie Becker, a fellow alumnus of the University of Pennsylvania's Wharton School and Stanford University's business school who unquestioningly carried out Kilgore's dictates, just as McCord carried out Hastings's wishes.

Kilgore's work ethic was legendary, and she expected the same level of sacrifice from every marketing team member. After learning that Blockbuster had created an in-store subscription program, which she considered a frontal attack on Netflix, Kilgore spent several evenings after work personally interviewing shoppers emerging from Blockbuster stores near her Redwood City home to gauge interest in the program.

One marketing team member recalled spending the bulk of a friend's destination wedding in an expensive hotel room completing projections that Kilgore had urgently demanded. Underlings marveled at her terrifying ability to spot minor flaws in multipage spreadsheets from merely glancing at them. More than one of her employees sought counseling for job-induced stress.

Kilgore anticipated an inflow of cash from the IPO and planned a multichannel marketing and advertising campaign designed to cata-pult Netflix beyond the reach of bricks-and-mortar competitors. She drew on her experience as a brand manager at Procter & Gamble to plan a full-scale campaign—online, radio, and television ads, as well as direct mail and retail partnerships—to broaden Netflix's reach beyond early adopters to mainstream middle Americans.

Kilgore realized what valuable advertising real estate she had in the Netflix mailer and set about making it as eye-catching as possible. With the help of an outside advertising agency she redesigned the logo and color scheme and, rather than following her own intuition, can-vassed subscribers and would-be subscribers to determine which branding scheme resonated best. The tests produced a clear winner: an arched, black-and-white rendering of the company name, with a lower-case F to preserve the symmetry, placed on a curtain of cinematic red. The look was reminiscent of the serials of 1930s cinema and, most important for a company with low brand awareness, it screamed for attention from mailboxes, the tops of subscribers' televisions, and coworkers' out-boxes.

NETFLIX WAS READY to launch on the national stage, but the dot-com meltdown that started in spring 2000 stopped the planned adver-tising push in its tracks. Wall Street began to shun companies with an e- prefix or a .com suffix, and Hastings and McCarthy were forced to withdraw the IPO.

In a lucky twist, Netflix's existing investors had topped up its balance sheet with additional capital ahead of the planned IPO; they bought shares in anticipation of a pop in the stock price when the company went public. That cash would sustain operations in Netflix's most difficult year yet, as Hastings and McCarthy sought some path to profitability amid ever-deeper losses and little prospect of new capital. They got a much-needed break on inventory costs toward the year's end, when Lowe's overtures to the studios bore fruit, and Warner Home Video and Columbia TriStar Home Video agreed to the first online DVD revenue-sharing agreements.

The deals cut Netflix's cost of buying DVDs to between three dollars and eight dollars per disk and put two to three times more product in the company's warehouse just as DVD player penetration levels soared to thirteen million U.S. households.

Losses of $57.4 million loomed in 2000, so Hastings and McCarthy decided to approach Blockbuster again to try for an alliance that would give Netflix a ready source of customers and a link to an established rental brand. It was a bit far-fetched, McCarthy thought, but he admired Hastings for having the guts to pitch it to the company they considered their top rival.

Hastings got a call, during a staff retreat in the faux Dutch town of Solvang, that his contact at Blockbuster, Ed Stead, was ready to meet. He boarded a rented private jet that belonged to former game show hostess Vanna White early the next morning, along with McCarthy and Randolph, and flew to Dallas.

The summons was unexpected, and none of them had brought business attire along to the retreat. John Antioco stopped in for a few moments to shake hands with them all at the glass-and-steel Renaissance Tower in downtown Dallas, and made a crack about McCarthy's Hawaiian-style shirt and jeans. McCarthy still retained enough East Coast banking decorum to feel slightly mortified.

Hastings laid out his proposal: Why not turn Netflix into an online arm of Blockbuster? The win-win, as he saw it, was that Blockbuster would be spared the expense of converting its huge VHS inventory to

DVDs and Netflix would get access to Blockbuster's twenty million active store users, and pay a fee for the privilege.

Netflix would concentrate on back catalog and niche films, leaving Blockbuster with the new-release trade that made up about 80 percent of its business. He envisioned putting Netflix promotional materials and a sign-up computer in every Blockbuster store.

Antioco expressed skepticism about the viability of Internet companies and groused that the market had grossly overvalued unproven business models, a sentiment with which McCarthy secretly agreed. They weren't surprised when Stead essentially laughed at Hastings's alternate proposal—that Blockbuster buy Netflix for $50 million.

Talk on the flight back to California was tinged with bravado: Blockbuster was making a mistake that it would soon regret. Antioco was kidding himself if he thought Blockbuster could replicate Netflix's technological innovations. They now had no choice but to kick Blockbuster's ass, Randolph vowed.

CHAPTER FOUR

WAR OF THE WORLDS

(2001-2003)

THE DOT-COM BUST WAS SILICON VALLEY'S version of the Dust Bowl. Young software engineers, paid in now worthless stock options, haunted a wasteland of abandoned office parks, looking fruitlessly for work before many returned to school to become lawyers or accountants. The stock market lost $5 billion in asset value, and many blamed inexperienced, free-spending Internet entrepreneurs and investors' "irrational exuberance" for sinking the economy. The rate at which new Web sites sprang up dropped to a fraction of the growth of the late 1990s' go-go years, as the New Economy mantra of "get big fast and never mind profits" was repudiated.

Hastings now was on a mission to prove to Wall Street that Netflix's survival of the dot-com meltdown was more than a fluke. In interviews in early 2001 he confidently predicted that Netflix would reach five hundred thousand paying subscribers and positive cash flow by the end of 2001. Data gathered by Kilgore's marketing department showed that customer retention was finally headed in the right direction.

The executive team made the rounds of the entertainment and financial media to make other predictions, too: Kilgore and Hastings told *Billboard* in March 2001 that Netflix projected a subscriber base of ten million by 2004, and that a robust catalog of streaming online video would be available to mainstream consumers within ten years. By the time the company reached one million subscribers, Hastings added, independent filmmakers would probably bypass the movie studios and distribute their films online through Netflix. When that happened Americans would already be used to renting online—at Netflix.

What he did not say was that Kilgore's marketing data also showed that Netflix still was not connecting with ordinary Americans—80 percent of its subscribers were still high-earning young males with better than average computer skills, i.e., computer geeks. Before they made another stab at an IPO, Netflix had to broaden its appeal to mainstream consumers.

THE MAIN THING Joel Mier loved about Netflix's Web site was the data it spit out every day telling him who his customers were: where they lived; how many times and when they shopped on his site; which pages they clicked on and for how long; and what they rented.

He had to strike close to home to kill his customers' habit of renting movies at Blockbuster—their homes. Mier and his staff often called new subscribers living within a short radius of Los Gatos to ask how they used the Web site: why they clicked on certain objects; why they signed up on a particular day and not a day or a week earlier.

If the conversation went well, Mier or his researcher would ask, "Hey, could we come over and visit with you, and watch what you're doing?" More often than not the startled subscriber would say yes, and a researcher would drive over with carry-out Starbucks drinks and watch as the subscriber searched for movies on the Netflix Web site. Mier, at an imposing six-feet-five-inches tall, generally assigned home visits to members of his staff, so as not to intimidate his customers.

They learned that Netflix was preaching to the choir, and that that was not bound to change quickly. Their male, educated, and well-heeled subscribers had a lot of opinions about how Netflix should improve its site. Mier mused that their Usenet banter provided a useful running commentary about what had to be fixed before the service could appeal to a less tech-savvy audience.

"If one were to judge Netflix solely on the basis of newsgroup postings, one would come to the conclusion that this is a service not worth spending good money on," a poster named Mark V. from Cincinnati wrote in 2001.

> My personal experience with them during the past 10 months has been mostly positive, however, especially now that they have improved their turnaround time on returns. I believe true movie buffs would be quite satisfied with their service.

Another poster had canceled his subscription after all thirty-five movies in his Queue had been listed as unavailable.

> Among them was Titus which had been sitting in my cue [sic] for 3 months. This is completely ludicrous and indefensible. If I see from this group that Netflix has picked itself up out of the slag heap I will return but not until.

The target Mier was aiming for was small but growing quickly. By 2001, about 60 percent of U.S. households—mainly upper and middle-income earners—had a home computer, and a slightly smaller number had Internet access, U.S. Census data showed.

Many U.S. Internet households confined their Web surfing to the curated universe of America Online, even though the revolutionary search engine Google.com, launched the same year as Netflix, was already available in twenty-six languages. On the e-commerce front, Amazon was still not profitable, and Apple's online music store, iTunes, and its revolutionary portable music player, the iPod, were still closely guarded secrets. No one had ever heard of Facebook, because the social network's founder, Mark Zuckerberg, was still in high school.

The mainstream customers that Netflix needed were still renting at Blockbuster, Hollywood Video, and Movie Gallery, so Hastings and Kilgore decided to take the battle to their rivals' turfs. The idea wasn't so much to get the bricks-and-mortar chains' attentions as to define Netflix by contrasting it with better-known opponents.

A true contest with Blockbuster, which had fifty million registered users (twenty million of them active) to Netflix's three hundred thousand, seemed ludicrous, but it was a great storyline—if only Hastings could get the rental giant to simply acknowledge a potential threat from online rental, thereby legitimizing the business in the minds of consumers, investors, and the media.

Throughout the spring and summer Hastings and other executive team members took swipes at Blockbuster in interviews and advertising.

"There are ten thousand movies on DVD, and we stock them all. That's more than ten times the selection of the largest Blockbuster," Hastings told *USA Today* in June 2001. "Everybody hates late fees. We never have late fees."

The contrast between the old-world giant and the agile young comer was irresistible to the media, and soon a David-and-Goliath tale emerged that Blockbuster could not ignore.

BLOCKBUSTER'S JOHN ANTIOCO may have looked a bit like ancient coin portraits of Augustus Caesar—deep-set eyes, a receding wreath of hair, and an aquiline nose—but he had an uncanny feel for what regular people wanted and liked. Antioco had an almost languid demeanor that could be misread as inattentive, until he pulled one of his startling, bet-the-ranch moves. He was a gifted storyteller and a good listener, the latter a quality that won him tremendous loyalty from his employees and the customer bases of several major U.S. corporations that he had turned around by the time he landed at Blockbuster at age forty-six.

Antioco was a people person, and he knew how to play favorites in a way that made employees want to work harder for him. He rewarded big wins with big prizes—African safaris, cash bonuses, and promotions.

His first job out of college required him to turn delinquent or underperforming 7-Eleven franchisees in New York City out of their stores—sometimes risking bodily peril from angry store owners—and return them to profitability for the parent company, Southland.

He discovered a knack for reading his customers—for putting thought into improving their shopping experience and finding the right mix of products for the stores in each neighborhood. In two decades he rose to vice president of marketing at Southland. He left in 1990 to find his own company to run.

Antioco developed a reputation as a reliable turnaround specialist while hopscotching among a roster of America's best-known brands. He brought the Circle K convenience store chain out of bankruptcy and took it public, did a stint at the Pearle Vision eyewear chain, and rescued PepsiCo's Taco Bell fast-food chain from cost cuts that went too deep. He was waiting to hear whether he or David Novak, head of KFC and Pizza Hut, would run the restaurant division that PepsiCo planned to spin off as Yum! Brands when Viacom chairman Sumner Redstone came calling in 1997.

Redstone had bought Blockbuster three years earlier primarily for the $1.25 billion in cash reserves on its balance sheet and its large, steady cash flow, which he used to offset the $10 billion he paid for Paramount Communications in a highly leveraged deal.

At the time, Blockbuster was near the end of a growth spurt fueled by its rapid acquisitions of smaller, regional video-rental chains. In those glory days of its near monopoly Blockbuster also had made ill-advised and expensive forays into music sales and an "entertainment convenience store" concept called Blockbuster Block Party that featured restaurants, rides, and games.

The competitive threat posed by DVDs and video on demand prompted Blockbuster's then chief executive, Bill Fields, to try to diversify his stores by selling clothes, magazines, books, and candy as a hedge against what he believed would be an irreversible decline in store revenues. The costly initiatives failed.

Fields, who knew the DVD ecosystem intimately from his time as chief of Walmart's stores division, told Redstone and Blockbuster's own managers that the big chain would never again see positive store revenue growth.

Redstone, who wanted Blockbuster off Viacom's books but could not find a buyer, went looking for new leadership. He had a headhunter contact Antioco to arrange a meeting in Beverly Hills.

It was the second time he had been approached to run Blockbuster, and Antioco still wasn't sure about moving to Dallas. He was even less keen on a proposal by PepsiCo chairman Roger Enrico that he and Novak run Yum! Brands together. Antioco didn't know much about the entertainment industry, but he was an expert at rehabilitating franchise-based retail businesses, and he liked movies.

He met with Redstone at the Beverly Hills Hotel and took an immediate liking to the seventy-four-year-old billionaire who had built his family's regional movie theater chain into a media empire.

Redstone offered to beat Antioco's already prodigious PepsiCo salary, which Enrico had stuffed with stock and cash incentives while bidding for Antioco's services against the private equity firm that owned Kinko's. More importantly, they agreed that after Antioco righted Blockbuster, he would take it public as its chief executive.

BLOCKBUSTER HAD WHAT Antioco considered a fatal flaw: an arrogance born of being the only game in town for too long. Its business model, which the company internally described as "managed dissatisfaction," had produced a wellspring of consumer resentment toward the big chain over late fees, poor selection, and bad customer service. Blockbuster's own research showed that customers had to visit stores for five consecutive weekends to get the video they wanted. Antioco found that, to add insult to inconvenience, the stores were dirty, the merchandise mix was often wrong for their neighborhoods, and the goods were overpriced.

What other business treats you like that? he thought.

Confounding the search for ways to fix the stores were Blockbuster's mulish franchisees, who owned a collective 20 percent of the U.S. store base and felt burned by Fields's attempts to turn them into entertainment convenience stores. He also encountered a demoralized, entrenched bureaucracy in the corporate-owned stores.

Antioco focused on what he could fix right away, like cleaning up the stores and, with Redstone's help, pursuing revenue-sharing deals with the movie studios that would allow Blockbuster to cut its inventory costs and triple its hot new releases. He tapped store managers and staff for ways to improve morale and, by extension, customer service. Lastly, he let customers know what he had done with a nationwide advertising campaign starring animated characters, a guinea pig and a rabbit named Carl and Ray, who delivered Blockbuster's new mantra: Movies were now "guaranteed to be there."

Customer satisfaction improved at a rate that surprised Antioco as a result of these measures. Rental revenue rose by 13 percent, and active memberships were up 7 percent a year after he stepped into the executive suite. Viacom's stock price more than doubled in the same period. Redstone, who had overpaid for Blockbuster and was still taking a lashing for it in the financial press, was thrilled, but he still wanted to pull Viacom's money out of the chain before the cable companies' new gambit—video on demand—started to erode its market share.

The plan was to spin off 20 percent of Viacom's Blockbuster stake in 1999 to make a market in the stock, and to sell off the rest when the share price stabilized. Viacom sent Antioco and Blockbuster's new chief financial officer, Larry Zine, who had served as Antioco's number two at Circle K, on a road show to present the plan to investors.

Zine was a slight and quiet man, and he became fast friends with Antioco when the two men worked to bring Circle K out of bankruptcy. Over the years, Zine, whose tranquil solemnity provided an interesting foil for the more dynamic Antioco, had learned to anticipate Antioco to the extent that he could often finish the CEO's sentences.

The road show turned out to be an exhausting ordeal. In some seventy meetings with suspicious investors, Antioco, Zine, and Viacom senior vice president Tom Dooley had to explain how Blockbuster would survive competition from video on demand and pay per view, and why Redstone's desire to sell his stake was not a vote of no confidence in the video-rental company.

Zine swore that some of the fund managers took the meeting simply to argue with them about why Blockbuster was doomed. Toward the end of their tour, in Paris, Antioco fell asleep on his feet while giving the presentation.

The August IPO was considered successful—just—by raising $465 million at a share price that fell $1 below the $16 to $18 target range. Antioco, now CEO of a publicly traded company valued at $2.6 billion, went to work to put Blockbuster on a strong competitive footing against its emerging competitors, including video on demand and the other U.S. store chains.

He meant to keep his road show pledge to investors that Blockbuster would control 40 percent of the video rental market within three years, up from the 31 percent it served with its sixty-five hundred U.S. stores.

The plan that he used to turn around Circle K had centered on cutting the store count, categorizing areas in the stores to better analyze sales, and cosmetic improvements, such as putting in better lighting, card readers, and canopies over the fueling areas.

Although he had little capital to spend to improve the bankrupt convenience store chain, he had also filled the stores with high-margin food items, such as fountain drinks. Since Antioco couldn't raise the wages of his severely underpaid Circle K store staff, he used his prodigious charisma to improve morale and rally them around his initiatives.

He and Zine went back to that playbook after the Blockbuster IPO to answer the questions he felt were critical to its future: What are we supposed to be doing for customers? What can we give them that is going to make them come back?

Antioco and Zine had arrived at Viacom at an ideal time. The corporation's management had tried and failed to solve Blockbuster's problems, so they gave the two executives a fairly free hand.

Since Fields had been unsuccessful at increasing store traffic by diversifying merchandise—a play that Antioco might have tried—he focused instead on customer loyalty programs such as store memberships and coupon giveaways, and he eyed video game sales, rental, and trading as potential growth businesses.

Under Antioco, Blockbuster also began investing in producing and distributing movies through a wholly owned subsidiary called DEJ Productions, after deciding that the digital future may call for exclusive content like that offered by the premium cable movie channel Home Box Office.

Antioco had mentioned Netflix among potential threats to store-based rental during the 1999 road show but had thought little about the online rental chain since that time. But, in 2001, as Netflix looked sure to surpass five hundred thousand subscribers, and DVD households surged toward twenty-five million, he took another look.

He devised an in-store subscription offer to counter Netflix—an unlimited number of movies, two at a time, for $29.99—and enlisted Blockbuster's cartoon mascots, Carl and Ray, for television ads. Blockbuster wrapped the buses in Netflix's Los Gatos hometown as part of the advertising campaign. Netflix—still unrivaled online—was thrilled to be publicly acknowledged as a threat.

"Blockbuster is about a hundred times bigger than us, but they're coming after us," Hastings told *USA Today*. "They're definitely out for a fight."

Netflix struck back a couple of months later with an offer of free service for the consumers who filed twenty-three class-action lawsuits against Blockbuster over what they alleged were unfair late charges. This exchange occurred as a group of young men inside Blockbuster's business development arm began to agitate Antioco and Stead to address the lack of a plan for online rental.

Despite being painted as technologically inept, Blockbuster actually was further ahead in 2001 than Netflix in realizing Hastings's utopian rental scenario of movies piped through broadband fiber optics into American homes.

When they rejected Hastings's offer to buy Netflix a year earlier, Stead and Antioco were already intending to bypass DVD by mail entirely and go right to the big prize—movies streamed directly to America's televisions from a central server. Besides, they had it on good authority, in the form of a report by media industry analyst Kagan Research, that the universe of online rental contained 3.6 million users, tops. In light of Blockbuster's now 65 million U.S. account holders (and 100 million worldwide renters), Stead and Antioco thought the online market was not worth considering.

Gartner analyst P. J. McNealy expressed the prevailing view in a 2001 interview, describing Netflix as a good niche business, but "whether everybody will pay that kind of premium remains to be seen. I don't know whether Joe Six-Pack is going to shell out $240 a year."

McNealy set the bar for legitimacy at one million subscribers—or 1 percent of U.S. households—for Netflix. "That's a goal, but they're not there yet," he said.

Antioco had cut a $50 million deal in 2000 with network provider Enron Broadband Services (EBS), a subsidiary of the Houston energy conglomerate Enron, to deliver Blockbuster movies into consumers' homes via a new type of high-speed data lines called DSL, or digital subscriber lines. The twenty-year exclusive video-on-demand (VOD) deal was supposed to commence by year's end with a selection of five hundred movie titles to which Blockbuster had obtained digital rights.

The high-speed data was to be carried to televisions and PCs over DSLs that Enron could access as a result of its relationships with Verizon Wireless, Qwest Communications International, Covad Communications, TELUS, and ReFLEX. Movies would be priced the same as on cable VOD services. But less than a year later—after completing a three-month trial—the companies broke off the joint venture, with EBS complaining about the quality and selection of the movies and saying it wanted to pursue its own offering.

It turned out that EBS's infrastructure did not exist. Antioco and Blockbuster had dodged a bullet.

A federal investigation of financial misdeeds at parent Enron, which would lead to its collapse, included a grand jury appearance by the president of EBS later that year and the sentencing of its chairman, Ken Lay, and two other executives to prison.

Antioco next hooked up with RadioShack to sell set-top boxes that would deliver Blockbuster's digital content to televisions. But market tests showed that the two retail chains served vastly different consumers, and they amicably pulled the plug on the VOD project a few months later.

In the summer of 2001, Antioco watched with interest as a federal court in California shut down the peer-to-peer music-sharing site Napster for infringing on copyrights owned by musicians and record companies, further obscuring the fate of digital content.

Consumers' reactions to the infringement lawsuits and subsequent ruling by the Ninth U.S. Circuit Court of Appeals sent ripples of fear through Hollywood. The lawsuits had prompted tens of millions of angry consumers to flock to video-sharing sites to exchange pirated files in protest. It was the first open public rebellion against companies that would try to manage digital rights tightly.

The studios realized that high-speed Internet connections and consumers' demands to use digital content where and when they wanted would lead to a spike in movie piracy unless a legal alternative emerged, so they got serious about finding that alternative. The first stab was a download venture sponsored by every major studio, except for Disney, called MovieFly, which faced significant technological obstacles—the least of which was the forty minutes it took to download a movie.

The Napster phenomenon made the studios more amenable to issuing online distribution rights, and Antioco obtained the rights to download movies from a number of film libraries, including those owned by Vivendi Universal's Universal Pictures, Metro-Goldwyn-Mayer, Artisan Entertainment, Trimark Pictures, and Lionsgate.

Antioco suspected that Blockbuster's digital ambitions had to wait for technology to catch up, so he at last turned to converting his enormous VHS inventory to DVD—reluctantly. The chain took a $450 million charge in late 2001 to eliminate a quarter of its inventory of videotapes and start stocking DVDs. He calculated that despite the huge cost of converting the inventories of fifty-two hundred corporate-owned stores, the cheaper cost and greater durability of the new format would boost Blockbuster's profit margins by as much as 3 percent in the near term. In the long term, however, DVD spelled troubles for Blockbuster stores, and he had to find a way to fix them.

NETFLIX WAS BEING swept along by the record-setting pace of DVD adoption and having no trouble signing up subscribers. But as Hastings rounded the third quarter of 2001, the burn rate at which Netflix was spending investor cash was too great to meet his goal of a 2001 IPO. The company was looking at a net loss of nearly $40 million for the year. He had to cut costs—drastically.

Hastings did not believe in spending money on high-end office space or other luxuries as a way to boost Netflix's image—that was the kind of thinking that had sunk so many dot-coms just a year earlier.

The new University Drive headquarters, a dank, low-ceilinged build-ing with a steamy atrium, was only a couple of steps above seedy. The floor plan featured staff cubicles grouped in egalitarian clusters designed to promote their sharing of, and openness to, data and ideas. Movie posters and an old-fashioned popcorn maker in the tiny lobby provided the only décor. Nearly everyone kept a NERF gun loaded and ready to repel random aerial attacks from rival departments.

As McCarthy saw it, Netflix's problem in getting an IPO off the ground was not cash. They had plenty to run the business, and every important marker of success—such as subscriber growth and DVD adoption—was trending in the company's favor. But appearances mat-tered to the financial community: specifically, the appearance that Netflix could pare its overhead, conserve its cash, and become nimble and lean enough to fight off the likes of Blockbuster and Walmart immediately if the smaller company's IPO attracted competition to the fast-growing online rental sector.

Another factor weighing against them was that there was no proven financial model for a subscription-based online entertainment rental company, because no one had ever done it. If they wanted to go public, McCarthy argued, they had to get the head count down.

Hastings decided to carry out the layoffs personally. The decision was wrenching, and he wrote every terminated employee a personal note of thanks for his or her contribution.

Every Friday morning he gathered the staff outside Netflix's office for rousing meetings to revel in progress on new engineering and tech-nology projects, dissect mistakes, and tout new partnerships. They met in a small paved patio area that had picnic tables and was bordered on one side by a knee-high wall that staff members used as a bench. Once a month the company rented the Los Gatos Cinema and brought in pizzas from the Round Table pizzeria two doors down. These gath-erings always began with the "initiation" of new employees—many of them shy immigrant software engineers—who were required to dress as characters from a movie of McCord's choosing, using costumes she kept in a large closet next to her office.

The meetings generally centered on two topics—a report on the state of the company's finances by McCarthy and a view of marketing initiatives and customer data by Mier. One Friday morning in September 2001, Hastings sent out an e-mail asking the staff to meet on the patio immediately. The summons sent whispered rumors racing among the workers, who quietly filed outside. Hastings attempted the same inspiring tone he assumed every Friday, in spite of the message he was about to deliver.

Their mission was to build the world's greatest entertainment service, to help consumers get movies they love, and to beat the competition, he told them. Netflix needed to cut costs to do that, and to go public.

"Here's what's going to happen today: A lot of you are going to lose your jobs, and for that, I apologize," Hastings said. "But I thank you for your time and for your commitment. And for those of us who remain, we're going to continue to move forward and fight with you in spirit."

Everyone returned to their cubicles and waited for the tap on the shoulder from his or her manager. By the end of the day about 40 percent of Netflix's workforce had been dismissed. Hastings took many of the newly jobless to lunch.

Randolph and Mier remained behind, too shell-shocked to work. Randolph stretched out on a cream-colored leather sofa opposite his cubicle and tossed a volleyball to himself, over and over. A marketing employee who had just been laid off came over to where they were sitting. "Hey, I just wanted to come in and say thank you, and just check in," the man said. "Are you guys okay? How are you feeling?"

Several others dropped by over the course of the afternoon to deliver their versions of the same message: "It's been great. Now keep going, keep up the fight."

The layoffs and their aftermath claimed the last members of the original team. Vita Droutman, tired out from years of working and reworking the fulfillment and shipping systems, and disappointed that Netflix seemed to be losing its quirky magic, felt a sense near relief when Hastings tapped her on the shoulder.

Having cut expenses to the bone, and holiday DVD sales likely to boost Netflix's subscriber base above the promised half million, Hastings and McCarthy decided to try again for an initial public offering: to raise at least $80 million, sometime in 2002.

McCarthy had an additional data point this time to entice investors. Netflix would finally be profitable, when it reached one million subscribers sometime in 2003. Investors were still stunned by the September 11, 2001, terrorist attacks on New York and Washington, D.C., when McCarthy and Hastings hit the road to pitch a pared-down business plan that focused laserlike on one thing—DVD rentals by mail. Perhaps because Netflix was one of the few dotcoms to survive the bust and stock market crash that followed the terror attacks, they had surprisingly little trouble securing commitments from the investors they had pitched by early the next spring.

A day or two before the May 23, 2002, IPO, Randolph and his nine-year-old son, Logan, rode a private jet to New York with Hastings, McCarthy, and Netflix board member Jay Hoag. They all stood on the trading floor at Merrill Lynch on the morning of the IPO, waiting for the new symbol, NFLX, to appear on trading monitors, and on the giant stock ticker of the NASDAQ exchange.

The opening was delayed that day because of an order imbalance. McCarthy watched the head trader halfway across the room—and suddenly the float went public, at fifteen dollars a share. The price held and climbed a bit.

The offering raised $82.5 million. Netflix had come a long way from the day in April, more than four years earlier, when Randolph had been thrilled to see his Web site crash under traffic that generated just 150 orders.

From a taxi that evening, headed for a celebratory steak dinner, Randolph looked out at a different world. He felt strangely disconnected from the ordinary cares of the masses of pedestrians hurrying past on sidewalks and in crosswalks. He was suddenly wealthier—at least on paper—than he ever imagined he would be. *So this is what it is like to have a dream come true,* he thought.

LOWE AND RANDOLPH'S last collaboration at Netflix turned out to be persuading the Smith's grocery chain to let them test a new concept for a rental kiosk called Netflix Express inside one of its Las Vegas stores. The two had been toying with ideas about how to counter the immediate gratification of Blockbuster's store subscription program with physical Netflix locations. They tried out different types of vending machines at Netflix's offices before deciding to field test the idea without investing in the expensive touch-screen kiosks that they liked best. In lieu of a machine, Lowe designed a store-within-a-store concept manned by a single employee, who had a catalog of about two thousand DVD titles on site. Randolph had a sleek surfboard-shaped Netflix Express sign made out of fiberglass for the booth. He and Lowe moved into a Las Vegas apartment together for a month to set up the kiosk at a Smith's in the suburb of Summerlin.

The location boasted a higher than predicted volume of rental activity during the short test, and people appeared to love the concept. But when Lowe excitedly reported his findings, Hastings and McCarthy shut him down. The kiosks would plug a hole in Netflix's convenience proposition, but they were geared toward new-release titles, and the inventory costs were just too high. McCarthy argued that Netflix could not afford to invest in another outlet for distributing DVDs when the future of the business was clearly digital distribution that would require expensive content deals and cash for software and technology development.

That summer, a strategy executive from McDonald's approached

Lowe to ask if Netflix would partner with the fast-food chain in testing DVD vending machines at McDonald's restaurants. Lowe loved the idea and recommended that Netflix participate, but Hastings nixed it, saying he did not want Netflix to be associated with McDonald's.

The free-spirited Lowe felt strongly that the time for the kiosk business he had been dreaming of for twenty years had finally come—and his experiment with Netflix Express proved it. When he left Netflix in January 2003, he called the McDonald's executive to see how the kiosk project was going. He subsequently flew out to Bethesda, Maryland, to meet with Gregg Kaplan, the strategy executive in charge of the project. The two men hit it off immediately. Kaplan brought Lowe on as a consultant for the kiosk project, which they later named Redbox.

THE LAST YEAR or so of Randolph's career at Netflix was a time of indecision—stay or go? He had resigned from the board of directors before the IPO, in part so that investors would not view his desire to cash out some of his equity as a vote of no confidence in the newly public company. Randolph landed in product development while trying to find a role for himself at Netflix, and dove into Lowe's kiosk project and a video-streaming application that the engineers were beginning to develop.

But after seven years of lavishing time and attention on his start-up, Randolph needed a break. Netflix had changed around him, from his collective of dreamers trying to change the world into Hastings' hyper-competitive team of engineers and right-brained marketers whose skills intimidated him slightly. He no longer fit in.

Shortly before Randolph and Lowe left for Las Vegas to test the kiosk idea, Hastings assigned Randolph's product development duties to chief technology officer Neil Hunt.

"What if this pilot doesn't pan out?" Randolph asked. "What happens then?"

"Then you will leave the company," Hastings said. And to Randolph's surprise they began discussing the terms of his severance.

The going-away party took the form of a roast done in Randolph's favorite form of verse—the limerick. When the others' had all been read, Netflix's cofounder turned the tables on his roasters with his own long and well-metered offering;

> I'm almost surprised
> I expected some toasts and instead I get roasts
> Well, two can play at that game. . . .

Randolph began. The limerick went on to good-naturedly skewer his coworkers. Finally, he turned to Hastings.

> And to Reed, well the guy can't be beat.
> Whether pitching to us or the Street.
> But that late-returned movie?
> *Apollo 13*—Phooey.
> It was actually *Teen Vixens in Heat.*

More than one person watched this exit with sadness, wondering whether Randolph and Lowe's departures would rip the heart and soul from the company.

CHAPTER FIVE

THE PROFESSIONAL

(2003–2004)

THE FINANCIALS WERE THERE IN black and white for all to see: reliable, triple-digit growth in a mature industry where single-digit revenue increases were the norm; the devoted subscribers; the growing market share.

When Netflix announced it had reached one million subscribers in March 2003, John Antioco realized he had made a mistake in trying to bypass online DVD rental, even though Blockbuster's own studies continued to show limited consumer appeal and Wall Street still scoffed at Netflix as a niche player.

But with another round of investor meetings scheduled in anticipation of Blockbuster's pending split from Viacom, and Viacom chief operating officer Mel Karmazin denying all requests for capital-intensive projects until after the split off, Antioco kept putting off a decision about how best to shut down Netflix for good.

Certain that they could buy their way out of the problem—and still believing that Hastings's $50 million asking price for Netflix was preposterous—Stead, who oversaw Blockbuster's business development operations, found and purchased an Arizona online DVD rental outfit run by a father and son for $1 million in 2002. The company, called DVD Rental Central, had about ten thousand subscribers.

Stead handed the information about DVD Rental Central to Sam Bloom, whose job as vice president of business development was to find start-ups that had developed technology that could advance Blockbuster's digital ambitions.

Bloom served on a charity board with Stead's wife and had met Blockbuster's irascible general counsel through her. Stead had previously spent eight years as Apple's general counsel but had come away without learning much about online technology, then in its infancy.

Bloom and Shane Evangelist, the vice president of strategy, who occupied the office next door, often joked that Stead had never actually figured out how Google worked. Nevertheless, Stead knew enough to realize that Blockbuster had to have an online strategy.

Bloom was keenly interested in the new digitized video and video-on-demand technologies, and he leafed through the packet of information on DVD Rental Central and checked out the little company's Web site with growing dismay. The Web site worked, but its Microsoft-based code would never accommodate more than a few thousands users.

"We just bought this company, and you're going to run it," Stead told him. "Tell me what you need to make this beat Netflix."

"Ed, this is never going to beat Netflix," Bloom said, startled. "You need to use this as an experiment to learn about the business: about turnaround time; customer behavior; and costs to acquire customers. That should be the ultimate goal of this." Bloom and Evangelist took the data from the company, which they renamed Film Caddy, and combined it with store data to see how customers were shifting between the two forms of rental.

A key piece of information that emerged from the Film Caddy tests—customers who rented online still liked to rent movies in stores. These movie lovers went online for back-catalog titles and used the stores for impulse rentals of particular titles. Bloom later reflected that the Film Caddy tests failed to reveal nuances about online rental that could have helped Blockbuster assess how big a threat Netflix actually posed.

First, the test run of about one year was too short to pick up on the fact that a significant percentage of subscribers cycle in and out of their online subscriptions—quitting the service and coming back later in the year. Blockbuster counted these as straight cancellations and miscalculated the average revenue per subscriber, making the online business look less lucrative than it was. Second, Bloom and his colleagues underestimated how valuable word-of-mouth recommendations would become on the Internet and how strongly consumer evangelizing would drive Netflix's growth.

Antioco still took the position, as late as 2003, that the online DVD rental market was limited. His instincts and every data point his team had developed showed that Netflix would not be a serious or long-term challenge to Blockbuster's market share.

The Blockbuster executive team could not fathom what customers saw in Netflix: The older titles that drove most of its business never moved at Blockbuster stores; renters had to wait days for movies; and the big chain's research showed that a large segment of its customers had no interest in going online to rent movies.

In mid-2002, Bloom listened in with rising alarm on a Netflix conference call with investors that highlighted the online DVD rental company's growing penetration into the San Francisco Bay Area. Bloom knew that Blockbuster store traffic in the same area was ebbing. The penetration charts that Hastings shared that day made it clear to Bloom: Wherever Netflix offered overnight delivery, its market penetration grew rapidly. Stead had been pestering Bloom for a report on Film Caddy, and Bloom decided it was time to do battle with Netflix.

Bloom doubted that Blockbuster could win in a head-to-head matchup against Netflix's superior Web site and customer service—it would be too expensive and far outside the company's core strengths.

"Blockbuster has a long history of sucking at technology, and people don't think of it as an online brand," he told Evangelist. And Viacom was keeping such a tight rein on cash expenditures that Antioco was having trouble investing in the stores.

They settled on a hybrid store-and-online rental program that would cost far less than building their own Netflix. They would use the existing Movie Pass store subscription program and add a Web site to it through which members could order movies from Blockbuster's vast inventory. The Web site would assign available DVDs to customers from inventory in stores, whose employees would ship out the orders each day. Blockbuster could boost lagging store traffic and tear customers away from Netflix by allowing Movie Pass subscribers to exchange movies they rented online in their local stores. *As a value proposition, it could not be beat*, Bloom thought.

Bloom set up a meeting to discuss the fate of Film Caddy with Stead and Antioco. When he showed up at the appointed time, they were headed out the door.

"Let's do this over lunch," Stead said. "Meet us down in the parking garage."

Antioco pulled up in his Porsche convertible and invited Bloom to shoehorn his burly, six-feet-two-inch frame into the tiny backseat, clutching the report he hoped to walk them through close to his chest so the wind wouldn't take it.

Antioco screeched out of the Renaissance Tower to a Bass Pro Shop, where he and Stead perused deer feeders, cattle troughs, and other supplies for their neighboring ranches as Bloom tried in vain to focus their attention on his proposal.

Frustrated, Bloom handed the idea off to Evangelist and told him to run with it. If anyone could get an online service going at Blockbuster, it was Evangelist, he thought.

Evangelist, then twenty-eight, was a rising star at Blockbuster whose audacity and preternatural financial savvy had immediately commended him to Antioco. The Blockbuster CEO had aroused plenty of veiled jealousy among his senior executives by showing the younger man every mark of favor and indulgence.

A former college student body president and gymnastics champion, Evangelist displayed a drive for success expected in an ambitious young man of modest upbringing. His parents both worked as gym teachers in upstate New York. He had grown up a gifted athlete in the competitive household despite his wiry build.

Evangelist had suggested a vice president's title when Zine expressed interest in hiring him, having interacted with Blockbuster's vice presidents as an IBM consultant and knowing that the title conferred the authority he needed to get things done at the big chain. Besides, he was easily as smart as his older counterparts.

One of his mentors at IBM, where he had started his career as a client representative for Blockbuster, once warned Evangelist to control his tendency to pretend to know more than he did. But overconfidence would serve him well as he plunged headfirst into online commerce—a field about which he knew almost nothing—cheerfully learning from each disaster as he rectified it.

Evangelist embraced the need for an online rental service, correctly seeing it as critical to protecting Blockbuster's market share. Market tests he conducted on Netflix customers showed off-the-charts levels of loyalty to the service—a metric that alarmed him.

But the testing also showed that Film Caddy customers were still renting, on average, three times a month at Blockbuster stores. There was no doubt in Evangelist's mind that he could come up with something better than Netflix.

He set up a cross-functional team within Blockbuster to lay the foundations for an integrated subscription program that would divide the country up into online fulfillment zones, each with its own distribution center.

He tried, over a six- or seven-month period in 2003, to get each Blockbuster department—store operations, marketing, merchandising, product, and franchise—to come up with specifications for participating in the online plan. The project hit roadblock after bureaucratic roadblock. Every department wanted to put its spin on it, or held it up with deal-breaking conditions.

Part of the problem centered on Antioco's demand for store tests of several other nationwide initiatives at the same time. Manpower was stretched in every department, as Blockbuster rushed to meet to-market deadlines on retail, gaming, and trading programs that their chief executive wanted to test.

AT A LATE 2003 planning meeting in Phoenix, the company was divided into two camps. One faction, led by chief content officer Nick Shepherd, responsible for provisioning the stores and in charge of relationships with the studios and vendors, pressed Antioco to make a choice between the integrated online/in-store subscription service and the store initiatives. Shepherd argued that there was no doubt the Blockbuster brand was tarnished but the company still had huge equity in its nearly 9,000 worldwide stores—and they needed to figure out how to fix them instead of throwing up their hands. The other, led by Evangelist, argued that poor initial results for all of the proposed store programs called for focusing the company's efforts into the integrated subscription plan.

Zine confirmed that they had all the cash they needed to fund all the proposals under consideration—but Antioco had to winnow the initiatives to a handful that the executive team and store managers could test effectively. It was up to Antioco to decide. Facing a rebellion among his trusted and battle-hardended store operators, Antioco turned to Evangelist.

"Shane, how much money do you need?" he asked.

"I need twenty-five million dollars," Evangelist said.

"All right—you've got it. Now leave, and don't bother the store operators," Antioco said. "You can take three people with you."

Evangelist tapped two analysts from the corporate strategy group and a technologist to help him put the plans on paper. He brought in programmers from technology consultant Accenture, and spent the first month working out specifications for the business. Instead of the original plan to charge one monthly fee for a hybrid in-store/online service, he was forced to replicate Netflix's online-only rental model, adding coupons for free store rentals as an incentive.

He planned to build and launch the Web site within six months, as a clone of Netflix called Blockbuster Online, and open it in least ten distribution centers. Once they launched and got it operating smoothly, they would figure out how to integrate it with the stores.

Evangelist found office space on two floors of an old red-brick pile called the Paramount Building in Dallas's bohemian West End district. The new offices were within walking distance of Blockbuster's Renaissance Tower headquarters but a world away from the upscale business district. The Paramount Building's lobby adjoined a sandwich shop, and often the smell of lunchtime cooking wafted into the atrium shared by all of the floors. The train stop about a block away attracted strange characters who frequented the tree-shaded benches at all hours of the day and night.

But it also was surrounded by some of Dallas's hippest restaurants and bars, where Blockbuster Online's young staff went regularly to ease the effects of working sixteen- and twenty-hour days.

One of Evangelist's first hires was Ben Cooper, a twenty-eight-year-old Internet marketing specialist who had worked for JCPenney.com and had helped Bloom publicize Film Caddy to customers who bought DVD players from JCPenney. Cooper was tall and slim, and had curly brown hair and a soft Louisiana accent; he became chief of subscriber acquisitions for Blockbuster Online after essentially writing a launch plan for Evangelist during his job interview in September 2003.

While he and Evangelist finalized the plan, Cooper continued to report to a marketing manager at Blockbuster's corporate offices. At his first lunch his new boss assured Cooper that he would easily find another job at the corporate headquarters when the online service fell through.

"We have a history of getting excited about projects like this, and they kind of don't pan out," his supervisor said.

"I didn't come here to do marketing for Blockbuster. I came to launch a business to compete with Netflix and revolutionize the industry, and if that's not what I'm doing, then I'm not going to be here," he told the man.

Cooper's father had owned a small video-rental chain in Lafayette, Louisiana, and Cooper himself had grown up behind the counters of those stores—serving customers, listening to their opinions, observing the stores' demand patterns, developing an intuition for how the business worked and made money. He worked at a Blockbuster store in high school, in the pre-Internet era when the clerks were mostly movie geeks who regarded the VHS screeners the stores received as the job's main perk.

Unlike Evangelist and Antioco, Cooper was comfortable with the technology underpinning the user interface that Blockbuster Online needed to build. He was not intimidated by Netflix's advantage in development time and subscribers, but he realized that its attention to detail and the recommendation engine would be difficult to replicate with the time and budget allotted to build their service.

Antioco's command that they develop Blockbuster Online separately from the Blockbuster stores meant that the stores' customer mailing lists were totally off-limits to the online marketing department, and that any online activities couldn't steal the spotlight from the stores. Blockbuster Online's ads could not mention, for instance, that the service did not charge late fees, as Netflix did in its advertising, because the comparison could cast a negative light on Blockbuster stores. Evangelist and Cooper had to establish their own relationships with movie studios and negotiate their own terms for buying inventory. When it became clear that corporate headquarters' benign neglect would not kill the online business, Blockbuster's franchisees threatened to sue to stop it from going live.

It seemed to Cooper that the store operations wanted the online service to fail as quickly as possible so Antioco could turn the focus away from the latest fad and back to his core business. Their myopia was understandable: Corporate employees received free rentals in any of the scores of Blockbuster stores in the Dallas metro area. There was no reason for them to consider renting anywhere else.

In late 2003, Cooper moved to the Paramount Building with Evangelist and a team of four other young executives who headed the as yet unstaffed retention, marketing, Web site, and IT departments. At first the entire founding team interviewed every job applicant to select the strong-willed, competitive types they would need to beat Netflix.

Cooper shared a large, oddly shaped office with Evangelist's second in command, a former Blockbuster business development executive named J. W. Craft. The office, which was furnished with beanbag chairs, a NERF football goal, and a dartboard on which they had pinned up a photo of Hastings, became a haven for Evangelist to come and brainstorm about the day's problems.

Craft, a twenty-seven-year-old Oklahoma-born Yale graduate, had helped Evangelist salvage the online project at the Phoenix meeting by backing up his boss with facts and statistics. In five years Blockbuster would have nothing else, they warned, if it did not invest in online rental. At Blockbuster Online he oversaw finance and distribution as well as content acquisition; Evangelist had charged him with acquiring at least twenty-five thousand titles for launch day so that they could advertise that Blockbuster Online had more titles than Netflix.

First he worked with post office data to settle on locations for ten distribution centers and used a minidistribution center he had set up at the Paramount Building to test equipment, floor plans, and processes. In contrast to Netflix's slow, organic growth, Blockbuster Online planned to spread its tentacles fast and far into the online rental industry.

Craft then turned to finding enough movies to satisfy Evangelist's mandate, spending hours squinting at long inventory lists from DVD wholesalers. He ordered every film title available on DVD, plus oddities like disks featuring wood-burning fires and fish swimming in aquariums, and still came up short, so he hired a couple of guys to sit in front of TV monitors all day and screen the treasure trove of unrated independent films for sex and nudity that ran afoul of Blockbuster's family-friendly policy.

Evangelist wanted a full complement of cross-promotional deals done with high-profile online affiliates like MSN, AOL, and Yahoo! to drive traffic to the service, starting on launch day.

Before the Accenture engineers wrote too much code, he, Cooper and Bloom met with Yahoo! and Amazon about online rental partnerships that envisioned Blockbuster providing the operations—DVD inventory, fulfillment, and subscription management—in exchange for using Yahoo! or Amazon's sophisticated Web site as a portal to the business. A partnership with a well-known Internet name could help consumers embrace Blockbuster Online as a cool new brand separate from its conventional parent and equal to hot and hip Netflix, Evangelist thought. But Blockbuster's legal team proved to be a stumbling block to it—Stead, by walking out of a meeting over terms he considered too steep, seemed to have torpedoed talks with Yahoo!. Deals with other prospective Internet partners faced similar roadblocks from Blockbuster's lawyers, with contracts returning to the Paramount Building with demands the online marketing team felt were not germane.

To finalize a cross-promotion deal with AOL, which owned online movie information and theater ticket purveyor Moviefone, teams from the two companies spent a week in the Paramount Building on separate floors sending the contract back and forth to keep it out of the hands of Stead's and AOL's legal departments. But Internet companies for the most part were wary of Blockbuster Online, because of its parent company's poor track record in technology, and deals were hard to come by.

Amazon founder Jeff Bezos clearly wanted an online DVD rental offering as a bridge to digital delivery, but his terms proved too onerous for Blockbuster Online, which already faced a steep path to profitability and worried about violating the federal Video Privacy Protection Act by sharing its subscribers' rental history data with the online retailer.

Evangelist had heard that Bezos was also talking with Netflix. He fervently hoped Amazon would buy Netflix and force the rental operation to take a backseat to the online retailer's growing and lucrative DVD sales business.

THE WEB SITE and distribution system were taking shape fairly quickly as Cooper labored over the marketing plan. Rick Ellis, an Accenture consultant acting as operations manager, took over Craft's initial work on the distribution system and translated it into a network of fully staffed warehouses. Ellis, who had worked in operations for international shipping company DHL, hosted a three-day tour to select warehouses near postal-processing facilities that would operate with no automation and eight to ten workers. That's how they would fulfill orders until it was clear the business was viable.

He found dealing with the U.S. Postal Service unexpectedly challenging, considering that Netflix had pioneered and perfected a rental-by-mail operation. Rather than revealing Netflix's procedures, which it deemed confidential, post office officials insisted that Blockbuster had to invent its own.

Ellis tested a fulfillment system in the mini–distribution center at the Paramount Building that he likened to a fast-paced lending library before deciding to use an identical layout in all ten locations, even down to the shelving positions for each title. As the launch neared, he drilled the teams at each site, using dummy data and real DVDs to meet Evangelist's productivity targets. Ellis started the project in December and had all ten distribution centers functioning smoothly enough by the July 4 deadline to earn a performance bonus.

Although Ellis was curious about how Netflix ran its warehouses, he never thought about spying on his competitor or asking his employees to do so. Evangelist, on the other hand, was not quite so principled. He and Cooper recruited consumers in several cities to become Netflix subscribers for the purpose of dissecting the rival service in regular questionnaires sent by the marketing department.

The Blockbuster Online team located most of Netflix's distribution centers on the new consumer blog HackingNetflix.com and studied videos of its warehouse operations that they found on YouTube to figure out how the complex system worked. They encouraged friends and family members to visit the facilities posing as confused subscribers asking to drop off DVDs and have a look around

At first Netflix warehouse personnel did not suspect anything, willingly giving informal tours and allowing the visitors to take photos. But when word got out about the rash of "subscribers" showing up at the distribution centers, Tom Dillon stopped the tours and took down signs identifying the warehouses as Netflix facilities. He also took great glee in disguising the provenance of the custom-made sorting machines in the San Jose warehouse by painting an invented logo, "M&J Automation of Dillon, South Carolina," on them. "M&J" stood for Mutt and Jeff, the nicknames Dillon had given to the two salesmen from NPI, the Dallas company that had sold Netflix the machines.

In coming years, Evangelist and his team would keep a close eye on where and how quickly Netflix expanded its distribution network, knowing that the centers represented new growth frontiers that Blockbuster Online and its parent had to defend.

IT WAS NO secret to McCarthy and Hastings that Blockbuster was close to launching its online service. In fact, through a chance encounter between a friend of Hastings's and a loud-talking consultant, they thought they knew exactly what shape that service would take. In October 2003, Hastings's friend had sat in front of the Blockbuster consultant on an airplane and taken notes on the conversation the consultant had with his seatmate, which he forwarded to Hastings. The consultant had revealed the budget and the number of people working on the project, its launch date, and the fact that subscribers would be able to return their movies at any Blockbuster store.

The consultant had described an integrated in-store/online DVD rental plan that, had it been carried out as described, would have posed a lethal threat to Netflix by giving Blockbuster Online access to the twenty million active customers of Blockbuster's stores. The convenience of getting a movie in the stores combined with the selection of online rental was something that Netflix could not match. But Hastings was so confident that Blockbuster could not master the complicated technology to integrate the two that he went out of his way to dismiss the service.

"In terms of their online efforts, we expect Blockbuster.com to be approximately as successful against us as Barnes & Noble was against Amazon," Hastings told investors in early 2004. "Until we are sure, however, we plan to watch them closely."

After enduring three years of reflected disgrace from the dot-com bust, Internet stocks had rotated back into favor in early 2004, and Netflix was suddenly the darling of the postbust era. Its share price had risen nearly 400 percent, and its steady average revenue growth of more than 100 percent each year was starting to attract attention.

Even though they'd had no real competition since launching the subscription plan, Netflix had nevertheless continued smoothing out kinks in its subscription business and was pushing ahead in all areas: consumer satisfaction was high; cancellations were low; and finally the service was being noticed by regular Americans, who were signing up at a clip of nearly three thousand per day. The potential online rental market was huge, maybe as large as twenty million subscribers, based on the penetration they were seeing in their first market, the San Francisco Bay Area, where more than 5 percent of residents were members, Hastings told investors.

In early 2004, Hastings and McCarthy boasted that Netflix would more than double its revenue in 2006, reaching $1 billion a year earlier than they had predicted. They announced plans to expand internationally—to the United Kingdom and Canada—and to present consumers with a movie download service in 2005.

Kilgore added television commercials to their marketing plan for the first time in early 2004, and subscriber sign-ups went through the roof. Netflix announced a month later that a planned quarterly loss would be three times wider than forecast, because a promotion for a free month of service was proving more successful than expected— more people were trying it out than they had predicted

Netflix's stock price soared past seventy-five dollars from a low of five dollars in 2002, and investors enjoyed a two-for-one split in February 2004. With the wind finally at their back, McCarthy announced that he would leave Netflix at the end of the year to find his own company to run. Hastings had no plans to step down, and McCarthy, now fifty, had no intention of playing second fiddle indefinitely.

McCarthy wanted to put the company on a solid cash footing before he left, and so he championed raising prices for Netflix's primary plan—the three-out plan—and investing the proceeds in more inventory and an upgrade for the Web site. He believed the resulting increase in customer satisfaction and decline in cancellations would compensate for subscribers who dropped the service because of the higher prices.

At its launch, Blockbuster Online surely would follow Netflix's lead and price its plans to take advantage of the boost in profit margins, especially since it faced higher costs to acquire subscribers.

"Why would the business with the higher cost structure start a price war?" McCarthy reasoned. It would make no sense.

In April, Netflix raised the price for the three-out plan to $21.99 from $19.99.

The move seemed to Evangelist like a gift Hastings had handed to him personally. He had, in fact, planned to price Blockbuster Online's subscription plans the same as Netflix's, and to give an added sweetener of two coupons for free in-store rentals.

Evangelist was elated by his rival's mistake: Blockbuster Online's market research showed that customers balked at paying more than twenty dollars per month for online rental, and below twenty dollars was where he planned to stay.

Blockbuster Online's Web site was not exactly ready when a test version quietly went live on July 15, 2004—the day Netflix announced its second-quarter earnings—but it amused Evangelist to screw with Hastings and McCarthy, whom he felt had been unaccountably condescending and dismissive of his new service.

The Blockbuster Online team issued sign-up codes for the site for each employee and offered a prize for the person who could recruit the most testers. Cooper ended up winning after the e-mail he sent out to friends touting the arrival of his "baby" went viral.

By the time their earnings call ended that afternoon, Netflix executives had discovered the Blockbuster Online beta site and began logging onto it. Cooper and Evangelist laughed when a URL tracing program showed e-mails with Netflix domain names—including rhastings@Netflix.com and bmccarthy@Netflix.com—signing up for a free test of the service and trickling onto Blockbuster Online for a look around.

CHAPTER SIX

SOME LIKE IT HOT

(2004–2005)

MCCARTHY SAT STEAMING IN NETFLIX'S conference room. The earnings call he had just presided over had ended, and the Netflix team had clicked onto Blockbuster Online's beta test as soon as it was over.

The site was practically identical to Netflix.com. They had copied it all—the user interface, the back-end functions, even the Queue. McCarthy had to hand it to them—no one at Netflix had perceived Blockbuster Online as a threat. But Netflix was not competing against bloated, slow-moving, technologically inept Blockbuster. Netflix was competing against itself—its own patented business model had been turned against them.

Hastings pointed out that, although Blockbuster had copied the look of the Netflix Web site, they couldn't see the algorithms under-pinning it. Without the ongoing optimization of costs, the matching algorithm, and the market research platforms, Blockbuster Online had only half of the whole picture.

The first thing that happened, as word of the Blockbuster Online beta spread, was that Netflix's stock price tanked—again. Netflix investors, now enjoying a brief honeymoon, were notoriously wary. In mid-2002, Netflix's stock dropped to five dollars on the news that

Walmart planned to launch an online DVD rental service. When Walmart launched the site in late 2002, and Netflix's marketing and analytics staff had had a chance to dissect it, they were underwhelmed.

Even before Walmart rolled out its service, at one dollar below Netflix's subscription price, Netflix had predicted that any entrant into online rental would struggle to replicate the pioneer's customer experience and functionality.

The tiny graphics, the lack of flow, and the clunkiness of the Walmart site revealed its creator's failure to grasp the idea that an online store had to be more than an animated catalog—it had to engage customers' imaginations and spark longings strong enough to compensate for the lack of a tactile shopping experience. The market had apparently reached the same conclusion, and slowly bid Netflix's stock price back up to past its IPO price, to nearly forty dollars a share by early 2004.

When intelligence reached Netflix's then chief analyst, Paul Kirincich, that Blockbuster was testing Film Caddy in 2003, he ran market tests to learn whether the little service was affecting Netflix's adoption rates. The tests detected not even a ripple in the market from Film Caddy, which made it easy to discount Antioco's announcement in April 2003 that Blockbuster would bring its own service to market in about a year.

"Whenever a competitor says that next year they'll have a better offering, to me that's a sign of weakness, because you're telling competitors what you're going to do, and you don't have the service to offer consumers," Hastings said a few days later.

For all Hastings's bravado, the market experienced a crisis of faith as soon as analysts took a look at Blockbuster Online's beta test. A round of selling started the following day that sent Netflix's share price careening off a cliff and into "sell" status for some analysts for nearly four years. The company lost nearly 60 percent of its market capitalization in a week, as its share price settled back at its IPO level of fifteen dollars.

In ongoing meetings and phone calls with investors and analysts, McCarthy and Deborah Crawford, Netflix's director of investor relations, explained that the young MBAs from Blockbuster Online faced a seasoned team in McCarthy, Hastings, and Kilgore, and that their new competitor would cause an expensive drain on Blockbuster's stores' inventory. It was useless. Most of Wall Street thought they were in denial, or plain stupid. It was exasperating, but a new threat was developing that demanded immediate attention from Netflix's executive team and its board.

A COUPLE OF days before Blockbuster Online launched its beta test, Hastings, McCarthy, and others at Netflix heard reports that Amazon had at last taken concrete steps to set up its own DVD rental service. McCarthy heard about it from a hedge fund manager, and chief content officer Ted Sarandos, who liaised with the entertainment industry at Netflix's Beverly Hills office, learned that studios were in negotiations with the giant e-retailer over inventory purchases for movie rental.

This news alarmed Hastings and McCarthy more than the specter of competing with Blockbuster or any other bricks-and-mortar retailer. Amazon, with thirty-eight million unique visitors flowing through its site each month, had the technological know-how to build a service to equal that of Netflix and the brand might be able to blow them out of the water.

Sarandos said he would try to confirm the somewhat cryptic reports, and for the time being, they decided to watch and wait.

UNLIKE THE BUSINESS-AS-USUAL attitude that accompanied Netflix's launch, the debut of Blockbuster Online on August 20, 2004, was an event. Cooper and Craft organized a movie-themed party in the Granada Theater in Dallas, complete with celebrity impersonators who mingled with guests.

An oversized button sat on a podium on the stage, ready for Antioco and Blockbuster president Nigel Travis to use to officially push the Web site to the Internet. Store personnel mingled with the 180 or so Blockbuster Online employees and Accenture programmers. Cooper, dressed in jeans and a black-and-white T-shirt imprinted with a screen shot of Blockbuster Online's home page, made sure the program went smoothly.

Throughout the beta test period Antioco and Zine had nervously cautioned Evangelist not to launch the site unless it was relatively bug-free and ready to show to customers. Evangelist assured them everything would be ready—he did not want to miss the start date he had promised Antioco. He did not share some misgivings he had about whether the site would support a huge influx of users.

The lights went down, and Cooper cued up the program. White words appeared on a black background on the theater's huge screen. A thumping electronic beat accompanied the video.

" 'Blockbuster's track record in online technology and marketing is less well developed.'—Reed Hastings, CEO, Netflix," the screen read.

" 'We find it unlikely that Blockbuster will promote their online service effectively.'—Reed Hastings," a second graphic read.

The crowd booed and made catcalls as the video cut back and forth between famous scenes from macho-themed movies like *Rocky, Braveheart, Taxi Driver,* and *Fight Club.* They went crazy as the screen lit up with yet another quote, this one from Antioco: "You have officially awakened a sleeping giant. Now let's go kick some ass."

A roar went up, and the video continued, cutting between movies scenes and graphics showing the monumental achievement that Evangelist and his team had put together in six months: six million mailers printed; 750,000 lines of code written; a half million Web pages created; twenty-five thousand titles purchased; fifteen thousand days of labor accumulated; one hundred–plus legal contracts signed, ten distribution centers created.

"The Giant Is Awakened," the video concluded, with a shot of

Blockbuster Online's yellow-and-blue mailer and the logo "Blockbuster Online: The Movie Store at Your Door."

Amid cheers and applause, Antioco and Travis walked onstage and said a few congratulatory words to Evangelist, who had been promoted that day to senior vice president, and to his team. Then they pressed the button.

Travis and Nick Shepherd had been invited to the bash as a gesture of inclusiveness, even though the suspicion between the two camps continued unabated. Shepherd, however, did not attend. Evangelist and Cooper got a good laugh when they heard a rumor going around Renaissance Tower that the online staff had filled its Paramount Building offices with the trappings of dot-com luxury—foosball tables and expensive office furniture—and that they enjoyed free meals as a perk of their supposedly sumptuous budget.

In fact, although Viacom's Karmazin supported the idea of an online rental service, he had balked at the potential expenditure of the $200 million or more that Evangelist estimated it would cost to build and run the service before it started making money. In the meantime, he was stretching the $25 million Antioco had allotted him nearly a year earlier until Blockbuster completed its split-off from Viacom in late 2004.

Cooper had rigged the button on the stage at the Granada to actually make Blockbuster Online go live, and it worked like a charm. Back at the Paramount Building, however, a coding error cropped up almost immediately. and as traffic built, the bad code threatened to take down the site. The programmers had to "bounce," or restart, the servers almost once an hour for nearly a week to keep the system running before they could fix the problem.

The meme cache error was the first of a litany of technical problems to dog Evangelist and his affable chief programmer, Aaron Coleman, throughout Blockbuster Online's sometimes painfully quick growth.

Coleman, a thirty-year-old Bay Area technologist, was not sure he was interested in that lead job when his girlfriend Jenny, who worked for Cooper at Blockbuster Online, persuaded him to meet with Evangelist. But Evangelist's personal charisma, coupled with the prospect of working for a well-funded start-up backed by a world-famous brand, won him over.

His first day on the job, in February 2005, ended at 3:00 A.M. The days that followed were equally packed with battles to keep the Web site functioning while Blockbuster Online brought new distribution centers onto the system, hit daily subscriber sign-up records, and added thousands of new titles to their inventory each week.

Within months, Coleman was fine-tuning the Web site applications and databases to process several thousand orders per second—making sure subscribers were matched with the next available movies in their queues, and then locating the DVD in the nearest distribution center—from a launch day average of about a dozen orders per second.

In the coming three years, Coleman and his programmers would completely rewrite the code supporting each system to accommodate growth, and to evolve the site to match Netflix, metric by metric and feature by feature, and to eventually surpass its performance.

The Blockbuster Online team looked at Netflix from the beginning with a mix of admiration and rivalry, and because they were young, they meant to balance their hard work with some fun.

The voices of Hastings, McCarthy, and Kilgore wafted through the Paramount Building on speakerphones each time those executives gave a presentation to analysts or talked to the press after an earnings report. Any mention of Blockbuster Online by Netflix was usually greeted with catcalls and sarcastic comments.

Sarah Gustafson was just four years out of college and typical of the full-time staff that Evangelist began hiring soon after the launch. She was bright and idealistic, and had followed Evangelist to the online service from Blockbuster's business development division to run customer analytics. She gathered the metrics that informed their pricing and purchasing decisions as well as the shape of the products it would offer subscribers.

While she relished the challenge of competing against a company she considered revolutionary, Gustafson had no illusions about the battle that lay ahead. Getting customers to try out the service was no problem, especially with cheaper prices and a better-known brand. Keeping them proved harder. When she dug into the cancellation data, Gustafson learned that two factors were responsible—delivery speed and availability of titles.

The biggest complaint that surfaced on consumer blogs and reviews of the service was the shortage of inventory that showed up as "long wait" notifications in subscribers' queues. While praised for relatively quick delivery, the fulfillment system frustrated subscribers by often delivering disks from the bottom or middle of their queues first.

In their haste to finish the project by Evangelist's deadline the Accenture team had had to build the Web site's main functions—its consumer interface and DVD allocation and distribution systems—on separate platforms. The arrangement got the site up and running but made it difficult to grow. Capacity was a constant problem that kept Michael Siftar, the software developer who Evangelist hired to transition Web site maintenance from Accenture to a permanent team, busy for the first few months of his tenure.

Siftar, an easygoing, articulate thirty-year-old from Broken Arrow, Oklahoma, who had most recently worked at Priceline.com, set up his office in a dark hallway, sat his staff at card tables outside, and went to work on the complex algorithms that decided which movie a subscriber would receive next and which warehouse it would come from. Siftar divided his programmers into three smaller groups that acted as sort of computer SWAT teams, putting down problems across the balky systems and reconfiguring them to meet an ongoing schedule of price changes, product rollouts, and consumer tests.

For all the problems with service levels, and in spite of their lack of experience, the Blockbuster Online team knew there was just one metric that counted to the financial press and to Netflix, and that was the size of its subscriber base. Evangelist made it everyone's business—twenty-four hours a day, every day—to make sure nothing impeded its growth.

He had Cooper rig their BlackBerrys to receive hourly reports showing subscriber sign-up levels. If any unexplained fluctuation in those numbers appeared, Evangelist would call—often late—and Cooper would slip out onto his back porch to talk to avoid waking his wife, Jess. He'd set the ring tone for Evangelist's calls on Darth Vader's theme music from *Star Wars*, and he only realized how obsessed with the reports they both had become after noticing that his dog ran to the backdoor every time it heard the ring tone. At the time they were signing up a few hundred people an hour—about three thousand a day.

The numbers provided the tech and marketing teams with constant alerts to choke points in the system—a link on an affiliate's page that wasn't clicking through, or a problem with a particular browser, or a software glitch that was preventing sign-ups. As ingenious as it was, the alert system essentially turned every job at Blockbuster Online into an on-call gig.

Evangelist set the tone for their work ethic and attitude: They were not Blockbuster crushing a smaller company; they were a start-up trying to catch a technologically superior and far more experienced competitor.

His discipline was remarkable, the result of a lifetime of sporting competition. He did not drink alcohol or smoke, played amateur-level golf, and maintained his college gymnastics physique; he could still do a back flip from a standing start. He adhered to what his Blockbuster Online colleagues described as a hummingbird diet: It consisted almost entirely of processed sugar—Hostess CupCakes, Dr. Pepper, and candy bars—and he would consume four or five plastic cartons of Tic Tac breath mints at a single meeting. The sugar fueled his innate ambition and athletic prowess, making Evangelist extremely intense to work for, but he also had something of Antioco's touch with people. His employees learned to simply roll their eyes at his more bizarre demands and find their own ways to accomplish what he wanted.

He set a strict schedule of goals and meddled minutely in every department to make sure objectives were met on time and on budget. Everything at Blockbuster Online was data-driven—Evangelist loved market research and used it to back every product decision—even if the research consisted of polling people waiting at the streetcar stop down the block from the Paramount Building.

The Blockbuster stores team steered clear of the West End operations, but Antioco and Evangelist exchanged e-mails or phone calls every night between 10:00 P.M. and midnight—a time the younger man prized as more valuable than his MBA from Southern Methodist University.

Although Evangelist's goal was to launch the online service separate from Blockbuster, to keep it from getting entangled in the rental chain's bureaucracy, and then to quickly integrate it with the stores, Blockbuster Online first had to overcome a major technological hurdle. In 2004, Blockbuster stores still were not connected to each other or to the Internet. Every night the stores still used satellite technology from the 1980s—the same system Cooper had used at his high school Blockbuster job—to upload cash register and inventory data and download software patches. Wiring the stores to communicate with the online service would be costly and complicated.

Antioco and his store managers also had bigger issues to face, with the spin-off from Viacom underway and ominous forecasts of declines in store-based video rental business. Evangelist put plans for the integration to the side and did what every kid playing catch-up does: Run hard.

CHAPTER SEVEN

WALL STREET

(2004–2005)

JOHN ANTIOCO WAS THE GUY from the wrong side of the tracks. He grew up not exactly poor, the son of a penny-pinching milkman who would die many years later having amassed a secret stock portfolio worth almost $1 million. He lived on a blue-collar block of walkups in Brooklyn, the youngest child and only son of his Italian American parents.

Johnny, as his mother called him, was a troublemaker at the Catholic elementary school he attended, which was on a leafy street with buckled sidewalks and had a tiny walled playground; he developed a reputation in the neighborhood for petty misbehavior as he approached adolescence. His father, a taciturn man, moved the family to a neat bungalow in the Long Island burg of Mineola when Antioco was twelve, to separate him from his bad-seed friends.

The upheaval of the 1960s mostly passed by Antioco. He avoided service in Vietnam thanks to a high draft number and attended the Woodstock festival only because a friend happened to be going and Antioco didn't have anything better to do.

The one thing that fired his imagination was making money. His father's miserliness was a topic of neighborhood gossip in Brooklyn and Long Island, and the constant corner cutting and patch jobs made Antioco swear that one day he would have enough money to never again have to live with half-broken things.

His landed his first real job at a Baker's shoe store in the Roosevelt Fields Mall on Long Island, where he discovered that he was good at selling things and loved working on commission, where his success or failure was toted up each night on a chalkboard for his fellow salesmen to see. He found it exhilarating.

Part of the attraction of coming to Blockbuster in 1997 was the chance to run a publicly traded company and join the top echelon of America's CEOs. By 2004, Antioco had fulfilled his mandate from Sumner Redstone—to make the giant rental chain healthy enough to split off from Viacom—and his promise to investors: to claim a growing share of the $8 billion movie rental industry. Blockbuster's annual revenue had grown to $6 billion, and its earnings topped $600 million.

But Viacom chief operating office Mel Karmazin, who came to Viacom in its 2002 merger with CBS, liked the cash Blockbuster reliably generated, and he convinced Redstone to rethink the decision to split it off.

Antioco was now saddled with the regulatory requirements of a public company and a parent company. He began to explore his options. He had been denied the chance to run Circle K and Taco Bell, and he did not want to mark time at Blockbuster if it was going to remain a subsidiary of Viacom.

Besides, Blockbuster faced a fast-changing competitive landscape, and Antioco believed he needed more autonomy to confront it. In 2003, Antioco brought several initiatives to Karmazin intended to beat back challenges to Blockbuster's market share from online rental and video on demand. When Karmazin saw a price tag totaling hundreds of millions of dollars in expenditures, he realized Viacom had to let Blockbuster go.

TO KEEP ANTIOCO onboard Redstone had cut him an even more impressive compensation package than the generous executive remuneration for which Viacom was known. The performance-based package brought Antioco's stake in Blockbuster to 3 percent and had the potential to total as much as $50 million in salary and stock-based compensation, assuming a healthy rise in Blockbuster's share price each year. Redstone also built in a $54 million severance package to protect and reward Antioco for bringing Blockbuster back from the brink of bankruptcy and taking it public that he could claim if he lost his chairman title or was fired without cause.

The contract he signed with Blockbuster gave Antioco everything he had ever dreamed of in his work life. Johnny Antioco from Brooklyn had arrived.

Redstone went ahead with plans to split off Blockbuster in a stock swap. Under the complex transaction that was announced in February and completed in September 2004, Viacom shareholders received 5.15 shares of Blockbuster stock plus a $5 special dividend for each share of Viacom stock they relinquished. Blockbuster took on $1.2 billion in debt to finance the special dividend, including paying Viacom $738 million to buy back its Blockbuster shares.

To satisfy its creditors' terms Blockbuster had to maintain a strict debt-to-income ratio—a challenge for a company in a mature industry that was forecasting eroding store sales and struggling to find a future in e-commerce.

Once the split-off was completed Antioco turned to three initiatives he believed would secure Blockbuster's future. First, he had to correct the overbuilding of video stores: He wanted to buy the Hollywood Video chain and shut down about half of the combined store base. Cutting underperforming stores would buy time for healthy ones as the industry transitioned to digital delivery. He figured it would cost about $700 million to buy the number two chain, which was controlled by its founder, Mark Wattles, and a group of private investors—if federal antitrust regulators did not object to the match.

Second, Antioco wanted to drop late fees to lure disaffected consumers back to the stores to try the new programs he was pitching: game and DVD trading and reselling and the in-store subscription that was similar to Netflix's all-you-can-watch rental plan.

The End of Late Fees, as Blockbuster named the program, would cost the chain a steep $250 million to $300 million a year in operating income, but their market research showed no better way to turn around dwindling store traffic than eliminating the strongest argument for online rental and other forms of distribution that promised greater freedom.

Consumers' ability to create, manipulate, and share their own videos online made them impatient with rules governing how, when, and where they watched rentals or purchases. Antioco saw this and knew Blockbuster had to distance itself from punitive late fees and other tenets of its managed dissatisfaction strategy.

Finally, he planned to make major investments of money and staff in online rental and the digital delivery system he had been hunting for over the past five years.

In October 2004, Antioco proposed a Blockbuster–Hollywood Video merger. Since 2001, movie rental revenue had shrunk by 19 percent, and the once mighty U.S. store base of seventy thousand locations—including Blockbuster, Hollywood Video, Movie Gallery, and other chains, as well as mom-and-pop stores—had winnowed to eighteen thousand, according to a report by media analyst Tom Adams. Blockbuster had to seize control—of its own fifty-two hundred stores, Hollywood Video's two thousand superstores, and Game Crazy's seven hundred–plus locations—before store rental revenue got too thin to support its far-flung U.S. store base. Federal antitrust concerns had prevented the sale of Hollywood Video to Blockbuster in 1999, but Antioco figured that the emergence of strong rental alternatives, including Netflix, would now force the agency to a different conclusion.

A buyout firm, Leonard Green & Partners, had already offered Wattles $10.25 per share to take Hollywood Video private in August—a transaction Wattles backed, put the number two U.S. rental chain in play, and allowed Hollywood's board to consider other offers. On November 12, Blockbuster made a tender offer of $11.50 per share to Hollywood Video's shareholders. A successful merger would give Blockbuster control of 45 percent of the U.S. store-based rental market. A week later, Dothan, Alabama–based Movie Gallery, the number three movie rental chain, entered the bidding with an undisclosed offer that analysts estimated was worth at least $760 million.

A week after that, Blockbuster said it would sweeten its offer in exchange for a look at Hollywood's books. Wattles, however, would not turn over the information to Antioco unless his rival agreed not to tender an offer directly to Hollywood Video's shareholders. Wattles said publicly that he welcomed the offer, but he privately expressed doubts to the Blockbuster executives that U.S. antitrust regulators would approve the deal.

The proposal had drawn the attention of billionaire investor Carl Icahn, a former corporate raider and self-styled shareholder activist, who then planned to profit on both ends of the Blockbuster–Hollywood Video merger. Icahn sank $150 million into Blockbuster shares and about $60 million into Hollywood Video. In a securities filing Icahn said he might seek to participate in, and influence the outcome of, any proxy solicitation and the bidding process involving the owner of the Hollywood Video stores.

Icahn, sixty-nine, had made his $8.5 billion–plus fortune twenty-five years earlier by taking over corporations in leveraged buyouts, pulling them apart, and selling the pieces off. He had perfected the art of greenmail—secretly accumulating a big stake in a target company, either by himself or with a cadre of like-minded investors, and demanding a premium to sell back his shares and go away.

Although he had worked to rehabilitate his image since the days when he was grouped with Michael Milken and Ivan Boesky as a parasite on the financial world, his tactics remained the same. Icahn maintained an office in the General Motors Building in Midtown Manhattan, overlooking Central Park and the Plaza Hotel. The decor, with its rich, bold colors and original artwork depicting famous battles, conveyed a sense of power and state. The conference room, where Icahn had hung framed news clippings detailing the companies he had raided and the CEOs he had fired, drove the point home. He ran a $2.7 billion fund that boasted a stratospheric 30-plus percent annual return on investment most years.

Icahn liked to purchase big stakes in undervalued stocks and use his leverage as a major shareholder to force management to make changes he outlined. Often these meant cutting costs, selling off assets, and replacing top executives or board members. Icahn's initial instinct had been to short Blockbuster's stock, thinking that it was sure to slowly bleed to death as video on demand and online businesses like Netflix came to dominate the movie rental market.

But Michael Pachter, an analyst at the financial services firm then known as Wedbush Morgan (now Wedbush Securities), who viewed Netflix as a sort of rental Ponzi scheme, convinced Icahn that Blockbuster was a stock to hold. Its strong brand, huge network of stores, and healthy revenue, would lead it to either eventually buy Netflix or put it out of business by starting its own online rental service.

Icahn quietly bought up shares for his own funds, and his interest in the stock spurred purchases from a number of hedge funds that followed the billionaire investor's moves in hopes of benefiting from what was known on Wall Street as the Icahn effect—an immediate rise in any stock Icahn bought.

He called to introduce himself to Antioco, who knew right away that trouble was here. Though Icahn liked to cast himself as a shareholder advocate, the changes that he forced on management generally benefited himself and other hedge funds that assisted in his arbitrage plays in the form of forced share buybacks and board seats for himself and his designees. Antioco's first instinct was to win Icahn over by presenting the billionaire investor with his road map for Blockbuster, but Stead advised against it: Regulatory rules prohibited such disclosures to a single investor.

Antioco was determined to resist Icahn's meddling, and he had a vociferous advocate in Stead, who made a point of being as rude to Icahn as possible every time their paths crossed. Stead related to his Blockbuster colleagues what happened when he and his spouse ran into Icahn and his wife, Gail Golden, at a charity dinner in New York. Golden looked at Stead when she was introduced and laughingly said, "Ah yes, so you're Ed Fucking Stead. I've heard all about you."

Alienating Icahn turned out to be a mistake that Antioco would regret. But in late 2004 he finally could turn to running his company without a corporate parent looking over his shoulder.

Antioco had known for a couple of years that late fees were killing Blockbuster's relationship with its customers. Late fees originally arose as a means to pressure customers to return rented movies quickly, so that stores could turn them around faster to make more money, and to avoid inventory shortages. Store operators were delighted when the fees unexpectedly became a strong and dependable revenue source. Franchisees were not about to give up late-fee revenue without a fight— even when Blockbuster's market research showed that the fees turned off existing customers and strangled the company's ability to attract new ones.

By 2004, active membership had been declining for several years, and Netflix's prolific ads promising "no late fees ever" were accelerating the losses. Antioco put Nick Shepherd in charge of changing the company's dialogue with consumers over late fees.

Shepherd was a robust-looking man, with close-cropped salt-and-pepper hair and translucent blue eyes, but his sturdy frame and hale complexion belied a somewhat high-strung and exacting personality. He grew up in England's rough northeast coal-mining district, Newcastle, the youngest child of the eight in his Irish-English, Catholic family. As a young boy he had dreamed of becoming a photographer, but his family was too poor to afford the equipment. Instead, he followed his older brother into restaurant work, eventually earning a degree in hospitality and business management.

He joined Blockbuster's UK operations shortly after Viacom bought the rental company in 1995, and had held a number of international operations and marketing posts before moving to Dallas in 1999, to work as head of international operations under Antioco.

Shepherd strongly supported resuscitating Blockbuster stores even though he knew that online rental in some form ultimately would undermine them. Still, he preferred losing store customers to Blockbuster Online than to Netflix or video on demand. Shepherd ordered market research on attitudes around late fees and discovered that, while only 20 percent of Blockbuster customers were paying late fees at any given time, more than 70 percent had paid them at one time or another, and most felt the stores were not consistent or fair about the way they were levied.

Intellectually he knew the brand was damaged each time a customer got into an argument with a Blockbuster cashier over unexpected late fees, especially as it frequently happened in front of a long line of customers waiting to check out. But the idea of wiping out an important source of revenue when store sales were declining made his gut churn.

Blockbuster's marketing department constructed a number of alternatives to the traditional late fees, such as returning to a per-day rental rate rather than simply tacking on another full rental charge for, say, seven days, as soon as the movie was late.

However, a test program conducted by a midwestern franchisee that removed late fees altogether convinced Antioco and Shepherd that all of Blockbuster would have to bite the bullet, too.

That Blockbuster franchisee, Mitch Kerns, had not only definitively reversed the slide in same-store sales, but also actually started building market share and revenue for his store. His program essentially gave his customers twice as long to watch titles and charged their credit cards for the price of the movie if they didn't return it within a month.

During a trip to visit Blockbuster's European stores in September 2004, Shepherd broached the subject to Antioco during an early morning walk beside a canal in the northwestern English town of Warrington.

"Do you seriously think, if we change the pricing structure and get past this late fees thing, it will make a big difference?" Antioco asked.

"I think it will fundamentally change the relationship with customers," Shepherd said.

Although Shepherd balked at killing late fees altogether, Antioco urged him to test such a program in a few U.S. markets. Shepherd chose to test in Chattanooga, Tennessee, a city where nearly every test initiative went wrong. He sent a second-string team of executives to launch the no-late-fees promotion—to increase its chances of failure.

To his surprise, the Chattanooga test replicated Kerns's results, so Shepherd ordered another city tested, and then another. The results were the same in every market: Consumers returned to stores more frequently and spent more money on rentals and other items. At the test's conclusion, Shepherd gathered managers in the test markets and asked for a show of hands: Which of four initiatives—including 99 cent per day rentals, game rentals and end of late fees—should they launch in January? They unanimously chose the End of Late Fees.

Although removing late fees would eventually spur store traffic and sales, Shepherd had to cut more than $400 million in costs out of the store business to compensate for the initial loss of revenue and to fund the growth of Blockbuster Online. He had kept Blockbuster's franchisees, who ran about eleven hundred U.S. stores, closely apprised of the market tests. When he revealed the results he faced a deep split between those who wanted to try the promotion and those who felt they couldn't do without the revenue.

"Do you want the business to go down the pound?" Shepherd asked. "Because that's where it's going to go. Or do you want to renovate the business?"

Although the franchisees accepted that the competitive landscape was changing for movie rental, Shepherd became aware of a deep animosity toward the online business led by one of Blockbuster's largest franchisees, Fred Montesi III of Southern Stores, who believed that Blockbuster Online would undermine the stores.

In the end, Shepherd convinced three quarters of the franchisees to try the End of Late Fees program, which Blockbuster would roll out in January with a big advertising push. The Blockbuster board approved the program in December, and the $50 million advertising campaign launched to the strains of Roy Orbison's "It's Over" and promised "The End of Late Fees . . . the New Blockbuster."

SHEPHERD HAD TO switch his focus in the midst of the End of Late Fees rollout and testify before the Federal Trade Commission, which had begun vetting Blockbuster's bid for Hollywood Entertainment. It was the second time that Blockbuster executives had trod the regulatory path in a proposed merger with Hollywood Video. The FTC's analysis of the proposed 1999 merger showed that sixteen hundred Hollywood Video stores lay within two miles of Blockbuster locations, and in many cases there was no other competitor in the area to maintain competitive pricing.

In the ensuing five years, Shepherd testified, the video rental market had diversified to include several new products that directly competed with store-based rental, such as video on demand, DVD sales, and online rental. But from the tenor of the FTC's questions at his first multihour session in Washington, D.C., Shepherd had the feeling that the regulators were no more open to the merger than they had been five years earlier. In an eleventh-hour attempt to save the deal, Wattles announced that he would buy as many Blockbuster stores as necessary to get it past the government.

Although Stead wanted Hollywood Video badly, Shepherd was not keen on it—he believed they could take out the number two chain without going to the expense or trouble of buying it. He and Antioco had identified about nine hundred Hollywood Video stores that overlapped with Blockbusters in markets that could not support both. These were the locations Blockbuster needed to eliminate.

On January 9, 2005, Movie Gallery revealed the details of its bid for Hollywood Video—$13.25 per share, plus the assumption of $300 million of debt—a price tag of $1.1 billion. Lawyers for Movie Gallery argued in a second round of FTC testimony that it was still too soon to say whether the newer movie distribution models competed directly with store rentals—after all, store rental prices had risen since their introduction. Data showed that renters patronized stores for new release titles that would not show up on VOD for months, and many used online rental subscriptions to access older content.

Antioco thought the FTC inclination to block the Blockbuster-Hollywood merger was wrong, and he was prepared to do the deal and take the government to court. But then Movie Gallery cofounder and chief executive Joe Malugen changed everything with his ridiculously huge offer. Antioco wanted to walk away from the deal and use his stores to attack Hollywood Video, but Icahn would not let the matter rest.

Icahn insisted in almost daily phone calls that Antioco raise Blockbuster's bid. The calls became acrimonious, as Antioco insisted that the chain wasn't worth what Malugen had bid, let alone another $1 or more per share. Cowed by Icahn's threats and bluster, Blockbuster's board of directors agreed to consider raising the amount of the offer, against Antioco's protests. He gave in in the end and launched a hostile bid on February 4 to take over Hollywood Video at $14.50 per share in cash and Blockbuster shares.

Regulators increased their scrutiny of the hostile bid and asked Blockbuster to provide a detailed list of pricing, discounting, and cost information. Investigators demanded e-mails and other documents that they believed proved the two huge chains viewed each other as direct competitors and not, as the companies were saying, potential partners with complementary markets.

Blockbuster turned over the documents in late February and stated in securities filings that it had complied with the regulators' demands. It had given Hollywood shareholders until late March to tender their shares, but again found itself facing uncomfortable media attention when the FTC discovered that the pricing information it had turned over was inaccurate.

The drama around Blockbuster's bid put off Hollywood Video's board of directors, which advised shareholders in a February 21 letter to vote in favor of Movie Gallery's bid. Although Blockbuster's bid was higher, it was clear that antitrust problems would likely scuttle or significantly delay that sale, the board wrote.

The FTC had not decided by mid-March on whether to clear Blockbuster's bid, and Antioco and Stead vowed to go forward with purchases of Hollywood Video stock until regulators stepped in to stop them. The FTC made it clear it would go to court to obtain an injunction to block the sales, and on March 26, Blockbuster stepped aside to let Movie Gallery complete its purchase of the number two chain.

"Given the current circumstances, in our judgment it is not in Blockbuster's best interest to continue to pursue the acquisition," Antioco said in a statement.

Icahn, now stuck with Blockbuster stock that had dropped in value, and a smaller than expected profit from the Hollywood Video–Movie Gallery merger, was furious, and he blamed Antioco for blowing the deal.

He called for Blockbuster's board to find a private equity buyer for the company; a move that Viacom had tried and failed at before splitting it off. Then Icahn demanded another special dividend for Blockbuster shareholders that would have totaled more than $300 million—again rejected by Antioco and the board. The tension between the two men rose, egged on by Stead, who vowed not to submit to the former corporate raider's tactics.

AS THE CRISIS with Hollywood Video unfolded, attorneys general in several states started looking into the End of Late Fees promotion with great interest—especially the policies under which Blockbuster charged a $1.25 restocking fee if consumers returned a movie or game outside the seven-day rental window, or the full sale price of the item minus the rental fee if they kept DVDs beyond a seven-day grace period. The state officials also complained that consumers were confused by the fact that several hundred stores owned by franchisees were not participating in the program, and that some of these even displayed End of Late Fees advertising.

The End of Late Fees ads prompted false advertising lawsuits in forty-eight states by mid-February, a development that proved more embarrassing than expensive. Blockbuster agreed a month later to change its advertising, to more prominently mention the fees, and to pay $630,000 to reimburse the states for the costs of their investigations.

Antioco began experiencing a crisis of confidence in the program that spring, wondering if Blockbuster should back away from it, as gross margins eroded and store costs proved more difficult to cut than expected. But Shepherd, who had started to see active memberships reversing their decline and slowly growing, dug in. He warned Antioco that he would stick with the program as long as he was in charge and reminded the CEO that the program had been his idea.

Antioco had warned investors before the split-off that Blockbuster would lose money in 2005, as it moved into new businesses, but the size of the losses from the End of Late Fees promotion, coupled with a steep industrywide downturn in DVD rental revenue, outstripped what analysts had forecast.

After growing by double digits since 2000, sales and rental of DVDs began cooling faster than expected. Retailers blamed the glut of product that studios had rushed to market to capitalize on DVD's high profit margin and a theatrical slate that wasn't connecting with consumers.

Although Zine had joked that the massive dividend payment represented "the price of exodus" from Viacom, he not been too worried about taking on the $1 billion–plus in long-term debt, because Blockbuster was still generating plenty of cash. The headline-grabbing losses that Viacom attributed to Blockbuster in previous years represented mainly noncash write-downs of the overpayment that the media conglomerate had made for Blockbuster. Zine believed the video rental giant was healthy enough to bounce back, as long as Antioco did not take on any more expensive initiatives.

AS SOON AS Blockbuster withdrew its bid for Hollywood Video, Antioco reached out to Icahn to try to head off a public feud over the failed deal. Icahn had a long track record of threatening proxy fights unless he got his way—usually in the form of an above-market payoff, management changes, or asset sales. Icahn had recently abandoned a threatened proxy battle at Kerr-McGee after the gas-and-oil company agreed to buy back $4 billion of its shares at a 15 percent premium. But Antioco didn't like to be threatened, and the discussions went nowhere.

On March 28, the day Blockbuster abandoned its pursuit of Hollywood Video, its stock price dropped 6 percent, to just under nine dollars—bringing its total decline over the previous year to 43 percent. Winning suitor Movie Gallery saw its shares rise by five dollars the same day. Icahn filed a letter with the Securities and Exchange Commission ten days later, criticizing Blockbuster's management in blistering terms for failing to close the deal.

Icahn lashed out at Antioco for taking the video rental chain on a spending spree with shareholders' money, and he vowed to change the company's direction by winning the three seats on Blockbuster's board that were up for election in May. In particular, Icahn also took aim at Antioco's $51 million pay package, which included a $5 million bonus, restricted stock grants worth $26.8 million, and options valued at $17 million. Icahn called the package "unconscionable."

Blockbuster spokesman Randy Hargrove shot back on Antioco's behalf, saying that the value of the stock grants and options, which made up most of the package, depended on the CEO remaining at the company and resurrecting the stock price. Antioco publicly called out Icahn for attempting to discredit Blockbuster's management with investors in order to press his own agenda for a payoff. Antioco warned that threats of a proxy fight would distract the company from the battle it faced to retain customers, potentially throwing away tens of millions already spent on new initiatives.

"The turmoil and uncertainty you have created threatens to destroy the organization, jeopardize our success and could prove damaging to shareholder value," Antioco wrote in a letter to Icahn that he filed with the SEC.

Just one month remained before Blockbuster's annual meeting in Dallas, and Antioco turned to protecting his company and his job from Icahn and his followers.

In Los Gatos, McCarthy and Hastings watched with interest. Their hope for a speed bump to derail Blockbuster Online had been answered.

CHAPTER EIGHT

KICK ASS

(2004–2005)

IT WAS CLUNKY AND PLAGUED with software and inventory problems, but in its first three months of operation, Blockbuster Online captured more than half of all the subscribers who were signing up for online rental for the first time. The two-dollar price difference helped divert traffic from Netflix, but persuading subscribers to stick to Blockbuster's service beyond the free trial period would prove challenging in the shifting competitive landscape that both companies faced in 2005.

Netflix felt the squeeze in new sign-ups almost immediately, but Hastings and McCarthy had bigger problems claiming their attention at almost exactly the moment Blockbuster Online launched. The rumors about Amazon entering their marketplace had grown louder over the summer of 2004, and then, in late September, proof surfaced that there was something behind them.

Jeff Bezos had seen forecasts that DVD sales would erode in a pattern suspiciously similar to the way music sales fell off with the advent of Apple's iTunes store. Like big-box retailers, Amazon was reaping healthy profits from DVD sales and wanted to protect that business until digital movie delivery became as lucrative as iTunes had become with music. Even though Amazon did not have a distribution system that could match Netflix's speed, it had all the ingredients it needed to run a DVD-by-mail service until digital delivery became a reality.

In late September Ted Sarandos, Netflix's chief of content acquisition, delivered solid proof from his studio contacts that Bezos was just three to six months away from launching a competing service, using his existing distribution centers. Amazon had purchased reader sorters to process the mailers and was close to completing deals to buy inventory from the movie studios, his sources in the industry said.

In early October 2004, venture capitalist and Netflix investor John Doerr set up a phone call between Hastings and Bezos in the hope that the two CEOs could reach a business arrangement that would keep Amazon out of their market. But the negotiations stalled a week later over Amazon's demands for steep fees for referring would-be renters to Netflix. "I talked to Bezos," Hastings told his executive team. "There is no working together that makes sense."

McCarthy scheduled a series of marathon board meetings for the following three days to come up with a strategy to either drive off Amazon or find a way to survive its challenge.

The company's major investors were incredulous and angry. How did Netflix not know Amazon was coming, some asked. The stock price surely would collapse again, others said. How could you do this to us?

Netflix's executive team began working from the supposition that Amazon would come in at a cheaper subscription price to try to spur sign-ups among its six million daily users, so they decided to carry out the most brutal price cut they could afford. Hastings told Kilgore and her team, and Kirincich, who modeled Netflix's financial forecasts in McCarthy's office, to figure out how low they could go on the monthly subscription price and still fund their marketing plan. Because Kilgore's husband worked at Amazon, they spent a weekend at Kirincich's house running numbers. On Monday they returned with a proposal to cut the three-out subscription plan by 18 percent, to $17.99.

Less than a week later, on October 14, 2004, Netflix tucked the news of the price cut into the bottom paragraph of a news release detailing its third-quarter financial results. Hastings divulged to investors and the media on a conference call an hour later that the new price, effective November 1, was intended to position Netflix for Amazon's imminent entry into the U.S. online rental market.

In a curt nod to Blockbuster Online, he acknowledged that the business environment had become increasingly competitive, but he barely mentioned that newest player in the space. McCarthy announced that he would abandon his plan to leave Netflix at year's end. He would instead stay on as CFO for at least two more years, and possibly indefinitely, until Netflix had weathered the competitive squall.

"There are very few challenges as exciting as the one we face, if in fact Amazon enters the marketplace," McCarthy said. "This is going to be epic, and it will be part of the lore of Silicon Valley."

"Besides," he added later, "you don't leave your friends in the middle of a knife fight."

After spending $10 million to open offices and a distribution center in the United Kingdom, Hastings decided to postpone the international expansion for at least a year, reasoning that he did not want a two-front war with Amazon, which had already launched its UK online rental service.

The raft of bad news sent the company's stock price sliding again.

"Look, everyone, I know the Amazon entry is a bitter and surprising pill for those of you that are long in our stock," he told investors on the earnings conference call. "This is going to be a very large market, and we're going to execute very hard to make this back for our shareholders, including ourselves."

Then Hastings laid out a scenario at once alarming and exciting: If Blockbuster and Amazon matched or beat Netflix's new eighteen-dollar price, video stores in America would be vacant within a few years. The $8 billion in U.S. store rentals would pour into online rentals, setting off a grab for subscribers, he said. The ensuing growth of online rentals would cannibalize video stores faster and faster, until they collapsed.

As video store revenue dropped sharply, Blockbuster would struggle to fund its online operation, he concluded. "The prize is huge, the stakes high, and we intend to win."

AT THE PARAMOUNT Building, Evangelist listened rapt as Hastings laid out his plans, wondering how Blockbuster Online should respond. The call echoed from speakerphones all over the office. A jeer had gone up when McCarthy made his knife-fight comment, and within minutes, one of the developers had photoshopped a knife-wielding McCarthy facing off against a gun-toting Antioco under a headline that read: "This dumb ass thinks he's in a knife fight."

As soon as the call ended, at around 6:00 P.M. local time, Evangelist was on the phone with Antioco. The Blockbuster CEO agreed to come over before having dinner with Shepherd and his thirteen-year-old son, James, at The Palm, a steak restaurant around the corner from the Paramount Building whose walls were covered with caricatures of its loyal patrons, including Antioco.

By the time Antioco and Shepherd joined them later that night, Evangelist and Cooper had decided to undercut Netflix by fifty cents— a price differentiation that preserved their ability to grow and turn a profit in the foreseeable future.

Antioco ridiculed the move as a timid half measure—like kissing your sister, he said. He argued for a deep chop—to $14.99—on the theory that their per-subscriber losses would be relatively small but Netflix would be seriously weakened if it tried to absorb the same losses from 2.2 million subscribers.

Shepherd didn't think a couple of bucks would change consumers' opinions about the online service, and he was worried about the short-term effect of a price cut on Blockbuster's financial health. But when he half jokingly asked James to weigh in, the teenager agreed with Antioco that a price drop was a great move.

"The kid says drop the price," Antioco said. "What are you going to do?"

He agreed to announce the smaller cut the next day. In Evangelist and Antioco's nightly conversations during that time they often entertained the idea of trying to pressure Netflix's share price low enough for Blockbuster to buy it. Evangelist mused that the price war they were about to set off could be just the catalyst needed for such a takeover.

The next day, Antioco and Karen Raskopf, vice president of corporate communications, made a series of phone calls to reporters at major financial news outlets, including me. As I spoke with Antioco, I pushed a few headlines announcing the details of Blockbuster's new pricing plan to Reuters's financial wires and watched as Netflix's shares tumbled.

"We were growing our business at a very nice clip but would not have elected to lower our prices," Antioco told me, clearly enjoying himself. "Having said that, we are determined that we are not going to be beaten from a price-value perspective." I hung up the phone and quickly called Netflix to get a reaction to what had turned into a price war. I was connected with Sarandos. After I explained why I was calling, a surprised Sarandos was silent for a moment.

"Do you have any comment?" I asked him again.

"We have to digest this a bit before we can make a comment," he said, sounding shocked.

McCarthy and Hastings had miscalculated badly, first by ignoring the threat posed by Blockbuster Online, and then by expecting Antioco and Evangelist to enter the online market in a way that made sense to Netflix. Since they also had failed to anticipate the Blockbuster chief's answer to their price cut, the Netflix team turned to what it understood—numbers—to find a way out of the price war they had set off.

Blockbuster Online was essentially Netflix in a time warp and would experience the same growth and usage patterns, they reasoned. McCarthy tasked Kirincich with modeling Blockbuster Online's business and growth trajectory using subscriber metrics they had gathered from Netflix's operations over the years—data that Evangelist had no way of knowing. Kirincich also created a financial model of Blockbuster's store operations to test the effects different price and spending scenarios in the online business would have on Blockbuster stores' balance sheets.

Since Blockbuster stores would have to fund the online business until it could break even—at about two million subscribers—it was critical to understand how many marketing dollars Antioco could put behind Blockbuster Online before he started to have budget problems. The $1 billion debt that Blockbuster had taken on in the Viacom split-off put a time limit on how long they would have to wait out Blockbuster Online if it continued to spend on marketing and price cuts, he told Hastings and McCarthy.

Among the advantages Netflix enjoyed were lower costs—they spent less to attract and keep subscribers, as their base aged, and on operations, which improved over time as the novelty of the service wore off and subscribers watched fewer films. Blockbuster would spend more to get its subscribers, who would turn over more quickly, and to service them for the first nine months or so, before their demand for movies flattened out.

Netflix's data also showed that an online service had to maintain a minimum level of marketing to attract enough subscribers to replace those who canceled. Cut advertising and public awareness campaigns below that magic number and the base would melt away.

McCarthy and his team believed that by running different price scenarios they could pinpoint exactly when Blockbuster would have to back off its marketing spending for the online service or risk violating its debt agreements with its lenders.

Another piece of luck fell into their laps fairly early in the battle that proved crucial to Kirincich's models. A Netflix investor pointed out to

Dillon that Blockbuster Online assigned sequential account numbers to each new subscriber, and those numbers appeared in the bar codes on its mailers. By having Netflix employees and their family members sign up for Blockbuster Online on a regular schedule—say, once a week—and noting down their customer numbers, Kirincich could calculate how effective its spending on marketing was, how quickly its base was growing, and how many movies the service had to ship. All of this data added up to the burn rate—how fast the online business was going through the budget provided to it by the store business. Kirincich believed that at the rate Blockbuster Online was growing, Antioco would be forced to back off, or possibly suspend marketing activities, by the second quarter of 2005.

The intricacy of their models and the accuracy of McCarthy's forecasts in the past made Hastings fairly comfortable about sticking to the pricing and spending plan they had announced in October. Their forecasts showed that Netflix's growth was still moving in the right direction, just a little more slowly with Blockbuster Online in the mix. Since only 20 percent of consumers were able to identify the Netflix logo, the company had plenty of room to grow. Blockbuster's ads were raising awareness of online rental, so the market would expand faster than they had anticipated.

They were still on course to finish 2004 with 3 million subscribers, and to add another 1 million in the coming year. Their models showed a base of at least 5.65 million subscribers in 2006—surpassing what market research had once said was the size of the entire online rental market.

A few days after the price war began, Hastings decided to approach Walmart chief executive John Fleming to see about joining forces to attack Amazon, which had become a Walmart competitor in a growing number of product categories. At an October 27, 2004, meeting he offered to refer subscribers to Walmart for DVD sales, with Walmart reciprocating by recommending Netflix for DVD rental. For all the fanfare of its launch, the Walmart site had managed to attract only about sixty thousand subscribers, and was not growing enough to dent Netflix, even at $4 a month less. Shortly after Blockbuster dropped its rates, Walmart cut its prices below both services, to $17.36 per month.

Hastings also wanted to gauge whether Fleming was open to a possible offer from Netflix to buy Walmart's meager subscriber base. The talks that night went nowhere, mainly because Fleming was trying to negotiate a partnership with Yahoo! in hopes of making the subscription business work.

As luck would have it, a young Netflix executive ran into a female acquaintance who worked for Walmart.com at a San Francisco Bay Area music venue. The two often joked about the rivalry between their two companies. One night the woman told him over drinks that Walmart's online service had little support from its corporate parent. Armed with this information, Hastings dug in to wait, and kept lines of communication open with Fleming.

AND THEN, ANTIOCO ratcheted up the pressure on Netflix again.

In late autumn, Cooper brought Antioco a plan to test a Blockbuster Online television spot in a few markets to see what effect it had on sign-ups compared to other advertising channels. They agreed to shoot two different commercials—one that Cooper and Evangelist liked and the other recommended by the ad agency for Blockbuster stores—and decide which explained online rental more clearly.

When he viewed the ads in the first week of January, Antioco loved the one Cooper had storyboarded so much that he decided to dispense with testing it.

"Let's run this on the Super Bowl," he told a surprised Cooper and Blockbuster's media buyer from Camelot Communications. "This is great, and we need to do something big. Forget the test market. Let's go with it." The spot featured a man who tells his wife he's going to return a movie and backs his car to the end of the driveway to put a Blockbuster Online envelope inside the mailbox. The spot was a perfect vehicle to rectify something that was still annoying Antioco—the price for the three-out plan. He wanted it cut to $14.99.

Following through on Antioco's directive, they purchased relatively economical ads that ran before the coin toss and after the last play of Super Bowl XXXIX on February 6 between the New England Patriots and the Philadelphia Eagles. Cooper and his wife, Jess, stayed home to watch the game without interruption. Shortly before the kickoff, Cooper's BlackBerry buzzed with the hourly subscriber report—two hundred sign-ups. At the hour after the first ad ran, the number was up to nine hundred. The Darth Vader ring tone emanated from his BlackBerry seconds later.

"Are you seeing this?" Evangelist asked. "This is big."

Cooper was cautious. "Let's wait and see what happens next hour," he said. When his BlackBerry chimed next, Cooper could hardly believe it—two thousand subs. The number kept climbing. Evangelist was ecstatic. That day, Blockbuster Online signed up about nineteen thousand subscribers—nearly four times their daily average. The next day, more than twenty thousand subscribers signed up.

The ad, which ran for several weeks, bestowed the double benefit of boosting customer awareness of the program and convincing skeptical business development partners that Blockbuster was serious in its bid to catch Netflix.

Hastings agonized over whether to drop prices further to meet Blockbuster's $14.99 holiday price cut, but McCarthy steadfastly objected. With Blockbuster losing even more on every subscriber, relief from its advertising juggernaut was even closer at hand. Kirincich checked his models again—and the outcome was the same. Blockbuster would have to raise prices by summertime. Because Netflix was still growing solidly, McCarthy wanted to sit tight and wait until the inevitable happened.

"They can continue to bleed at this rate of $14.99, given the usage patterns that we know exist early in the life of the customer, until the end of the second quarter," Kirincich told the executives.

The trouble was, the wait was excruciating. The holidays became a season of panic, as Christmas approached and Netflix had not reached the bottom of the range of subscriber additions it had forecast for investors. As staffers took off for the holidays, Erich Ziegler, the marketing analyst charged with subscriber forecasts, tried to calm Hastings, McCarthy, and Kilgore, who were concerned about the slow sign-ups. The adoption rate of the DVD format was expected to reach its pinnacle in 2005, when holiday sales of players went through the roof, he explained. In each DVD player box was a red Netflix coupon for a free trial membership. Most of these would be redeemed on or a few days after Christmas Day. That was the theory, anyway.

Ziegler then headed to the airport to fly to his parents' home on the East Coast, confident in his prediction. Kilgore arranged for hourly reports of subscriber additions to be sent to the finance and marketing teams' BlackBerrys, in case they needed to adjust the marketing mix. They were in the clear. By the day after Christmas, Netflix blew through its subscriber forecast with year-over-year growth of 118 percent. All the same, the uncertainty had been maddening.

POWERED BY HEAVY spending on advertising and in-store coupons, Blockbuster surpassed 750,000 subscribers in four months, a benchmark Netflix worked for four years to reach. The attack on Netflix's market share drove up both the cost of signing up subscribers and cancellations, as consumers played one service against the other.

Hastings acknowledged in a January call with investors that Netflix had to pay more attention to beating back Blockbuster. Although Amazon was a more formidable foe from a technology standpoint, Blockbuster was more motivated, because they were defending their core business, he said.

"It has been a serious effort, and one we clearly underestimated, a mistake we do not intend to repeat," McCarthy added.

Despite the aggressive attack, Blockbuster had not managed to interrupt Netflix plans to launch a modest download service, and to make a profit in the last three quarters of 2005, he said. Next McCarthy shared his department's forecasts, hoping word would get around of the dire financial straits in which Blockbuster would soon find itself.

"At the fifteen-dollar price point, based on our modeling, we expect their online business to lose money on every subscriber indefinitely, unless they slash their marketing spending, which will slow their growth," he said. "If we have to match Blockbuster's pricing to sustain our growth objectives, . . . if we end up in a war of attrition, our operating losses will increase as well. But I believe we are better positioned to survive the battle than Blockbuster."

Wall Street practically ignored the warning about Blockbuster's debt, but short sellers started borrowing large positions in Netflix stock, anticipating another plunge in its share price. Analysts played along by downgrading the stock. "For the third consecutive quarter, we were left with the impression that Netflix management is not acting upon, but reacting to, its competitive environment and subscriber sentiment," Richard Ingrassia at Roth Capital Partners wrote to clients in a note advising them to sell Netflix shares.

"Prospects for the business remain cloudy near-term as subscriber growth and profitability hinge on what Blockbuster and Amazon will do next," Youssef Squali at Jefferies & Co. advised his clients.

Mario Cibelli of Marathon Partners spent one of the more interesting days of his career as a hedge fund manager at a Netflix distribution center in Long Island, and came away with a different opinion. "There's not a snowball's chance in hell that Blockbuster can do this," he told his colleagues, when he returned to work later that day.

The warehouse manager, a former aerospace engineer, had shown Cibelli a series of charts posted on the wall; it had about two dozen optimum performance metrics. "As long as my performance is within this band, I won't hear from senior management," the man said, indicating the charts. "As soon as I move out of this band, I will get a call."

Hastings and his team had spent the time and thought to build a quality business, and management clearly was running Netflix for the long term, Cibelli thought. He laid out his reasons for taking a long position in Netflix shares in an internal memo:

> On the surface, Netflix is a massive video store; taking in cash for monthly renting rights and loaning out DVDs to the consumer. Beneath the surface, Netflix is akin to a think-tank, creating algorithms to maximize the long-term value of each customer that it enlists, orchestrating a complex distribution system and finding ways to reduce its costs of service.
>
> It is the unseen aspects of Netflix's business model, and its long head start, which differentiate it from the competition and may allow Netflix to retain the leading position in the industry for some time.

Although the online business seemed a natural extension of Blockbuster's core competency, "it is quite rare for a mature company to enthusiastically go after a new business that promises to cannibalize, in part, a corporate cash cow," Cibelli wrote.

Blockbuster would soon be "very tempted to raise price at its online unit in the face of the losses it is likely experiencing," he predicted.

Cibelli also dismissed the idea that Amazon posed an imminent threat, concluding that the big e-tailer would find it difficult and expensive to build a service to match that of Netflix. But the little company made a tempting takeover target for Amazon, "at an appropriate price," as long as tax issues related to assuming Netflix's distribution centers could be resolved.

No one but his clients and colleagues were privy to the details underpinning Cibelli's contrarian viewpoint, which was just the way he liked it.

HASTINGS HAD REMARKED on a conference call in April that Blockbuster had thrown everything at Netflix "but the kitchen sink." When he arrived at the University Drive headquarters the next day, a giant box from a home improvement store was waiting. Inside was a kitchen sink, courtesy of Ed Stead and the executives at Blockbuster. Hastings got a kick out of the gesture, but he had no intention of again underestimating the seriousness of the challenge that Blockbuster had laid down. Netflix was under siege, and Hastings knew he needed to rouse his company to its peak performance. His employees found on such occasions that he could be a stirring speaker and an inspirational leader they would follow to the limits of their endurance.

He relied on parables and props to make his points, once dressing as Muhammad Ali in a robe and boxing gloves to encourage his staff to roll with the punches in the fight against Blockbuster. Another time he handed out wooden harpoons to managers to exhort them to wait patiently for the whale that was Blockbuster to come up for air. He invoked Sir Edmund Hillary's lean-and-mean two-man climb to the top of Mt. Everest to explain how Netflix would vanquish better-funded brands with fewer resources.

The prospect of a full-on battle with Blockbuster unnerved some, especially in light of the bad press they were getting. Kirincich lost a newly hired employee after the man had second thoughts about join-ing embattled Netflix and decided to ask for his job back at the com-pany where he had just given notice. There was a sense at Netflix's headquarters of circling the wagons, buying as much of the stock as they could afford, and letting their focus and desperation do the rest.

Armed with financial and marketing models that showed Block-buster could not afford the game of chicken it was playing, Hastings maintained a steadfast answer to the criticism and takeover rumors circulating that spring. Netflix would run at break even—sacrificing profits and plowing all of its cash into growing its subscriber base as fast as it could to raise an impenetrable barrier to entry by Amazon and other challengers.

A subscriber-based business would lose a lot of money until it got large enough to defray fixed overhead costs. In early 2005, Hastings and McCarthy pegged the cost for a new competitor to enter the market at $350 million to $500 million.

Hastings restated his warning for Blockbuster at a Reuters conference in San Francisco in March. "How long are you prepared to run at break even?" I asked.

"As long as it takes to run off the competition," he answered.

"So—is that a year? Five years?" I asked.

"As long as it takes," he answered.

Part of Hastings's break-even strategy called for spending $90 million per quarter in an advertising arms race designed to force Blockbuster deeper into the red.

KEN ROSS WAS that rarest of creatures—a warm and endearingly enthusiastic New Yorker. He still delighted in his work as a corporate spokesman, despite having coped with vicissitudes ranging from Michael Jackson's hair catching fire during a Pepsi commercial shoot to the clay feet of the executives he served. Ross, fifty-one, liked Faconnable shirts, jeans and loafers, laughed a lot, and embraced reporters he liked as friends. Ross turned down the offer when Hastings and Kilgore first approached him to work at Netflix because it would entail moving from Los Angeles, where he had relocated from New York in 1999, to Silicon Valley.

Nor did Ross like the idea of reporting to Kilgore instead of directly to Hastings. Working as an arm of Kilgore's marketing seemed too constrained a role—he wanted to control press and investor relations plus internal communications. But he liked Hastings and Kilgore and Sarandos, and he saw the promise in Netflix—that he could help turn it into a defining lifestyle brand. The second time Hastings made the offer Ross decided that he'd have enough influence to do just that if he was any good at his job. He took the job as vice president of corporate communications in January 2005 and set out to remedy the yawning awareness gap between Blockbuster and Netflix.

He had taken over the head PR job at Netflix from Shernaz Daver, a fast-talking, energetic consultant who had suffered through a year-long drumbeat of negative headlines about Netflix since Blockbuster launched its competing service. Daver, an attractive, gregarious woman of Zoroastrian descent, first introduced me to Netflix's upper management during my first trip to the headquarters she jokingly called "the hole" in Los Gatos.

Daver had battled so many reporters over stories about Wall Street's gloom and doom predictions about Netflix's demise at Blockbuster's or Amazon's hands that she had almost no time to actually promote the service. By the time Ross arrived, she had made inroads into main-stream lifestyle magazines but the articles centered mainly on pains-taking descriptions of how the service worked.

As a result, Ross was working with a blank slate when it came to ordinary American consumers.

First he would find the soccer moms and NASCAR dads in the markets beyond New York, Los Angeles, and San Francisco, and he planned to do it by making sure the company and all of its execu-tives looked and acted like they belonged to an established leadership brand.

Second, he would establish Netflix as a newsmaker and a "must fol-low" company among the nation's top media outlets. Ross focused on journalists at just a few major media outlets—the *New York Times*, the *Wall Street Journal*, *Fortune*, *Forbes* and *BusinessWeek* magazines, and the Associated Press, Bloomberg, and Reuters newswires—since they set the business news agenda in the United States.

He chose forty-seven-year-old Steve Swasey for a second in com-mand, a seasoned PR man who, he reflected, didn't need directions to get to the *Today Show* green room. Ross found in Swasey a perfect foil—a bad cop who could unflinchingly deliver a firm company line and not back away in the face of intense journalistic wheedling and abuse.

Not that Swasey relished his power, as some company flaks do. He was a boyish-looking native Californian who wore his khakis and preppy buttoned-down shirts starched under immaculate blazers and peered anxiously over his frameless glasses when he talked. Swasey was parsimonious with any true scoops about the inner workings of Netflix or its officers but, when strictly necessary, delivered this information almost with shame, as if it had been pried out of him under torture.

Swasey's reserved demeanor masked a love of spectacle—especially the elaborately choreographed press conferences and lengthy television stories that he excelled at promoting, and later described with utter satisfaction as "glorious."

The first time Swasey saw the clockwork process of a Netflix distribution center, with red envelopes whipping through a postal sorter, the giant racks of movies, and the workers' hands moving in a blur to pack and unpack DVDs, he envisioned a sublime series of television and photographic events.

He convinced Ross to let him invite local media for tours of the distribution hub in Phoenix. The event, for which he had workers wear t-shirts with huge Netflix logos on front and back, generated so much positive publicity that Swasey's "hublicity tours" became a staple of Netflix's shoestring PR campaign. Swasey eventually won coverage of the humble facilities from the likes of *60 Minutes*, *Nightline*'s John Donvan, and Pulitzer Prize–winner Susan Sheehan, who wrote about her day packing disks for the *New Yorker*'s Talk of the Town column.

Ross had worked with press-shy chief executives, and he was relieved to find that Hastings was not one of them. Although abrupt and demanding with staff, Hastings was reliably pleasant and engaging around journalists, and he suppressed his impatient streak under even the most inane questioning. And he demonstrated early on in

Ross's tenure that he had the discipline to moderate his behavior for the good of the brand. During their second earnings call, Ross and Swasey kept a tally of the number of times Hastings mentioned Blockbuster—nearly three dozen—and compared it to his mentions of Netflix, which came in at about half that number. They showed him the scorecard at the end of the call, and Ross remarked, "A leader doesn't do that." It was the first and only time he had to tell Hastings to focus on selling his own brand.

Like most Silicon Valley moguls, Hastings had little interest in his clothing or appearance. Jeans and T-shirts were his workday uniform, and dressy was the bowling shirt he wore to a 2005 presentation for investors, known as an analyst day, at the posh Fairmont San Jose Hotel. As the plan to present Netflix as a company to watch succeeded, and photo shoots became a staple of Hastings's press schedule, Ross convinced him to hire a consultant to come up with a wardrobe for public appearances.

"When you are getting photographed in the New York Times or Fortune or the AP, you're making a statement about the company," he told Hastings. Hasting liked to be photographed with a fan of DVDs or behind a conveyor belt in the nearby distribution center. He stuck to company-related settings as a safeguard against the embarrassment he had felt after posing on the hood of his Porsche for a photo accompanying a 1995 USA Today article about Silicon Valley start-ups entitled "Boom! You're a Millionaire."

Hastings proved an adept and interested student of mass media, and held up well most of the time as Netflix's public persona. Occasionally Hastings's engineer brain would trump his CEO manners. At a 2010 event at the Churchill Club, hosted by former Walt Disney chairman and chief executive Michael Eisner, Hastings ended his ninety-minute appearance, rose, and walked off the stage before the moderator had finished a rather meandering concluding speech—eliciting an audible gasp from the audience.

But Hastings was a great interview, simply because (to Swasey's chagrin) he readily answered every question put to him clearly and succinctly, and he was better informed than many tech executives about his own business and the industries touching it.

MIKE KALTSCHNEE RODE a commuter train winding between Connecticut and Manhattan, watched the rising drama between Blockbuster and Netflix unfold in the financial press, and thought, *Here is something worth pursuing.* Kaltschnee was a software programmer by profession and a writer by avocation, and he became interested in Netflix at around the same time he decided to take up blogging. He decided to combine the two in a new type of online journaling called "brand blogging," in which a writer shares his enthusiasm (or hatred) for a particular company and invites readers to post comments or information about it, in the spirit of transparency. He was a tall, husky man with a geek's enthusiasm for taking things apart—especially businesses—to figure out how they worked. In 2003, when a red coupon for a free trial of Netflix floated out of the box of the DVD player he had purchased, he tried the service and was hooked. He loved the vast movie selection and the sleek Web site, of course, but he was equally fascinated by the delivery mechanics. How did Netflix coordinate mailings for more than one million Queues? Why did the turnaround time vary depending on where he dropped off the mailers? How did the company put away so many DVDs each day with so few employees? *I wonder how it all works,* he thought.

Kaltschnee had started a Web design firm with three other guys in the mid-1990s that became one of the first subscription services for graphics. They sold the company a few years later, and Kaltschnee stayed on to create a second subscription service for the buyers' stock photography collection. He knew about subscription businesses from that experience, and he wanted to learn how Netflix had been so successful. In November 2003, he launched the blog HackingNetflix. com, in keeping with his pledge to deconstruct the service and learn how it operated; its masthead was Netflix-red and its observations, gentle.

Kaltschnee was an unabashed advocate for Netflix from the start, and he'd joined a generation of bloggers who wanted to share their personal experiences with a product or corporation. He and his followers, who soon numbered a quarter million per month, ran commentaries on Netflix news, product launches, legal troubles, and just plain gossip, sometimes shared by anonymous insiders. Blogs were a gold mine of information for journalists about product and price tests, company gossip, and consumer sentiment. I read HackingNetflix devotedly and, eventually, so did most other mainstream journalists.

The bloggers and their followers gained exponential power in the rise of the social networking movement, as consumers learned to take both compliments and complaints online and publicly demand redress. The blogs' collective might spoke to and for consumers in a way that advertising could not match. They seemed to see everything. Companies may have looked down on them but certainly became too wise to ignore them, as both Netflix and Blockbuster soon learned.

At first, Kaltschnee posted about two or three times a week. His posts included short lists of newly released titles, cheerful links to news articles, and information about Netflix's financial or stock performance. He quickly built up a community of frequent contributors, as well as visitors who came to the site to check out how to work new features, to scope for answers about changes in service, or to share experiences.

The link to Blockbuster Online's beta test first turned up on HackingNetflix, courtesy of Cooper. Kaltschnee shared it with readers, but he noted that the new service appeared to be a poorly executed clone of Netflix.

As the online rental price war heated up, Kaltschnee wanted a way to communicate directly with Netflix to answer the hundreds of questions, comments, and tips he was getting about the competing services. The trouble was, Netflix wasn't interested. He couldn't even get on its media list. At first he took the rejection in stride, noting that the company's press materials were available from other sources.

In mid-2004 he again approached the company, asking for information for a proposed Ask Netflix column he was putting together for his now ten thousand monthly visitors. He also asked for a tour of a Connecticut distribution center, promising "to keep this friendly (I do like you guys)." The company's response was three lines long—again turning him down and wishing him luck with his site.

After much soul-searching, Kaltschnee shared the e-mails with readers.

"I know I'm not alone," he posted a day or two later.

> It's hard to get companies to take bloggers seriously. I really like Netflix, but they are slowly withdrawing, closing themselves off from their customers (they recently removed their phone numbers from the site). Instead, companies should be embracing these online communities, comprised mostly of the highly desired "early adopters" that evangelize products to the general population.

The reaction from the blogger community was instant—condemning the company and setting off a heated discussion in the mainstream media about the brand bloggers' place in the information ecosystem. Top outlets such as the *New York Times* and the *Wall Street Journal* began to quote Kaltschnee regularly, as a sort of consumer advocate. He was invited to be a panelist on an MSNBC show about brand bloggers.

Netflix finally contacted Kaltschnee a few days after his watershed posting. The company wanted to incorporate HackingNetflix and other blogs into its media plan, product marketing executive Michele Turner told him—it just wasn't sure how they fit. Ensuing conversations resulted in the reinstatement of a consumer service phone number on the Netflix site and on Kaltschnee's page, despite Dillon's objections about the costs of live operators.

Kaltschee also joined Netflix's affiliates program—and started getting a small bounty for each reader who became a Netflix subscriber. He saw his status at the company rise again early in 2005, when Ross and Swasey took over communications. While neither Ross nor Swasey had much to do personally with blogging or social networking, they understood the potential as an important communications channel.

At their first meeting, at a Starbucks in New York City's Union Square, Ross found Kaltschnee personable, dedicated, and professional. He decided to treat HackingNetflix as a new type of media outlet—different from but on the same plane as the *New York Times* or Reuters. He granted Kaltschnee's request for a tour of a distribution center, and he invited the blogger to interview Hastings in Los Gatos. Kaltschnee was thrilled. When he finally sat down with Hastings a few weeks later, with a long list of reader questions, Kaltschnee was so nervous that Ross had to stop the interview and urge him to take a few deep breaths to calm down.

But he was not shy about relaying his readers' pointed questions about one issue that kept cropping up among heavy DVD users, one that had even begun bothering Kaltschnee. He called it throttling.

It seemed that Netflix was intentionally slowing down movie deliveries to a subset of subscribers, who complained about it vocally and for months before Kaltschnee agreed they might have a point. These users learned from talking among themselves that they probably fit the profile of subscribers that Netflix internally labeled "pigs"—the service's heaviest users—who made up about 25 percent of the subscriber base.

"I am usually a very happy Netflix customer, but sometimes I get a bit frustrated with their allocation strategy," Kaltschnee wrote on March 22, 2004.

I've been on "Long Wait" for Sofia Coppola's hit *Lost in Translation* since it was released more than a month ago. Am I being punished for renting more movies than the average Netflix customer?

Two months later he was still waiting, but by this time, readers had started talking to each other about similar experiences. A poster named Eli wrote:

> I'm not sure they are being totally honest about how their waiting system works. It would be in Netflix's best interest to get the movies to people who just put it in their queue, rather than those who had been waiting.

The complaints, and the realization that certain subscribers were being singled out, spurred the late 2004 filing of a class action lawsuit by a San Francisco subscriber that eventually forced Netflix to admit that it gave priority to customers who rented fewer DVDs when inventory was tight. This system helped retain the infrequent renter, known to Netflix as "birds" while putting the brakes on renting by the expensive "pigs."

A few months later, Kaltschnee noticed that the Blockbuster store near his home in Danbury, Connecticut, was refusing to honor the corporation's End of Late Fees promotion. Dozens of his readers related similar experiences at nearby Blockbusters. It was their observations—amplified by the media—that captured the attention of attorneys general in forty-eight states who filed the lawsuits against Blockbuster alleging false advertising.

Both Netflix and Blockbuster settled their blog-incited lawsuits out of court by doling out free rentals to subscribers. Although they had made no admission of wrongdoing, the experience planted a strong incentive for both companies to pay closer attention to what their customers were saying online—a lesson that Kaltschnee later worried that Hastings had not taken to heart.

Hastings admitted to reading HackingNetflix, but he cautioned his executives against taking it too seriously. It overrepresented people with a passionate interest in Netflix, he said.

While this was probably true, Kaltschnee thought it was a mistake for the company to discount feedback from its most loyal followers; the way they used the Internet had a way of amplifying things until they were impossible to ignore, as Netflix's subsequent attempts to cancel two popular Web site features showed.

Practically every source of consumer data had shown marketing and analytics chief Joel Mier and product manager Chris Darner that Netflix subscribers wanted to split their queues so that each member of a family could manage separate movie selections. The idea made sense. Data from separate Queues made Cinematch recommendations more accurate and the subscriber experience better. Hastings resisted the idea, describing it as a barnacle that would impede every programming decision that followed. If subscribers wanted multiple queues per household, let them buy separate subscriptions, he said.

Following entreaties from Mier and Darner, Hastings allowed queue splitting, but he insisted that it be built as cheaply and simply as possible—the easier to disassemble when it failed. The feature, called Profiles, launched in 2005 with little fanfare, and as a result, first attracted a small subset of passionate users from the subscriber base.

At around the same time, Hastings incorporated a feature called Friends into the Netflix Web site as an answer to the rising popularity of social networks. Since federal privacy laws prevented Netflix from sharing customers' rental data publicly, any Queue sharing had to be done among subscribers. The feature was also thought to fill a customer retention role. Netflix's focus groups indicated that people were more likely to rent or purchase movies, and enjoy them more, when they shared the experience with friends.

Even so, Friends, like Profiles, gained only a small following—10 percent or less of subscribers—during its six-year existence, since many subscribers said they felt uncomfortable sharing their movie picks.

IN 2008 HASTINGS decided to deactivate Profiles. The company put users on notice with a curt post on the company's blog, and readers of HackingNetflix unleashed a vocal and unrelenting protest.

A poster named Lisa wrote:

> This is the most non-customer friendly thing I've seen Netflix do to date. No way is this an improvement to customers.

A poster named Mike wrote:

> Wow, what on earth are they thinking? I've been a member since 2004 and this is the first time I've considered switching.

The posters escalated their complaints, asking *New York Times* technology columnist David Pogue to investigate Netflix's decision. Pogue found Swasey's initial explanation—Profiles gummed up the Web site's programming—"uninformative and patronizing."

Ten days later, Netflix product manager Todd Yellin wrote on Netflix's blog that the company had reversed course on its decision to kill Profiles.

> Listening to our members, we realized that users of this feature often describe it as an essential part of their Netflix experience. Simplicity is only one virtue and it can certainly be outweighed by utility.

Despite Yellin's apology, Kaltschnee didn't think Netflix understood the message its subscribers were sending, and when the company abruptly canceled Friends twenty months later, in 2010, he was sure of it. The company eliminated the feature with no warning or explanation as part of a Web site redesign, and its small band of devotees turned to Kaltschnee to set things right. In the uproar that followed, Yellin again admitted to "fumbling the ball."

> We've read every blog post, Tweet, news article, call log to
> Customer Service by those of you who are upset about this
> decision. To you we apologize for not being more upfront earlier.

This time there would be no reprieve.

> We decided to move engineering development time and
> resources from a little used feature to support and maintain the
> things that benefit all Netflix members as the service evolves.

Kaltschnee was troubled to learn that Swasey had protested the decisions to kill both features without first relating the reasons—or even the news of it—to users and had not been listened to. Kaltschnee agreed that the features had to be eliminated for the good of the service, but he did not understand why the company had not felt the need to explain that to its subscribers.

"When people are really passionate about something, you have to tell them the story of why you're taking it away, and how that will make their lives better someday," he told Swasey.

The cancellations of Profiles and Friends exposed a growing fault line between marketing and engineering in Netflix's decision making. A drive for technological advance for its own sake seemed to have replaced the desire to understand customers' needs and meet them. Kaltschnee worried that the episodes reflected a hubris and stubbornness that led Hastings to turn a deaf ear to his customers when he became impatient with the pace at which his vision for Netflix was unfolding.

Hastings prevailed in the end, and quietly eliminated Profiles in

2010 with no explanation and no protest. By then, Netflix's video-streaming service had nearly eliminated subscribers' need to maintain Queues, and that feature died a natural death.

The news was disheartening for Kaltschnee. Was Hastings learning anything from the extraordinary access he had to his customers through forums like HackingNetflix? He hoped so, but he was starting to doubt it.

CHAPTER NINE

THE BEST YEARS OF OUR LIVES

(2005-2006)

AFTER ANTIOCO DROPPED BLOCKBUSTER'S BID for Hollywood Video, a furious Icahn immediately took aim in the press. Antioco began to ignore his demanding phone calls: When the irate billionaire placed his customary closing-time call to Blockbuster headquarters, Antioco had his secretary routinely say that he had left for the day.

The tactic backfired when Icahn vowed to add Antioco to his wall of shame—by stripping him of his chairmanship, and possibly his job, in a proxy fight at Blockbuster's May 11 annual meeting in Dallas. Antioco began to think he had made a mistake in not trying harder to placate Icahn, just to get rid of him. But it was too late; things had gone too far. A couple of weeks before the meeting, shareholder advisory services Glass Lewis and International Shareholder Services conditionally endorsed Icahn's slate—consisting of himself and media executives Strauss Zelnick and Edward Bleier—over Antioco and two sitting directors whose terms had expired. The firms advised shareholders to put Zelnick and Bleier on the board, but if possible, withhold votes from Icahn, as his patent animosity toward Antioco and Blockbuster's executive team would be detrimental to the company.

The tension came to a head on Blockbuster's May 6 earnings

conference call, when Icahn and Antioco got into a six-minute argument, as analysts and journalists listened in.

"Are you willing to agree that if these initiatives don't work, and things don't work out, that you would allow your whole board to be up for election next year, so that the shareholders would have the right to remove the board if they so wished?" Icahn asked.

"That's not up to me to make that decision. The board will make that decision, so that's the best answer I can give you," Antioco shot back.

Finally, Antioco had the operator cut Icahn off in midsentence.

Antioco enlisted corporate communications chief Karen Raskopf to do damage control—to respond to the Glass Lewis and ISS recommendations against him and his directors. Blockbuster's top management sought a compromise the night before the annual meeting, in negotiations that lasted until 2:00 A.M. and resumed at 8:00 A.M.—but it was too late.

In a stunning upset, Icahn and his two dissident directors captured 77 percent of the vote from Blockbuster's shareholders at the May 11 meeting, with a coalition of Icahn and his hedge fund cohort tipping the balance. Blockbuster employees who attended the meeting in the Renaissance Tower auditorium emerged shocked, some in tears. Antioco, who had been stripped of his chairmanship, vowed to trigger his $54 million severance package over the material change in the terms of his employment.

"I'd be lying if I told you this is a happy day, because it is not," Antioco said. "But we'll roll with the punches."

In response to Antioco's threat, the Blockbuster board voted to create an eighth board seat to restore the chief executive to his chairmanship. Icahn also reiterated that he and his directors would not attempt to block the online and late fees strategies.

Blockbuster's share price reacted by swinging upward, but the next day, the two main corporate-debt ratings agencies, Fitch and S&P, cut the company's credit rating deep into junk territory on concerns about its mounting debt and increased competition.

ERICH ZIEGLER WAS at a Super Bowl party in early 2005 when a Blockbuster Online commercial filled the screen at his friend's house in Silicon Valley. When it ended the other partygoers turned to him and asked if Netflix was nervous about Blockbuster's expensive advertising assault.

"I would have spent that money a million different ways," Ziegler said. "I'm not scared at all."

Ziegler had created a complex and sophisticated spreadsheet program that he called the FlexFile to keep up with demands from his boss, Leslie Kilgore, for information and projections about how well Netflix's marketing plan was working. The beauty of FlexFile was its ability to take a stub of data—say, a week's worth of responses to a particular ad—and extrapolate the projected results for a month, a quarter, and a year.

It broke down every marketing channel where Netflix ran ads—radio, TV, billboards, online—to project its cost per acquisition, lifetime subscriber value, and number of acquisitions. It calculated revenue, cancellations, and numbers of subscribers that Netflix would pick up from a particular configuration of advertising.

Using this tool, Ziegler would correctly predict Netflix's marketing costs and subscribers for sixteen straight quarters. FlexFile was better than a crystal ball, and in Ziegler's mind, it eased the pressure-cooker environment that Netflix executives lived in as the fight against Blockbuster grew even more intense. Ziegler used FlexFile to analyze Blockbuster's marketing plan and noticed what he considered costly mistakes—errors Netflix had made long ago and learned from. One of these was getting involved with affiliate coupon and rebate sites that took a high bounty for every customer they referred. The sites had terrible retention and high levels of fraud. He reveled in the fact that cash-strapped Blockbuster kept pouring money into them.

But for all their mistakes, Blockbuster was attracting a growing proportion of subscribers with its expensive ad campaign and generous coupon offers. Netflix had to have an answer for that value proposition.

Kilgore saw only one way to compete on price without sacrificing vital marketing dollars—rolling out a family of subscription plans with prices starting at $9.99 a month for a one-DVD at a time unlimited rental. That announcement, combined with McCarthy's disclosure in April that Netflix's return to profitability would be delayed by a quarter because of Blockbuster's stronger than anticipated onslaught, drew criticism from Wall Street analysts, who worried that Netflix subscribers would flock to the cheaper plans.

ANTIOCO AND ZINE had to go to lenders in early 2005 to renegotiate Blockbuster's credit agreements when they realized that business was not picking up as fast as they had expected as a result of the End of Late Fees promotion. Cutting costs also had proved more difficult than they had predicted. Blockbuster's creditors, who were familiar with Antioco's turnaround plans, quickly granted the chief executive more room in his credit agreements to run at a loss, in order that he could grow the online business and get End of Late Fees well under way.

Like the banks, the studios were fairly forgiving about Blockbuster's slow pay practices, having also seen theatrical revenues declining and sales of DVDs slowing. Zine and Shepherd made the rounds of home entertainment executives in the spring, asking for extensions to pay for DVD inventory and to release shared rental revenue.

But the proxy battle became an issue in the credit renegotiations, with lenders demanding assurances that Antioco—and not Icahn—controlled the company. Some studios saw the rental giant's financial troubles as a good excuse to end their revenue-sharing deals with Blockbuster. "Antioco has never negotiated in a win-win scenario. There is enormous animosity toward him, because he failed to realize that Hollywood is about long-term relationships," one home entertainment executive told a Hollywood trade paper. There was a sense that the studios finally had Blockbuster where they wanted it: Sales of DVDs reached $18.3 billion, and consumers' appetites for owning disks seemed inexhaustible. Overall rental revenue dipped to $8.3 billion from $8.9 billion.

WHEN HIS MARKETING program reached full swing, Evangelist's BlackBerry resounded with hourly notices of ten thousand subscriber sign-ups per week in early 2005. Blockbuster Online was on track to reach two million subscribers and thirty distribution centers by the end of the year, benchmarks that Antioco celebrated by pledging to invest $120 million in the online service in 2005.

Blockbuster Online's solid subscriber growth numbers concealed a serious problem with churn—cancellations that had dogged the young service since its launch. Evangelist had been wooing a former AT&T marketing executive named Lillian Hessel to tackle consumer retention. Hessel had quit AT&T after its merger with Cingular, hoping to find work that involved less travel and more flexibility, so that she could spend more time with her two young children.

Hessel, a tiny blonde with delicate features, wasn't sure after talking with Evangelist that she wanted the position at Blockbuster Online, which included overseeing customer service and analytics. The job seemed too big for one person, she told Evangelist, and she advised him on how to divide up the duties before he offered the post to someone else. Evangelist called Hessel again a few days after their meeting to press her to take the job, as she wrapped up work on a charity function at her children's school.

"I'm losing customers I can't afford to lose—I haven't even paid for them yet," he told her. "Can you help?"

The culture shock of working for a start-up, albeit backed by a major corporation, after her well-appointed office at AT&T hit Messel on her first day as Evangelist showed her to the office she would occupy.

"Okay, and who are all these other people?" she asked, indicating the room's half dozen other occupants, who were working at computers.

"Those are your office mates," he told her.

"And that smell is—"

"The grease pit from downstairs. It comes in pretty strong every now and then," one of her new colleagues said.

The fast pace and freedom to improvise quickly won Hessel over to her new job. She was a decade older than most of her new colleagues, and her knowledge of corporate process and adherence to proprieties provided stability and ballast. Hessel was proud to call herself an old-fashioned lady, but she could swear like a sailor when she wanted to make a point, and had no problem telling Evangelist when he had gone off course.

Like Randolph and Kish's, Hessel's approach to customer retention came from her direct-mail experience, which meant making customers' experiences as close to perfect as possible. She realized after studying Blockbuster Online's Web interface and back-end systems, that a few important details were missing. These issues ranged from the fairly complicated, such as how the fulfillment system selected which disk to send to subscribers when their first choice was not available, to the simple, such as whose job it was to check for scratches on DVDs.

Taken one at a time, as Netflix had done over seven years of careful optimization, the problems were easily solvable. Solving them all at once, in the heat of battle over market share, turned out to be a tangled process. Getting the distribution system right was crucial, because it was the company's only physical link with its customers. Most consumer complaints centered on long waits for popular DVDs to become available. Slow delivery times, the product of a smaller and hastily configured distribution system that did not take into account where Blockbuster Online customers were clustered, also weighed on customer retention.

The lower prices of Blockbuster Online's plans mitigated some of the customer service problems, but Hessel sometimes faced an uphill battle convincing Evangelist and Cooper to fix the service's holes before investing in more customer acquisition channels or new features for the Web site.

Another problem lay in the fact that they had copied Netflix's fulfillment system without really understanding how it worked. Netflix achieved overnight delivery quickly by letting its subscriber base dictate where the hubs would go, rather than just plunking them down in large population centers, as Craft and Ellis had done.

Slowly they learned the ebb and flow of supply and demand that governed the business. They figured out how to place advertising strategically, in markets where they had solid distribution, and to hold off in places where they would have delivery delays. The programmers tweaked back-end algorithms to make better calls about whether to send a customer the first DVD in his queue if it involved a long wait or a lower-order choice that would arrive faster.

Hessel learned to spot subscribers who were likely to cancel—usually those with few movies in their queues, and those whose queues concentrated on one genre or actor—and started an e-mail campaign to gently persuade them to choose a wider variety of films.

Slowly, retention rates rose and acquisition costs edged down. At last they were getting the hang of it, Hessel thought.

BY SUMMERTIME ANTIOCO could no longer shield the online program from the company's financial difficulties. Blockbuster's financial crisis unfolded just as McCarthy and Kirincich's models had predicted. The year's DVD releases had performed woefully so far, and box office revenue—a fair indicator of rental revenue—was down by 5 percent over 2004. It was clear that Blockbuster would miss its earnings targets, meaning that it was in danger of violating its debt covenants. Antioco directed Zine to again press Blockbuster's creditors for relaxed repayment terms, and broke the news to Evangelist that he would have to suspend marketing spending for a few months, and possibly raise prices to match Netflix's.

Shepherd was dispatched to the Hollywood studios to beg for more time to pay for the disks it needed to keep up with demand. Most agreed, but Universal insisted on keeping Blockbuster on a strict payment schedule. The result was that the chain and the online service decided not to carry a number of new Universal titles, and to stock their more popular titles lightly.

Antioco called Cooper and asked him to cut his marketing budget by more than half. The cuts were so deep that Cooper had to call some affiliates and apologize for having to turn off their links to Blockbuster Online, or to cut their bounty in half. The experience burned bridges with some of the service's advertising partners that, along with its vendors, were already annoyed with the parent company's slow pay practices.

The flood of marketing dollars that Antioco had committed to Blockbuster Online was crucial to keeping subscriber growth clicking along at record rates, and Cooper feared that cutting off that lifeblood would stop the momentum in its tracks. He was disappointed to be right. The result of the deep cuts to marketing was the same as letting up on a throttle. New subscriber additions barely kept up with cancellations, leaving Blockbuster Online treading water after a few weeks. While Netflix had zoomed past three million subscribers in March, Blockbuster had to abandon its goal of signing up two million by year's end.

To compensate, Evangelist and Cooper stepped up pressure on the store staff to tout the online service to their customers aggressively. It was a tough sell to managers who were seeing underperforming stores across the country close by the dozens and believed they were putting their jobs in danger. The sign-up rate at air card–equipped computers (Blockbuster stores still were not wired for Internet service) was so abysmal that Cooper and Craft decided to do some snooping around.

They set up "secret shopper" expeditions to a sampling of stores across the country and found that some store managers were actively discouraging their customers from signing up, using passive tactics like hiding the sign-up laptops, and even telling customers who inquired that the online service was no good.

Evangelist was furious. He took his complaints straight to Antioco. During a tense meeting with Shepherd and store operations manager Bryan Bevin, Antioco laid out his ultimatums: Shepherd and Bevin would start getting cooperation from the stores or people would be fired. The stores were losing revenue, and that would not change—but if Blockbuster's customers were going online and abandoning the stores, Antioco wanted them to go to Blockbuster Online rather than Netflix. That was an order.

Bevin, a taciturn man with a reputation as an enforcer, took Antioco's threats to heart and took off on a trip to Blockbuster's remaining five thousand company-owned stores to inculcate the message in store managers' minds. He and Shepherd devised a rewards system for the stores that signed up the most online customers, and with enthusiastic backing from them—the top two store executives—the initiative started producing results. Shepherd later compared it to a religious conversion.

Adding to Evangelist's frustration was Walmart's decision to shutter its online rental service and direct its customers to Netflix—an arrangement that Hastings won over dinner with Fleming by finally convincing the Walmart chief that he was in over his head.

Walmart offered its small online subscriber base the chance to continue their subscriptions at their current discounted price with Netflix, for a year. The retail giant also agreed to promote Netflix on its main Web site, and in exchange, the DVD rental company would remind its subscribers to buy their DVDs at Walmart.

Evangelist and Cooper were caught off guard, but put together a counteroffer the next day: Walmart and Netflix subscribers could get two free months and a DVD movie of their choice for switching to Blockbuster. Walmart ceding the DVD rental battlefield to Netflix and

Blockbuster did not do much for either company's subscriber base, but it did convince Wall Street at last that online rental was not as easy as it looked, and was not a cheap alternative to store rental.

"We believe Walmart's decision to exit the business and entrust it to Netflix reflects operational excellence at Netflix and high barriers to successful execution and profitability in the space," Thomas Weisel Partners analyst Gordon Hodge wrote in a note upgrading Netflix's stock to "outperform."

WITH THE DEBT crisis and proxy battle behind him, Antioco and his managers settled in to what would become a draining battle with an increasingly dysfunctional board of directors.

Antioco thought Icahn often seemed distracted and unprepared in board meetings—taking phone calls or rehashing issues that had been resolved in previous meetings. He insisted on having his own company's staff vet deals that Antioco brought to the board, often delaying action for months or until prospective partners walked away in frustration. A deal to stream movies in partnership with Hewlett-Packard died this way, and an opportunity to buy the studio-owned streaming service Movielink lingered for months before the board finally made a decision.

Eventually Icahn succeeded in having most of the board meetings held at his Manhattan offices—expedient for the now mainly New York–based directors and acceptable to Antioco, who enjoyed the chance to visit his hometown friends. However, meeting in Icahn's office basically put Icahn in charge, despite Antioco's status as chairman.

For the sake of the company, Antioco and Icahn papered over their differences, and in public at least appeared to be pulling in the same direction. The executive team at Netflix had remained mum in the press about the proxy battle, but they watched it delightedly as the mounting feud with Icahn distracted Antioco from his fight with Netflix.

With Blockbuster's marketing program quiescent, Netflix seemed to go from strength to strength—surpassing its forecasts and seeing its stock price soar back into the low thirty-dollar range—territory it had not seen since Blockbuster entered online rental.

Developments in the entertainment industry also seemed to be turning in Netflix's favor. Theaters suffering through the longest box office slump in twenty years were also fighting the rise in home entertainment systems. Only 22 percent of Americans surveyed in 2005 preferred to see movies in a theater rather than at home on DVDs, an Ipsos poll showed. Walt Disney chief executive Robert Iger angered theater owners over the summer by predicting that DVDs and movies would soon be released together, to save the studios marketing costs and to take advantage of much more lucrative DVD sales.

Billionaire Mark Cuban, founder of the HDNet television channel, vigorously advocated releasing movies in all formats—theaters, DVDs, and pay per view—at the same time, at tiered pricing, so consumers could decide whether they wanted to go to a theater or pay a premium to watch at home. The idea brought protests from the entertainment industry and garnered a wellspring of support from consumers.

Additionally, Mitch Lowe had resurfaced at a new subsidiary of vending machine company Coinstar called Redbox that was testing video rental kiosks inside McDonald's restaurants. Redbox was still working out glitches with the machines, but a test of twelve hundred kiosks was successful enough for the company to set a goal for installing as many as twenty thousand kiosks across the United States. Netflix managers viewed Redbox, with its one dollar per day rentals and an inventory that focused heavily on new releases, as a near-term challenge to Blockbuster and Movie Gallery.

Although the financial community continued to view Netflix with skepticism, the company aced a couple of consumer satisfaction surveys, beating out the better-known Amazon and QVC.

Netflix finally got the relief, in early April, from the price war that McCarthy had predicted the previous winter when Blockbuster announced it would raise the price of its most popular subscription, the three-out, from $14.99 to $17.99, bringing it in line with Netflix's prices. Elated, Hastings and his team figured they would soon start soaking up Blockbuster Online's departing customers.

By summertime it seemed clear that Amazon would not launch in the United States, and McCarthy started spreading the word among investors. Netflix's most feared rival had unveiled a German DVD rental service that priced its plans almost identically to Netflix—€9.99 a month for three rentals, one movie out at a time, and €18.99 a month for six rentals, three at a time. Amazon appeared to use the services to learn the online business internationally, where it stood a better chance of unseating Netflix.

Only Movie Gallery, occupied with digesting its oversized purchase of Hollywood Video, had completely ignored online rental, a decision that left Hastings equal parts amused and incredulous. Movie Gallery chairman and CEO Joe Malugen made it clear in an earnings conference call in August that he had no interest in entering the overheated online space.

"The online delivery model requires patience and days of planning and waiting. We know that the online model does not meet the needs of most of our consumers, because for most, renting a movie is not a carefully planned activity," Malugen told analysts. "I continue to believe that online rentals are a niche business that will appeal to only about 5 percent of the market. And I believe this fact is borne out by the recent financial results of both Blockbuster and Netflix, which reflects their ongoing price war."

Blockbuster's cash crisis became public a couple of weeks later, when the company said it would not pay a quarterly dividend for the first time since it went public in 1999. *Variety* reported Shepherd's urgent meetings with nervous studios and other product suppliers to again beg for extended payment terms, and to ensure Blockbuster would not have its supply of fall DVD releases cut off. The word that Blockbuster would forgo $400 million in revenue by abandoning late fees was getting around, as were stories that some studios were demanding cash up front.

Antioco described the bricks-and-mortar rental industry as "in the tank," and agreed that movie studios had a legitimate cause to worry, that the disastrous year for both theatrical and home rental revenues portended an upheaval to come.

"I am not trying to portray that everything is hunky-dory with the rental industry. It's not," he said in an interview in December. He still predicted, however, that Blockbuster would have a profitable fourth quarter, after losing more than half a billion dollars in 2005.

Meanwhile, Bear Stearns upgraded Netflix to "outperform" from "peer perform," and raised its price target, as it noted that rental industry statistics finally confirmed what Antioco and Hastings already knew: Mainstream consumers were drifting away from store-based rental. As analysts took apart Blockbuster's business model in notes to clients and in interviews, noting that its stores and overhead were too bloated, Antioco was busy divesting—jettisoning everything unnecessary. In late 2005, he put DEJ Productions, Blockbuster's movie acquisition and distribution arm, on the block for $25 million, and he put out the word that he was taking offers for Movie Trading and Video King, retail outlets that were taking the company's focus away from its core businesses, Antioco said. The company sold $150 million in convertible debt to fend off bankruptcy, and Icahn upped his stake in Blockbuster to 15 percent, at a cost of $38 million.

As a terrible year wound to a close, the numbers confirmed the bad news: Movie ticket sales finished the year down 12 percent from their peak in 2002, and overall spending on movie rental declined for the first time in twenty-five years. Sales of DVDs, however, were still growing.

Although its subscriber base had stalled at one million, Blockbuster Online had finally started making a contribution to the company's overall health, in the form of a growing revenue stream. It had been a rough year for Blockbuster—having to navigate a secular change in its business during a deep downturn—but, Zine told investors, 2006 looked brighter, with new programs like End of Late Fees and Blockbuster Online producing desired results.

NETFLIX ENDED THE year with no debt and 4.2 million subscribers, and it had earned the right to boast that its business, since it relied heavily on back-catalog titles, was impervious to the vagaries of Hollywood's movie release schedule. The two companies had traded places in market capitalization at about midyear: Netflix was now worth about $1.5 billion and Blockbuster, still more than $1 billion in debt, had dropped to $684 million.

CHAPTER TEN

THE EMPIRE STRIKES BACK

(2006–2007)

BY EARLY 2006, THE MEDIA and Wall Street were stepping over Blockbuster's presumably dead body to talk about what was to come next—Netflix or a video-on-demand format that bypassed DVD rental completely.

Broadband had reached enough American households to make the studios look again at distributing video over the Internet, as they grudgingly began accepting that there was no going back to the golden age of tightly controlling access to content by restricting its use to movie theaters, commercial television, and the nonportable (by digital standards) VHS format. The studios preferred the video-on-demand format, fearing that another Blockbuster would rise up to divert revenue from their coffers and hit on a digital delivery model that would liberate consumers from having to watch advertising or pay for cable. Premium cable programmers, such as HBO, Starz, and Showtime collectively shelled out $1.5 billion each year to the studios for exclusive cable rights to new movies, and the studios were not about to give up that revenue without a fight. Also, every major studio but Sony were part of conglomerates that owned cable channels or cable distributors.

Overall rental and sales of DVDs, which reached their zenith at $27 billion in 2006, were expected to begin a slow but definite decline starting the following year. Digital video delivery was growing by triple digits, year over year, but still made up just 1 percent to 2 percent of annual revenue from movie sales.

WALT DISNEY'S IGER was the first of the studio chieftains to embrace the Internet ethos of letting content be free—sort of. Disney, fresh from a merger with Steve Jobs's Pixar Animation Studios, was the first to sell movie and TV episodes on iTunes, the online music store affiliated with Jobs's Apple Inc. By placing blockbuster movies like *Pirates of the Caribbean: Curse of the Black Pearl* and hit prime time TV shows like *Lost* on iTunes, Disney signaled its acceptance of what tech companies had long known: Consumers would watch what they wanted, when and where they wanted, and there was nothing the content owners could do about it. Disney also began testing two of its own digital approaches: a download service called MovieBeam, to rent Disney movies through a set-top box, and an advertising-supported streaming Web site for its ABC television shows.

MovieBeam was cumbersome, requiring consumers to buy a two-hundred-dollar set-top box, which was similar to a digital video recorder, that trickled one hundred movies per month on a broadcast signal to subscribers' homes. Customers had to pay again for each movie they ordered, and had twenty-four hours to watch it after pressing play.

The ABC Media Player proved more successful, because it was free; it only required consumers to watch a couple of thirty-second ads per commercial break. The player application was easy to download to a laptop, and it delivered video streams fast and flawlessly.

MovieBeam sputtered after less than a year on the market, and Disney spun it off, while the ABC player grew steadily in popularity; viewers requested sixteen million streams during a two-month test.

Other studios invested in downloading sites that failed to take off, mainly because of the high costs and restrictions of their digital rental models. Movielink, a joint venture of five major movie studios (Metro-Goldwyn-Mayer, Paramount, Universal, Sony, and Warner Brothers) offered fourteen hundred titles for rental and one thousand for purchase via download or by burning to DVD. Vongo, a video download service formed by Liberty Media's Starz channel, Microsoft, and Sony, tried to interest consumers in both pay per view and subscription, but started with just one thousand titles.

Download services were also unattractive due to another temporarily insurmountable factor: the slow growth of U.S. broadband penetration. Just under 50 percent of U.S. households had access to broadband service as 2006 dawned, and those that had fast Internet access still had to wait a couple of hours to download a near DVD quality movie onto a laptop or computer. Even when the files were downloaded, the resolution and sound quality were not nearly as good as the new high-definition (HD) DVD and Blu-ray formats, and no one had yet figured out an easy way to get the movie from the Web to televisions, where most consumers preferred to watch them.

The download methods and business models were clunky, the Web sites not compelling, and the services as a whole could not compete with either Netflix or—even with all its flaws—Blockbuster Online.

Hastings and McCarthy watched the download services rise and implode, believing that a well-functioning, inexpensive streaming service could win against them but convinced that several fatal flaws had to be worked out before digital delivery could succeed. Getting a decent selection of titles would be difficult, because the studios had signed away the rights to rebroadcast their movies to premium cable companies like HBO, Starz, and Showtime for a decade. To buy those rights would require a bigger subscriber base than the six million Netflix was forecasting for the end of 2006.

Although Hastings and McCarthy insisted publicly that Netflix would roll out its own download solution in the coming year, they had by then decided instead to create a nimble media player like Disney's that would stream video straight from the Internet to any portable video-enabled device and, eventually, to the television.

Though not yet. They felt the cost of a separate set-top box would put digital delivery out of reach for a significant chunk of potential subscribers, and curtail the rapid growth in streaming they needed to convince the studios to cut them in on content deals. Hastings admired YouTube—its easy-to-use software and portability—and he realized that a free video player software program that could be downloaded to any video-enabled device would spread organically. Hastings also brought in digital video recorder designer and ReplayTV founder Anthony Wood to come up with an inexpensive and easy-to-use set-top box for streaming, to enable Netflix to travel that crucial last three feet from the Web to the television.

Hastings insisted to reporters that Netflix did not compete with the download sites, including Apple, because subscription rental attracted a specific kind of user—one who planned ahead and only occasionally required the spur-of-the moment convenience that the à la carte services offered. He saw the others as complementary to Netflix.

The six months of having virtually no competition while Blockbuster settled its debt problems left Hastings with the pleasant task of telling the market that his company would deliver better than expected revenue and subscriber growth in 2006. He told investors in April that as many as 20 percent of DVD householders in markets such as Boston and Menlo Park, California, were now Netflix subscribers, and the market showed no sign of saturation. Netflix's stock price had bounced back to thirty dollars, while Blockbuster's was marooned at around four dollars.

Yet Blockbuster Online remained a threat, despite its flatlining subscriber growth during the last quarter of 2005 and the first quarter of 2006, and Netflix did not want it resuscitated now that its parent's debt problem was under control.

Netflix sought the immediate shutdown of its nearly identical competitor. Following the Blockbuster Online beta release, when the resemblance was revealed, Netflix began sending cease-and-desist letters, without result. They went to federal court in San Francisco in April 2006 to seek an injunction to force Blockbuster to take down Blockbuster Online and rebuild it without infringing on two Netflix patents. In response, Blockbuster's attorneys contended that Netflix's patents—especially one covering the idea for a subscription DVD by mail service—were too broad. They filed a counterclaim alleging antitrust violations by Netflix.

Netflix filed its lawsuit shortly after the U.S. Patent and Trademark Office issued the relatively rare business methods patent. A violation of this patent would force Blockbuster to take down and reengineer its Web site or pay Netflix royalties to use it.

The dueling lawsuits dragged on for a couple of years, and they finally settled out of court with Blockbuster agreeing to pay an undisclosed sum. In exchange, Blockbuster demanded that Hastings stop publicly stating that he had incurred the late fee that prompted the idea for Netflix at a Blockbuster store. Blockbuster had searched its databases after hearing the story, and never found such a transaction. In subsequent interviews, Hastings quietly reset the story at a mom-and-pop rental store in La Honda, California, that had since gone out of business. (These terms were part of a sealed settlement, the details of which were related to me by several sources who knew about it. I did not see the documents. I was not able to confirm this with Netflix's communications department.)

THE HUMILIATING GROVELING to its bankers and its other creditors, mainly the movie studios and DVD wholesalers, had ended for Zine and Shepherd after a trip to each coast in 2005, but Blockbuster had a lot of catching up to do.

To satisfy lenders that Blockbuster was cutting noncore operations, Antioco put its international operations and video game and trading businesses on the block. Another two hundred employees were laid off at the corporate offices in Dallas and McKinney, including Stead, who parachuted out with a $1 million payday. Antioco also cut one hundred unfilled positions from Blockbuster's job rolls.

The brutal cost cutting seemed to put Blockbuster on a solid footing with analysts and investors, who reacted by boosting the company's stock rating and price. The decision to cut late fees finally appeared to be paying off. Antioco told investors with relief that Blockbuster's corporate stores, where late fees had been suspended for a year, had beaten the industry downturn in same-store revenue comparisons, and franchisees who had refused to participate were still in the doldrums.

Publicly, at least, relations improved between Icahn and Antioco. Icahn passed on the chance to embarrass Antioco further by running another dissident slate at Blockbuster's 2006 annual meeting, when he and two other directors were up for reelection. Investors reelected Antioco and longtime directors Robert Bowman and Jackie Clegg to new three-year terms without comment, in contrast to the previous year's fireworks. However, Icahn did step in—more subtly—to shape the board by holding up the replacement of a retiring board member that same month. Icahn discarded several possibilities for an independent director before agreeing to Los Angeles–based entertainment industry executive Jules Haimovitz. Although Antioco viewed Haimovitz's appointment as another attempt by Icahn to consolidate his grip on the board, he was satisfied with the choice. Icahn publicly expressed confidence in Antioco and his turnaround plan—including online rental—and seemed uncharacteristically loathe to create any more drama that would affect the stock or management's concentration.

In private, the power struggle between Icahn and Antioco moved to a passive-aggressive level that almost mired the board into inaction. Board members, cowed by Icahn's temper and billions, said nothing when he allowed his twenty-six-year-old aspiring filmmaker son,

Brett, to sit in on board meetings and offer his unsolicited opinions on business plans presented by Blockbuster's management team.

Icahn floated the idea of having Brett take over the online business, and actually sent him to Dallas to take stock of the service and advise Evangelist on how to improve it. Evangelist ostensibly welcomed the younger Icahn but warned that he could not run the online business from his home in Los Angeles. Blockbuster Online needed a full-time general manager who was present for the sixteen- to eighteen-hour days that it took to keep up with Netflix and weather the storms that Blockbuster's precarious finances were causing. Brett Icahn demurred, but he continued to weigh in on initiatives and attend meetings for both the store and online businesses, as he took on a larger role in his father's investment company.

The customers returning as a result of the End of Late Fees promotion had saved the Blockbuster stores from the worst of the 2005 downturn in rental but had not compensated them for the lost earnings. In response, Antioco shifted his marketing budget to Blockbuster Online for a barrage of advertising and coupons for as many as four free store rentals a month.

They had to do more, however, to catch Netflix, after the long dormancy with virtually no marketing. Evangelist kept his warehouses open on weekends and persuaded the post office to scan incoming Blockbuster Online envelopes with company-provided scanners, so that customers' next DVDs would clear for delivery as soon as they were checked in at the post office.

When customers noticed the faster Blockbuster delivery times and queried Hastings about it through an interview with HackingNetflix's Kaltschnee, the CEO said Netflix would not follow suit because of the cost—to his bottom line and his employees' psyches. "We will work as hard as we can on the five days when the distribution centers are open," he said.

Subscriber additions to Blockbuster Online lurched forward again, enlivened by the new spending. The uptake on the coupons was promising, with new subscribers citing the in-store rentals and faster delivery times as decisive in their choice of Blockbuster Online.

Netflix began actively investing in worthy low-budget films, hoping that the exclusive content would distinguish it from hit-driven Blockbuster. Most of these films would not get theatrical distribution beyond film festival appearances, so the exposure the filmmakers received by selling distribution rights to Netflix was beyond what they otherwise could have expected. By positioning itself in the burgeoning independent film movement, Netflix built cachet that was good for its image among its increasingly sophisticated consumers, and it built goodwill in the film community.

Blockbuster partnered with Weinstein Company, the independent movie studio, in what it touted as an exclusive deal to offer films like *Miss Potter* and *The Libertine*. The trouble was, once those DVDs hit the market, the First Sale Doctrine allowed Netflix and every other rental outfit to buy the same titles at retail and rent them to their own subscribers.

Blockbuster created a low-end tier of $7.99 for one-at-a-time limited rentals. Netflix squeezed below it with a $4.99 price for two movies per month.

The bargain basement prices alarmed analysts, who predicted that the services were encouraging subscribers to trade down to cheaper plans, decimating profit margins rather than boosting subscriptions. Wall Street watched closely as Netflix's subscriber additions climbed toward the six million Hastings had forecast for 2006. Surprisingly, revenue per user stayed fairly stable, showing that the new lower-priced plans were, for the moment, attracting new trade exactly as they were designed to do. As the second year of the price war wore on, with no decisive victory, Evangelist and Antioco started looking for a knockout punch before they again spent themselves into trouble.

FIVE MILLION SUBSCRIBERS—that was Evangelist's goal. If Blockbuster Online could get there, it would move past the expensive building phase and into profitability. Blockbuster was spending a worrisome fifty dollars to add each new subscriber for every thirty-eight dollars that Netflix spent.

After reviewing marketing studies he had done in 2003, Evangelist realized that Netflix had done a better job of retaining subscribers at the same point in its lifecycle, even with the giveaways Blockbuster Online subscribers were receiving. And Netflix's customer satisfaction, even among subscribers who had quit the service, sat at a maddeningly unassailable 65 percent, he noted.

But the data held a bright spot: Netflix subscribers could be persuaded to switch to Blockbuster for the added benefit of being able to rent at least once a month at a Blockbuster store. Since there would be no prying Netflix customers away from the service for anything other than an extraordinary offer, Evangelist knew Blockbuster Online had to blow their minds. The only way to regain momentum was to merge the online and store operations for a hybrid rental offering, but marrying the two separate businesses seemed technologically and financially insoluble.

"Before we go out and spend a whole bunch of money, let's go figure out how to make it fascinating," Antioco said of a combined in-store and online subscription. The problem lay in how to track online subscribers when they went into stores to return movies: Without Internet access, the stores could not connect to Blockbuster Online to track how many DVDs its subscribers had out and what they had returned, or to signal the distribution system to send the next disks in their queues.

One evening that spring, as they sat in the Renaissance Tower offices wrestling with how to use the stores to gain an advantage over Netflix, Antioco turned to Evangelist and said, "Put a free rental coupon on the mailer. Just print the coupon on the mailer and have them bring the mailer into the stores for free rentals." Instead of counting disks rented at the Blockbuster stores against a Blockbuster Online subscribers' rental plan, the stores would simply give them the free store rentals that they were already entitled to as part of their monthly subscriptions, when they returned a disk in its mailer. The coupon printed directly on the mailer would include a bar code with the subscriber's account information. When store employees swiped it at the cash register, the next DVD in the subscriber's queue would be released—after the accumulated data was uploaded in the stores' nightly satellite feed. The stores then would mail the DVDs to Blockbuster Online's distribution centers, where they would be checked back in.

The program wasn't exactly the integrated service Evangelist had envisioned, but it obviated a full-scale integration of the two systems and produced the hybrid offer that his studies and consumers said could beat Netflix.

Most important, the proposition was simple for consumers to understand: rent in the stores or online for one fixed monthly price.

A test conducted in July in Colorado Springs, Raleigh, and Fresno in spring 2006 produced the results they had been looking for—a melding of the deep online DVD catalog and stores' convenience that would drive traffic and online sign-ups past Netflix.

Four weeks into the test Evangelist and Cooper flew into Colorado Springs to observe the program in action. They pulled up to a Blockbuster store near the heart of the little mountain city early on a weekday afternoon to chat with the manager to find out what customers thought about the program. The store was a few blocks down from a Hollywood Video, and right away, before they even got out of their rental car, Evangelist noticed something strange and exciting.

The Hollywood Video store was nearly deserted—a normal sight on a weekday afternoon—but the Blockbuster store was hopping. A light but continuous stream of customers flowed in and out, all of them clutching yellow-and-blue Blockbuster Online mailers when they arrived. The store manager confirmed that what they were seeing was not a fluke. Since the promotion started, store traffic and sign-ups to Blockbuster Online from the store's laptop were soaring.

Evangelist was so astonished that he called Antioco, on vacation in

Mexico, to tell him about the test. Blockbuster's market research team considered Colorado Springs a bellwether market, and the tests underway in Fresno and Raleigh confirmed it—they were returning the same results. Antioco hopped a private plane to Colorado Springs the next day to see the spectacular midweek store traffic for himself.

The hybrid program, dubbed Total Access, addressed every problem Antioco had been trying to solve since 2001: the overbuilt store base; the store inventory problems; the struggle to win back market share from Netflix. It would come at a steep cost.

Antioco immediately ordered Total Access rolled out nationwide in time for the holiday season. Karen Raskopf hired one of Hollywood's most eye-catching yet relatable stars—Texan Jessica Simpson—to promote Total Access at an event on Hollywood's Walk of Fame, in front of the home of the Academy Awards, the Kodak Theatre (later renamed the Dolby Theatre). Blockbuster officially launched Total Access on November 2, 2006.

I never passed up an opportunity to see a CEO of a company I covered, so I made plans to talk with Antioco and Evangelist after the event. The blond and cheerfully plastic Simpson, whom Antioco declared "embodies entertainment," did her part, vamping for press cameras and soaking up the palpable adoration of fans and blue-shirted Blockbuster employees. She thanked Blockbuster for inventing two great ways for her to celebrate "movie night . . . with my girls and my girly guys and Daisy," her Maltese pooch.

Backstage, Antioco looked elated and relieved—like a man still absorbing his escape from certain death. He and Evangelist—who reminded me of almost a father and son in the similarity of their wiry, compact statures and barely leashed energy—were all smiles and swagger in our brief interview, and I came away reminded that, for all its recent woes, Blockbuster was more than capable of crushing Netflix.

Total Access was pretty simple, but ingenious. If Blockbuster had truly gotten its act together, this could spell trouble for Netflix, which had just surpassed six million subscribers. Blockbuster had had to abandon its stated goal of two million online subscribers the previous year, and Antioco wanted to use the engine of Total Access to make good on that forecast before the end of 2006, just six weeks hence. Shortly after the program was launched, he called in Nick Shepherd to talk about how to get there with the stores' help.

Shepherd's role at Blockbuster as executive vice president and president of international operations was finding practical ways to carry out Antioco's big ideas, and he was good at his job. He prided himself on curbing Antioco's more exuberant and expensive propositions, such as the plan Antioco now proposed: spending $6 million in incentives to encourage Blockbuster store managers to push Total Access over the crucial holiday quarter.

Both Antioco's and Shepherd's annual bonuses were riding partly on Blockbuster Online reaching two million subscribers by the end of the year, but Shepherd was sure he could meet the target for far less money.

"I don't like what you do. You don't want to spend money," Antioco told him during a morning jog along the Katy Trail, a hike-and-bike trail that winds through Dallas's posh Oak Lawn suburb. "Sometimes I'm not sure you're thinking big enough."

"Do you want the target met?" Shepherd responded.

Antioco agreed to let Shepherd use his own methods, and let the matter drop.

The integrated subscription program formed a two-pronged attack on both Netflix and Hollywood Video, by grabbing customers from both companies. In a roundabout way it would accomplish what Antioco had tried to do with his bid for Hollywood Video in 2004—winnow the U.S. store base down by almost 50 percent.

It had been a tough sell to store managers and Blockbuster corporate staff, who had seen store rentals dropping with no end in sight, and endured cost cuts totaling more than $450 million over three years to fuel the online business. The store staff finally appeared to accept what Antioco and Shepherd had been preaching for two years: The age of the video store was over. Hitching their stores to the online service and reaping fees from Total Access exchanges was their only play.

In the end, it cost Blockbuster only the price of the MINI Cooper that Bevin had demanded if he hit the target. Bevin stayed on the road from Total Access's launch day to Christmas Eve, touring corporate stores to cajole, exhort, and threaten managers to meet their numbers. In the end, customers decided the matter, responding in droves to Blockbuster's marketing blitz, which delivered 750,000 new subscribers in six weeks.

Shepherd bought the car with his corporate American Express card and delivered it to Bevin's house on Christmas Eve with a giant red bow tied around it. They had surpassed two million subscribers, and there seemed no limit to how fast they could grow

IT FELL TO Ken Ross to infuse Netflix with the credo that great brands had to connect with consumers on a personal level. Making an emotional bond with Netflix's subscribers would seal the deal that stellar service, Cinematch, and enthusiastic word of mouth teed up for the little company, Ross knew. As Randolph's influence had waned, Netflix's marketing efforts had focused on a rational connection with consumers—with the best software, logical interfaces, and a peerless DVD selection, why wouldn't consumers choose Netflix? It was a realm where Hastings and Kilgore ruled.

Ross's idea was to harness the allure of movies and movie stars to confer their magic on Netflix's brand. He produced Netflix's Rolling Road Show to dust loyal subscribers and the media with some of that magic: a series of movie screenings at famous outdoor filming locations. To persuade megastars like Kevin Costner, Bruce Willis, Kevin Bacon, and Dennis Quaid to lend their wattage to Netflix, Ross came up with a clever quid pro quo.

Each of the actors he selected also headlined his own rock band. In exchange for appearing at the screening, the Rolling Road Show would include a full-scale concert by each band. The temptation to play in compelling outdoor settings to their most devoted fans with banks of cameras trained on them was too much to resist—as Ross knew it would be.

The first event, in Dyersville, Iowa, celebrated the twentieth anniversary of *Field of Dreams*, a nostalgic baseball film starring Kevin Costner. The spectacle of Costner returning to the field where he filmed the iconic movie, picnicking and shagging baseballs with fans, and rounding out the evening by playing a concert with his band, Kevin Costner and His Band, was irresistible to the world entertainment press—and to local Iowans. The concert and screening attracted more than seven thousand people, and the Iowa State Patrol had to close the road leading to the venue.

Netflix screened *Jaws* on Martha's Vineyard and brought Willis to NASA's Cape Canaveral space center to celebrate *Armageddon* and play with his band, The Accelerators. Quaid and his band, The Sharks, serenaded fans of *The Big Easy* on the banks of the Mississippi in New Orleans, and Bacon celebrated his 1982 coming-of-age film, *Diner,* with a screening and concert with his band, The Bacon Brothers, on Baltimore's Inner Harbor.

When streaming became Netflix's sole marketing focus, Ross wound up the promotion with a concert and screening of *The Wizard of Oz* in New York's Central Park, in a partnership with Warner Brothers in which Netflix subscribers could stream the classic film for free for twenty-four hours after the event. Oscar winner Jennifer Hudson performed "Somewhere Over the Rainbow" on a concert stage in Central Park's Rumsey Playfield.

The Rolling Road Show and the press it generated did more than reinforce the positive feeling about Netflix that put the company on the tops of consumer satisfaction surveys year after year—it invested the brand with the excitement and sense of voyage that has always accompanied the experience of going to the movies. That visceral response to a company was hard-won and powerful—but not easy to quantify through algorithms or spreadsheets. Ross, perhaps alone among Netflix's executive team, understood that a customer's feeling about a company could decide whether she stayed and paid, month after month.

His was the voice now pushing back against the numbers and the logic.

He and Sarandos grabbed onto the burgeoning independent film movement—with its antiestablishment drive to democratize moviemaking—as a means to align Netflix with young indie filmmakers and stars, and to define the brand as hip yet serious and outside the mainstream. Consumers may not have noticed the unmistakable red logo in the backdrop—of red carpet photos of their favorite celebrities at the Independent Spirit Awards and the Sundance Film Festival—but Netflix was suddenly everywhere that the stars partied.

Ross kept improving on his strategy of doing good for Netflix by doing right in the eyes of consumers and the movie industry. He persuaded director Martin Scorsese to recruit four famous friends to design artwork for Netflix's mailers for the holiday season—in exchange for a donation to Scorsese's film preservation charity, The Film Foundation. The designs, by Scorsese and his eleven-year-old daughter, Francesca, actors Orlando Bloom, Charlize Theron, and Leonardo DiCaprio, and director Peter Jackson, debuted at a press conference at the Directors Guild of America in Los Angeles hosted by Kilgore. The glowing coverage tied the company ever closer to the magic of movies.

"The red mailer, which is one of the most visible expressions of our brand, was a natural way to showcase our partnership with the Film Foundation and express our holiday spirit," Kilgore told the entertainment press. "It's gratifying to us to support the important work of the Film Foundation, which, like Netflix, is committed to preserving the heritage of film and helping it find new audiences."

For all his success in positioning Netflix as a top underdog brand, cool and mighty with an ironic wink, Ross knew the company had a problem the moment he read about Total Access in a posting on Hack-ingNetflix in spring 2006. Netflix's own industry informants confirmed the results of the Total Access market test in Colorado Springs.

Ross had helped PepsiCo ease the number two cola brand away from a communications strategy that emphasized price instead of a camaraderie with young consumers during his long career there. Everyone knew about Pepsi and Coca-Cola; consumers were looking for reasons to embrace one brand over the other when the cola wars broke out in the 1980s. By positioning itself as "The Choice of a New Generation," Pepsi attempted for the first time to ally itself with soda drinkers instead of its own product—a bond that proved critical when Coca-Cola rolled out its New Coke formula in 1985.

Internal studies showed Pepsi that consumers liked the new, sweeter drink better than either Pepsi or Coke's original formula. With no answer to a clearly superior product, Pepsi set about trying to sabotage New Coke—to make it disappear from the marketplace. Fortunately, Coca-Cola had underestimated its customers' attachment to the idea of the ninety-nine-year-old original formula, and Pepsi fanned their outrage in ads showing Coke drinkers complaining, "They changed my Coke."

"I stuck with them through three wars and a couple of dust storms, but this is too much," grumbled one of the three actors costumed as old codgers sitting outside a barn, as he cracked open a cold Pepsi.

Pepsi never had to compete against the new formula, because Coca-Cola pulled it from the shelves just two months after its introduction.

In Total Access, Ross believed he had another version of that battle on his hands. Netflix had no answer for a consumer proposition that offered the convenience of stores with the matchless selection online delivered, but the cola wars had taught him that consumer sentiment would play no small part in the outcome.

Blockbuster Online's obvious strategy would be to paint Netflix as "The Wait Company," and if it somehow found the funds to sustain the free store rentals for more than a few months, Netflix was dead.

They had to find a way to make Total Access disappear, because Ross could think of no good way to counterprogram.

The subscriber growth numbers, when they began to come a few weeks after Total Access launched, confirmed Ross's fears. For almost as long as Blockbuster had been in online rental, Netflix reliably signed up 70 percent of new subscribers to Blockbuster's 30 percent. Total Access reversed that market share split in a matter of weeks.

Kirincich and Ziegler examined Blockbuster's costs and debt and concluded that Antioco could keep Total Access going for as long as two years without running into serious financial trouble. If Netflix kept shedding subscribers, its share price could collapse long before that, perhaps leading to a demoralizing death spiral.

Total Access was cleaning inventory out of Blockbuster stores, and Kilgore's spies—local marketing and DVD wholesalers—told them that store franchisees hated the promotion and were beginning to mutiny.

Inside Netflix, the atmosphere was grim. Hastings had hoped to move his base of operations to Rome for a year to be with his wife and children, who were studying abroad. Instead, he was flying back and forth to Europe once a month, and the exhaustion from those flights and the dilemma over Total Access began visibly to wear on him.

Kilgore began haunting the sidewalk outside her local Blockbuster store to interview Total Access customers. "They really like this," she told her team worriedly. It was clear that she was rattled—much more so than three years earlier, when Blockbuster had cut its prices to $14.99.

McCarthy urged everyone to stay calm. If they stuck to the task of optimizing their operations and executing their business plan brilliantly, they would win. They debated dropping their prices again on some plans, but the models did not show enough of a long-term benefit. McCarthy rolled out his financial models to argue for tabling the price cuts for at least a month. Hastings overruled him, tense about shareholders' reaction to Netflix's ceding its advantage in subscriber growth to Blockbuster for so long.

"Your spreadsheet math is bullshit," Hastings said. "We won't know 'til we know, so let's just try it."

McCarthy renewed his quiet talks with his own investors and with analysts who covered Blockbuster about the impact Total Access was having on the big company's balance sheet. Ross set up meetings for McCarthy with select financial journalists to try to get some traction on a story about Blockbuster's impending debt implosion.

The Total Access promotion generated significant attention from Wall Street analysts, who overlooked the program's steep costs and concluded that it finally would put Blockbuster back where it belonged—on top of store-based rental and ahead of Netflix. At Marathon Partners, Cibelli again staked out a contrarian view, warning his partners and investors in an internal note that "in its current state, the Total Access initiative is unsustainable over the long term." Blockbuster had converted in-store customers to less profitable online customers to meet its year-end targets and generate buzz for the program: "In-store customers are Blockbuster's most profitable patrons, so near- and longer-term profitability is sacrificed," Cibelli wrote.

The promotion would end either by driving Netflix out of business or with Blockbuster modifying the terms of Total Access to run it profitably, and Cibelli, who planned to hold on to his Netflix stock, was betting on the latter.

NETFLIX STILL HOPED to somehow make twenty million subscribers by 2012, but Hastings began distancing the company from that forecast. Netflix and Blockbuster would now split the $8 billion rental market, and there was plenty of profit for both, he now said.

With a feeling of dubious curiosity I traveled to Netflix's new Los Gatos headquarters in January 2007, along with journalists from other major outlets and HackingNetflix's Kaltschnee, for a demonstration of the long-awaited streaming feature. Steve Swasey had been warning me and the others—as Hastings had been warning investors—not to expect much in the way of title selection. I couldn't help thinking of the myriad download services I had seen come and go over the previous three years, mainly because there was nothing on them that anyone wanted to watch. They seemed little more than an inconvenient form of pay per view.

Hastings and Swasey, who had by now been promoted to vice president of corporate communications, gave me a quick tour of the airy, nouveau Mediterranean open-plan building. We stopped by a state-of-the-art espresso bar in the kitchen-dining area so that Hastings could make me a cappuccino—a ritual I later learned he performed for all the reporters he met with individually. Then we sat down in the main conference room, so that he could show me the streaming feature.

The conference room was cavernous and sleek, with a big skylight that let the winter sunlight pour in. When I remarked how much the company had grown from the dingy digs on University Avenue where I had first met him years earlier, Hastings looked around proudly and smiled, saying he could hardly believe it himself.

The "instant streaming" feature, which he demonstrated on a laptop with the eagerness of a kid with a new toy, was, like most Netflix software, a work of art that fit seamlessly into the Web site's suite of features. It took one mouse click to load it and about twenty seconds to begin playing a movie at DVD-quality resolution. The onscreen controls worked without a hitch—better than my DVD player, I thought.

It was puzzling, though, that they had launched with so thin a title selection—just one thousand movies—considering that Hastings had torpedoed his earlier download effort for the very same reason. I wondered how much Total Access was cutting into Netflix's growth and whether that had influenced the decision to go public with the feature so quickly.

Analysts generally liked the timing of the new offering as an answer to Total Access, but tech writers whined that tethering viewers to the Internet to watch a movie made Instant Viewing of limited value. And they brought up a valid point: How many subscribers would want to watch something as long as a movie or TV show on a small screen?

It seemed counterintuitive, but as with all his bold moves, Hastings had glimpsed the future and was steering his company toward it. Meanwhile, Netflix's market researchers had found the holy grail of customer feedback in the streaming service—real-time input about what customers thought about the movies they watched, based on how they behaved as they watched them. The system watched viewers as they screened films, noting the scenes where they stopped and rewound, how long it took them to abandon a film they didn't like, where they paused, what scenes they skipped. The resulting analysis of human behavior had the potential to be richer and more personal than any focus group could be.

Netflix no longer needed to connect with subscribers through its movie ratings system to know what they liked, but Ross knew that if the company could not make Total Access disappear like New Coke, they would have to call on consumers' sentimental attachment—and hope it was enough.

CHAPTER ELEVEN

THE INCREDIBLES

(2006–2009)

FROM NETFLIX'S BEGINNINGS IT HAD been paramount to make every movie seem enticing. That wisdom, handed down by Randolph from his direct mail bible, had been critical to Netflix's survival when the DVD universe was new and the title selection slim, and tending toward the old and obscure.

Helping subscribers find movies they loved—not just liked—ensured that they kept returning to the catalog to find some hidden gem, paid their fees each month, and told others about the service. At its most engaging, the Cinematch algorithm acted as a guide leading subscribers down fascinating and unexpected paths through the huge catalog.

Nearly 70 percent of the titles that ended up in subscribers' queues resulted from a Cinematch recommendation. The recommendation engine was so compelling that Netflix used it to predict and control its inventory needs—it helped smooth out a steep demand for new releases and directed subscribers toward older films with better rental economics. The fact that the voyage of discovery captivated subscribers was gravy in the early years, but in the throes of Netflix's war with Blockbuster, it had the potential to be a game changer.

At first Cinematch sorted and presented lists of movie titles that users were likely to rate highly, based on how they had rated other films in the past, along with themed lists created by Netflix's content editors. The more movies subscribers rated, the more accurate the system became. As the Web site functionality grew more sophisticated, Cinematch would present only titles that a subscriber was likely to enjoy—meaning that every subscriber saw a different Web site each time he or she signed on to the site. Along with software created by Amazon, Cinematch represented the world's best collaborative filtering system.

Over the years, Hastings had augmented his software engineers with mathematicians, to improve the algorithm, and had tinkered with it extensively himself. The idea of boiling down human behavior and tastes to a set of equations fascinated him: Was it really possible to capture so much chaos within the confines of numbers?

He later would describe how his obsession with the matching algorithm took over his free time—how he had once spent Christmas closeted with his laptop at his Park City ski chalet working on Cinematch while his wife, Patty, complained that he was ignoring their children and frittering away their vacation.

By 2006, Hastings and his team had wrung all the advances they could out of their approach. Taking in outsiders seemed pointless—he had hired the best he could find. Just as his great-grandfather had set up his Tuxedo Park laboratory to attract the world's finest scientific minds to the greatest physics mysteries of his day, Hastings decided to hold a $1 million science contest to push for breakthroughs in the algorithms that powered Cinematch. Alfred Loomis had enticed world-famous scientists to his physics lab by dangling cutting-edge equipment, luxurious accommodations, and generous stipends. Hastings would attract machine-language scientists to his contest by offering a real-world data set larger than that community had ever seen.

Scientists at the Loomis lab raced to make breakthroughs in radar and nuclear fission that would change the course of World War II; Hastings hoped the results of the Netflix Prize would come fast enough to put an end to the war with Blockbuster. He favored a contest along the lines of the 20,000-pound Longitude Prize, awarded in 1714 by the British government to the developers of a method for measuring longitude at sea, or the $10 million Ansari X Prize awarded in 2004 to the developers of the first reusable civilian spacecraft.

The $1 million cash prize would go to the first team to improve Cinematch's predictive powers by 10 percent, with $50,000 Progress Prizes awarded to the leaders at each anniversary of the contest's start date. The contest would be open to anyone of any educational level and background, from any country allowed to do business with the United States. Netflix would provide a database of one hundred million subscriber movie ratings (stripped of personal identifying information), so that contestants could test their equations with real data. Netflix would keep a running tally of the teams' progress on a public leaderboard, and the winner would own the algorithm—but had to grant the company a license to use it.

The improvement of 10 percent was equivalent to consistently predicting a subscriber's movie ratings to within one half to three-quarters star on Netflix's five-star system. The task of implementing the contest fell to James Bennett, vice president for the recommendation system, and Stan Lanning, a former Pure Atria engineer who, along with Hastings, had refined Cinematch and presided over the movie ratings system.

Lanning, a genial man with a bald head and a long, gray beard, shared a dark cave of an office with a bank of computer monitors and a life-size plastic skeleton riding a pogo stick in one corner.

Steve Swasey and Ken Ross planted a story about the Netflix Prize in the *New York Times* and were surprised when a page one story appeared on the contest's launch day—October 2, 2006. The U.S. and international press ran the story widely, and before the day was up, more than five thousand teams and individuals had registered for the contest. For Swasey, whose assessment of his day was inextricably bound up in the tenor of Netflix's press coverage, media reaction to the announcement was as thrilling as watching election results roll in and knowing that his candidate was winning by a landslide. Swasey later compared the prize to the a combination of the Preakness, World Cup, and Super Bowl for geeks.

More than forty thousand teams from 186 countries registered for the $1 million contest in the ensuing three years, attracted by the largest data set ever released and the open and generally friendly nature of the competition. As they began posting their results on the live leaderboard maintained by Netflix, and talking about their progress in the discussion groups, the scientists, mathematicians, and interested amateurs slowly built the world's most accurate recommender engine from scratch.

Among them was a team of statisticians looking for new ways to predict human behavior.

AT&T Shannon Laboratory lies in a gentle fold of green fields bordered by large lush trees in Florham Park, New Jersey, about a ninety-minute train ride from Manhattan. The complex is square and geometric, and has a clean, unpretentious, and uncluttered lobby from which anonymous hallways radiate into the distance. One wall features a gallery of photographs of AT&T scientists, famous in their insular world, and artifacts such as early telephones and antique electronic equipment stand in as decor.

Each floor has a cozy lounge furnished in Arts and Crafts–style couches and chairs set up around old-fashioned blackboards that are used for brainstorming. The network of hallways gives onto relatively spacious offices, each with a huge whiteboard on the hallway side and a wall of windows overlooking a neatly kept green on the other. The furnishings are utilitarian, and many offices, including that of researcher Robert Bell, have piles of papers stacked neatly along one wall, waist high.

Bell, a shy California native who came to AT&T Labs in 1998, heard about the Netflix Prize in an e-mail that AT&T's executive director of research, Chris Volinsky, sent around to about twenty researchers in

Florham Park a day or two after Netflix announced the contest. Volinsky led AT&T's data-mining group, which had worked for more than a decade on large-scale predictions of how customers were likely to behave: which customers were likely to buy an iPhone; which were likely to set up fraudulent accounts; what were the evolving risks associated with the U.S. customer base?

Data mining is the process of finding predictive or meaningful patterns in huge sets of data: the instant sorting and sifting through billions of Web sites that produces the ranked results of a Google search; the detection of abnormalities among normal cells in a computer-aided medical scan; or suspicion over the comings and goings of a group of visa holders that could indicate a potential threat against the United States.

Scientists mastering data mining have to write algorithms that examine a data set for important patterns but also discard associations that may seem compelling but lead nowhere.

Volinsky was a gregarious man whose childhood passion for baseball statistics evolved into a career as a data-mining expert; he loved contests not only to showcase what AT&T Labs could do but for the excitement of competing against the world's best minds in their emerging field. Volinsky also loved movies, and both he and Bell, who also found his vocation in baseball stats, were excited about the chance to experiment with Netflix's huge trove of real-world data—a set of customer ratings that was a hundred times larger than any they had ever seen.

Bell had entered and won contests before the Netflix Prize, but the $1 million and the open-door nature of the competition—anybody with a PC and an Internet connection could enter—gave the contest a special allure. It quickly became a leading topic of conversation in the research and academic communities that Bell traveled in, and he relished the chance to see how he stacked up against his peers.

About fifteen people showed up for a brainstorming session Volinsky organized shortly after the Netflix Prize was announced, but active members dwindled after a couple of weeks to just three—Bell, Volinsky, and their younger Israeli colleague, Yehuda Koren.

At first they watched as the Netflix-sponsored leaderboard lit up with a couple of hundred solutions—at least two of which bettered Cinematch within a week. A month later there were several thousand teams, the best of which had wrung a 4 percent improvement over Cinematch using all-original solutions. The chase after the $1 million prize drew not just the elite of data mining, but also from the machine language and mathematics communities, as well as brilliant amateurs from software development, and even from psychology.

Each team was limited to one submission per day, but a lively conversation was taking place all day and all night, as participants from all over the world signed on to the discussion board maintained by Netflix.

For Koren, this informal conclave of brilliant minds homing in on the same problem was captivating. He spent hours at home and at work tinkering with their equations and trying to stay ahead of the surging progress on the leaderboard. Each adjustment of the equation could take a week or more of time stolen from regular work tasks—a day to write the proposed solution, several hours to run the enormous data set through powerful computers, more time to analyze the outcome and make adjustments, and another set of hours to run the data again. Each man found himself thinking of the contest at odd hours, perhaps waking in the night with an idea for an incremental improvement.

They were ready to post their own entry on the leaderboard by the contest's fourth month, as team BellKor. After Netflix used a confidential set of test data to verify their results, team BellKor entered the contest in the twentieth slot. From then on, Koren was obsessed, pushing Volinsky and Bell to try to drive their way up the leaderboard. Let's see if we can get into the top ten, he'd say. Then, the top five, and the top three.

In April 2007, they landed briefly in the top slot, only to be knocked out a few days later. For weeks they flirted with the lead against Dinosaur Planet, from Princeton, and Gravity, a team of four Hungarian researchers. BellKor again took the lead at the eight-month mark, and this time they held it. They collected the first fifty-thousand-dollar Progress Prize for an 8.4 percent improvement to Cinematch. The big prize seemed well within their grasp as they entered the contest's second year.

WHEN NETFLIX'S FOUNDING software engineers, including Hastings, contemplated building a recommendation engine in 1999, their first approach was rudimentary and involved linking movies through common attributes: genre, actors, director, setting, happy or sad ending. As the film library grew, that method proved cumbersome and inaccurate, because no matter how many attributes they assigned each film, they could not capture why *Pretty Woman* was so different from, say, *American Gigolo*. Both were movies about prostitution set in a major U.S. city and starring Richard Gere, but they were unlikely to appeal to the same audiences.

Early recommendation engines were unpredictable: In one famous gaffe, Walmart had to issue an apology and disable theirs after its Web site presented the film *Planet of the Apes* to shoppers looking for films related to Black History Month.

Netflix's software engineers next turned to a "nearest neighbor" algorithm, one with a focus on grouping customers together according to their tastes in movies, rather than associating the films with each other.

By the time the Netflix Prize was announced, subscribers had made one billion ratings of sixty thousand movies and television shows—a rich data set but one whose subtleties were not being plumbed by Cinematch.

BellKor and the other teams wrote their recommendation algorithms from scratch, and they experienced in a matter of months the learning curve that had taken Netflix years to traverse, and then they transcended it. The algorithms they created found eddies and whorls in the huge data set that were completely unfamiliar to Volinsky, Bell, and Koren. The algorithms analyzed the patterns created by the subscriber ratings and assigned its own descriptors to films that were richer and more subtle than labels like director, actor, and genre but had no real meaning to the human mind.

For example, Bell noticed that the algorithm "learned" that subscribers who liked Woody Allen movies often cared only for particular types of film that Allen had made—perhaps made during a particular era of his career or in a peculiar setting—and did not recommend the director's other works.

Progress came slower in the contest's second year, especially after BellKor divulged its methods in a paper required by Netflix Prize rules, and the team watched others come close to overtaking them by using their own methods. They became stuck at an 8.6 percent improvement over Cinematch.

Toward the middle of the contest's second year, Koren took a job with Yahoo! Research in Israel, and unsure of what his future contribution would be, pushed hard to try to solve the puzzle before he departed. Their momentum slowed to a half percent here and a tenth of a point there, so Bell and Volinsky turned to the leaderboard for fresh blood to propel them out of their doldrums.

A new team, called Big Chaos—two young Austrian mathematicians who had built on BellKor's first-year foundations and were soaring through the rankings—caught Bell and Volinsky's attention. In a sort of scientific blind date, to see whether their approaches to the problem and their personalities would dovetail, Bell e-mailed the team—Andreas Toscher and Michael Jahrer of Commendo Research—to explore the possibility of a hookup. The BellKor team felt assured by a series of e-mails that Toscher and Jahrer would hold nothing back, and they agreed over a transatlantic phone call to combine forces, as BellKor in Big Chaos.

They next went looking for environmental and psychological factors that affected how and why people rated movies the way they did. Were subscribers more or less generous when they rated on weekends versus weekdays? What effect did rating a lot of movies at one time have? Did people rate movies differently according to their moods, and if they did, how could that be quantified? Did a person's propensity to be a tough rater or a generous one change over time, and if so, how and why?

Each of those questions became an equation of its own to be tested and, if the results were consistent and relevant, added to a stew of equations that made up their winning formula.

As the improvements to Cinematch piled up in painful halves and tenths of a percent, a small subset of films eluded classification and emerged in the second year as a major barrier between the Netflix Prize contestants and their $1 million payday. These movies generally were of an ironic or polemic nature, and they sharply divided audiences and critics on whether they were masterpieces or crap.

Chief among this group was the quirky independent film *Napoleon Dynamite*—the title that accounted for the largest error rate in all of BellKor's models—as well as politically polarizing movies like *Fahrenheit 9/11*, Michael Moore's documentary about the terror attacks on New York and Washington and the second Iraq war.

Predicting which side of the ratings gulf subscribers would come down on when rating films like *I Heart Huckabees*, *Lost In Translation*, *The Life Aquatic with Steve Zissou*, and *The Passion of the Christ* was a crapshoot. There was just no telling from previous ratings how people would feel about these films.

Bell reasoned that the solution to the *Napoleon Dynamite* problem lay not only in finding neighbor films but in teaching the algorithm when it did not know enough about a subscriber to make a prediction at all. The result was an equation that discounted a subscriber whose ratings were too paltry or who gave too many ratings for one type of film or a meager number of consistently high or low ratings.

Despite seminal insights in the second year, the teams squeezed out just an additional 1 percent improvement over the previous year's progress. BellKor in Big Chaos collected another fifty-thousand-dollar Progress Prize to add to a growing prize trove that included a kitschy replica of a Hollywood Walk of Fame star that they won the previous year and placed in the lobby at AT&T Shannon Laboratory.

Netflix's Bennett, who retired in 2009, wondered if the $1 million prize would ever be claimed. The contest started up again in earnest in January; the leaderboard leaped to life as teams struggled to close the gap of less than 1 percent improvement over BellKor in Big Chaos's results to capture the big prize.

Teams began combining on a grand scale in hopes that marrying their methodologies would help them bridge the last few tenths of a percent and carry them over the 10 percent threshold. BellKor in Big Chaos also went looking for fresh ideas. They found two French Canadian software programmers, Martin Chabbert and Martin Piotte, who were charging up the leaderboard by combining the Progress Prize–winning formula with their own, unorthodox, solutions.

Neither Chabbert nor Piotte, who called themselves Pragmatic Theory, had any formal training in data-mining methods, and they had purposely refrained from studying the research stemming from the prize during its first two years. They preferred, they said, to approach the problem by finding patterns in the data or psychological aspects of the subscribers and translating them into working software models. They rejected external movie data and concentrated on predicting ratings rather than on trying to explain them with their formulas.

"The algorithms that find actual patterns in the data, in infinite shades of gray, are much more powerful than any sort of meta-data, which assigns to black-and-white boxes," Chabbert said.

Their creativity moved the needle for their combined team, now dubbed BellKor's Pragmatic Chaos, a crucial 0.65 percent—bringing them over the 10 percent threshold on June 26, 2009.

The Netflix Prize rules called for a thirty-day last call period for competing teams to match BellKor's presumably winning submission—a period that they all found nerve-racking. Several top-ranked teams combined as The Ensemble, and on July 25, 2009, they submitted a solution that bested BellKor by 0.04 percent.

In the frantic twenty-four hours before the competition closed for good, Koren and Big Chaos were in constant touch, trying to eke out another tenth of a percentage point or two from their combination of equations. They finally turned in their last and best solution and waited in four separate countries for the contest to close. Twenty minutes later it appeared that the Ensemble's results had bested BellKor by one-hundredth of a percent.

For about an hour after the contest closed, Netflix went dark. Volinsky, at a family vacation in Seattle, sneaked away periodically to check his e-mail. Nothing. When they had won the two Progress Prizes, Netflix had notified them that they had won within minutes.

A dejected Volinsky conferred with Bell back in New Jersey and the other team members and decided to turn off his cell phone. He couldn't resist hitting the refresh button one more time, and as the e-mails loaded he saw it: a message from Netflix.

They had won.

The members of BellKor's Pragmatic Chaos met in person for the first time when they picked up the medals Hastings awarded them at a press conference at the Four Seasons hotel in New York City attended by the director of AT&T Laboratory, Hastings, Netflix chief scientist Neil Hunt, members of The Ensemble, and a phalanx of journalists.

Hastings had not wanted to travel to New York for the press conference, preferring to have it in Los Gatos, but Swasey insisted. He knew the prize and the people who had vied for it for nearly three years had captured the attention of the world's scientific community as well as a decent number of ordinary people. What they had accomplished was worth celebrating with an all-out, formal ceremony with speeches, gold medals bestowed on the winners, and a wide-ranging dialogue with journalists.

After the ceremony, the winning team held a technical briefing to show how they had won. Swasey, who had been thrilled by the turnout, was amazed that nearly all of the media stayed to hear the extremely arcane hour-long talk. The event punctuated three years of steady behind-the-scenes work by Swasey as he ginned up media interest in a science contest. He celebrated the bonanza of headlines he had generated that day by going around the corner from the Four Seasons for an expensive and mediocre sushi dinner alone—feeling slightly forlorn that all the fun was all over.

The format for the Netflix Prize press conference, with its branded banners, eye-catching props, and high-tech hardware, later became the template for the normally low-key Netflix's barnstorming rollout of its international services.

Bell and Volinsky did not keep the prize money, but each designated a charity where they wanted the funds donated. As required by the contest rules, AT&T granted a license for the winning algorithm to Netflix and applied it to its own U-verse television service to monitor users' television habits and suggest programming they might like.

The contest resulted in a recommendation system so sophisticated that it could read peoples' movie tastes from behavioral clues and no longer needed much input from the ratings system—especially when it was paired with a video streaming application. For example, the system could soon determine that a particular subscriber watches comedies on certain weekday evenings, or binges on episodes of a TV cop drama on the weekends, or rewinds when a particular actor or scene appears.

"We're getting information about what you like without you having to do anything," Volinksy told me after the contest. Subscribers no longer even have to rate movies, because a program embedded in a set-top box or on the Netflix Web site, monitored what shows and movies they watched and how they watched them to figure out whether the selection was memorable, and how to duplicate the experience with films available in the streaming library. If the algorithm chooses hits more often than misses, it captures the essential ingredient for a successful brand—our trust.

The Cinematch algorithm represents the marriage of marketing and technology that conferred such extraordinary success on Netflix. Because consumers found what they wanted among a limited DVD library, they left the video store and followed Netflix online. The trust they placed in the company—fostered by Randolph's intuitive user interface and peerless customer service and coupled with Hastings's beautiful algorithms—allowed it to smoothly shift the movie rental paradigm to streaming, where so many others had failed.

CHAPTER TWELVE

HIGH NOON

(2007–2008)

A WEEK AFTER THE INSTANT Viewing launch, Hastings and his team arrived at the Sundance Film Festival, where both Netflix and Blockbuster customarily held court with independent filmmakers in snowy Park City. For the first few years after Netflix's launch, Hastings shut down the company and flew every employee to Park City for the festival. Staffers would go to screenings and hang out at the old church Hastings had converted into a vacation home. It was his way of emphasizing that they were part of a great company that was doing important things.

That Sunday Hastings sat alone in his church-turned-chalet and waited for his rival to arrive. It was a gray and cold January afternoon. The snowy lane outside the modest redbrick meetinghouse echoed with the voices and boots of festival-goers meandering down the hill to the little town's makeshift screening rooms to watch movies, make deals, and be seen.

In a few hours Hastings would follow them down to the invitation-only party that Netflix sponsored every year in a warehouse fitted with a red carpet for celebrity arrivals, a constellation of open bars, and a dance floor. The party had become rather famous, and the year before,

Evangelist and the Blockbuster Online crew had posed as Netflix employees to try to crash it. They had been stopped at the door and turned away when one of the twenty-somethings had claimed to be Hastings.

This year's party celebrated *Little Miss Sunshine*, which had debuted a year earlier at Sundance and now was up for four Academy Awards. The Netflix marketing team had decorated the warehouse's interior to recall the film's suburban desolation—from the gaily-patterned plastic tablecloths to the buckets of Dinah's Chicken featured in the film.

The decorators had even parked an ancient yellow VW bus, like the one Greg Kinnear drove in the movie, in one corner. The party was designed to echo the ironic cool that appealed to consumers about Netflix, and that the now ten-year-old company had carefully cultivated.

Sundance was the top marketing event of the year for Netflix partly because the festival's antiestablishment yet glitzy vibe echoed Netflix's journey in the entertainment world, from dark horse to suddenly significant. Hastings went all out to get the Netflix logo seen by the right people in the movie industry—studio chiefs and filmmakers whose power to grant streaming rights would be crucial to fulfilling the company's appeal as the place to go online for movies.

In 2007, Hastings recruited dozens of his young employees and turned them out on the streets of Park City outfitted in red parkas bearing Netflix's red-and-white logo, like walking billboards. The company's marketing department sprinkled Netflix beanbag chairs, ball caps, scarves, and other promotional items into swag bags and hospitality suites.

Evangelist took note of the near saturation of Park City's streets with the red Netflix logo from the rented chalet where he was staying with Craft and Cooper and counterattacked by hiring half a dozen models to strut around in tight jeans and white parkas bearing the Blockbuster Online logo.

Hastings had an urgent and confidential mission. On this trip one of his main concerns was finding the right time to approach Antioco about doing a deal to save Netflix—by making Total Access, or preferably Blockbuster Online, disappear.

NEARLY A MILLION new subscribers joined Blockbuster Online in the two months after Total Access launched, and market research showed consumer opinion nearly unanimous on one important point—the promotion was better than anything Netflix had to offer. Hastings figured he had three months before public awareness of Total Access began to pull in 100 percent of new online subscribers to Blockbuster Online, and even to lure away some of Neflix's loyal subscribers.

Hastings had derided Blockbuster Online as "technologically inferior" to Netflix in conversations with Wall Street financial analysts and journalists, and he was right. But the young, hard-driving MBAs running Blockbuster Online from a Dallas warehouse had found the one thing that trumped elegant technology with American consumers—a great bargain.

His momentary and grudging admiration for Antioco for finally figuring out how to use his seven thousand–plus stores to promote Blockbuster Online had turned to panic. The winter holidays, when Netflix normally enjoyed robust growth, turned sour, as Hastings and his executive team—McCarthy, Kilgore, Ross, and chief technology officer Neil Hunt—pondered countermoves.

Models created by Kirincich and Ziegler showed that Blockbuster faced financial ruin if it continued giving away two-for-one rentals for much longer than a quarter or two. In the end, the Netflix team agreed that Hastings had to try to convince Antioco to wind down the promotion before it killed both companies. The Sundance meeting was his chance to do just that.

THE COMMUNICATIONS REQUIRED to bring the two chief executives together on January 21, 2007, were almost as complex as diplomatic hurdles in a visit between two heads of state. After intermediaries at their companies finally connected them via three-way text messaging, Hastings and Antioco agreed to meet later the same day at Hastings's chalet.

Neither Antioco nor Shepherd had to ask what their rival wanted to discuss. Since arriving at Sundance a few days earlier, the Blockbuster team had heard in meetings with studio executives that the Total Access promotion had hit Netflix hard in the fourth quarter. Antioco decided to go alone, to keep things informal and give Hastings privacy to say what was on his mind. He and Shepherd agreed to meet up for lunch as soon as Antioco wrapped things up with Hastings. Shepherd was disappointed to miss hearing what he hoped would be the admission that Netflix was in trouble because of the Total Access promotion.

As Antioco rode up into the hills above Park City's crowded main streets to the address Hastings had indicated, he thought about the three years of gambles, sacrifices, and bravado it had taken to finally gain the upper hand against a foe whose success was riding on the demise of the video store. Still, it had cost him upwards of $500 million to rectify his mistake in not buying Netflix at $50 million when he had the chance. Netflix had gone on to spend a nearly equivalent amount to build and market its service in the ensuing years, but there was no disputing that its superior platform was the product of years of testing and tweaking and perfecting. The cab arrived, and Antioco paid and stepped out onto the porch of the steepled redbrick building where he had been let out. The Netflix chief answered the door himself. As soon as they sat down with their drinks, Hastings cut the pleasantries and turned serious.

He congratulated Antioco for the success of Total Access and admitted that the promotion had definitely gotten Netflix's attention over the holiday quarter.

It was a great proposition—and Netflix couldn't really match it, Hastings continued, but his analysts had calculated that each in-store trade was costing Blockbuster two bucks. With no limits on the number of movies Total Access subscribers—now three million strong and growing—could check out each month, Blockbuster's debt would add up fast, Hastings observed.

Antioco waited for Hastings to come to the point.

The growth Total Access had created was phenomenal, but the only way to keep it up is by spending yourself into a corner, Hastings added. The minute you stop the free trades and raise your prices to make a profit, you lose your advantage, and we start growing again.

So what do you suggest? Antioco asked.

Let us buy your subscribers, Hastings said. We're better at online rental—more technologically proficient.

Hastings made the proposal sound like he was doing Blockbuster a favor, but Antioco knew it was the closest he'd get to an admission that he had won.

I don't know, Antioco said. I think we're doing all right. Besides, I don't know how we get a deal like that past the Federal Trade Commission's antitrust department. Hastings tossed out the idea of forming a joint venture to buy the subscribers, to get around regulatory hurdles, and idly discussed other scenarios, but never mentioned money. They parted after agreeing to have their teams confer.

Antioco left the chalet with a sense of exultation.

SHEPHERD RETURNED FROM Sundance with his stomach in knots. His debrief with Antioco following the meeting with Hastings had evoked dueling emotions. The thrill of having Netflix admit that it could not compete with Total Access battled the dread of keeping the cash-burning promotion going indefinitely while Antioco and Evangelist figured out how to make it profitable.

The two months he had spent the previous year riding the company jet back and forth to Los Angeles with Zine to beg the studios to keep Blockbuster provisioned with newly released DVDs that it could not pay for had been extremely stressful. He did not want to repeat the experience.

He had to somehow force Antioco and Evangelist to confront the looming liquidity crisis posed by Blockbuster Online's explosive growth.

With both companies pouring hundreds of millions of dollars into marketing online rental, the universe of online subscribers was expanding faster than anyone thought possible, to more than twelve million by the end of 2007. While Evangelist and Antioco crowed about having Netflix on the ropes, Shepherd wondered how Blockbuster would maintain quarterly earnings while handing out unlimited free rentals to two million new customers and suffering a painful contraction in store rental that was killing the Movie Gallery and Hollywood Video chains.

The next few months will be tough for Blockbuster, Shepherd thought.

HASTINGS RETURNED TO Los Gatos after Sundance to confront bad news from his market research team and worse news about quarterly earnings. Hastings and McCarthy reported to Wall Street that Netflix was already feeling headwinds from three months of Total Access.

Walmart was about to go live with a video download-to-own service that had the backing of all of Hollywood's big studios and undercut Apple's iTunes and Amazon's new video download service, UnBox, in price. The marketplace for digital delivery, although small, was getting crowded. And Redbox, now with more than ten thousand kiosks nationwide, was growing into a potential threat. The last thing Netflix needed was another destructive battle with Blockbuster.

Nothing Blockbuster Online had done in the past three years—price cuts, free coupons, massive advertising spending—had substantially diminished Netflix's superiority when it came to luring new subscribers. The year-over-year subscriber growth numbers each quarter were enviable—74 percent, 76 percent, 60 percent, and 51 percent in 2006. The growth forecast for fiscal 2007 had dropped to a comparatively shocking 17 percent.

Netflix's share of new subscribers looked likely to waste away to nothing by summertime if Antioco carried through on his post-Sundance pledge to spend another $170 million on the program.

Netflix was under siege. For the first time, Hastings had to take down his forecast for annual subscriber growth. He and McCarthy reminded analysts of Blockbuster's crushing debt and the effect that Antioco's spending was likely to have on the company's credit agreements. Netflix had zero debt and plenty of cash on its balance sheet to wait out Blockbuster as long as that took, they pointed out.

But the seriousness of the threat posed by Total Access wasn't lost on Wall Street.

"I don't know how Netflix can win this thing," Pachter, the Wedbush Morgan analyst, said after hearing the bad news on Netflix's first-quarter conference call. "The only way they get back to growth is if Blockbuster goes away."

That was exactly what Hastings feared.

After Sundance, Hastings sent over an informal bid to buy Blockbuster Online's subscribers. The offer was $200 per subscriber, or about $600 million total, and growing, plus fees paid to Blockbuster stores to service Total Access subscribers after the takeover.

Shepherd saw the figure as a starting point and believed that they could command a much higher price through continued negotiation. He thought of the freedom from debt that amount of cash would bring. But Antioco and Evangelist were insulted by the low-ball per subscriber price and, convinced they could do better after Hastings watched his customers flee for a few months, advised the Blockbuster board of directors to turn it down.

The Blockbuster board took up the Netflix offer at a February board meeting at Icahn's office in the General Motors Building in Manhattan.

Evangelist presented the directors with the pros and cons of selling Blockbuster Online, whose subscriber base was growing at a rate of twenty thousand to twenty-five thousand per day and would surpass four million by summer's end. The analysis is simple, Evangelist said. We don't want to sell for what Netflix is offering. Let's see what they'll pay when they've started losing subscribers. Why sell now, when Blockbuster Online had all the momentum?

Icahn and the board agreed.

After the Sundance meeting with Hastings, Antioco had gently broached the potential sale to Evangelist, who now faced the prospect of losing his job just as the business finally bore fruit. Evangelist's initial reaction was exultation. When the board voted down Hastings's offer, however, he was relieved at having a little longer to bask in his success.

The board then turned to a routine agenda item that would affect Blockbuster's future more profoundly than the decision not to sell Blockbuster Online to Netflix. It was the approval of annual bonuses for the company's top executives, including a doubling of Antioco's $3.8 million performance-based bonus. Antioco's relationship with Icahn remained uneasy, but he had hardly thought about the outcome of his performance review and the bonus vote. Netflix's offer to buy Blockbuster Online, and the spiraling down of Movie Galley and Hollywood Video, had validated his strategy. When the board came to the long list of bonuses, they voted to approve each award without much discussion, until they arrived at the last name on the list: John Antioco.

As Icahn peered at the bonus amount printed on the page—$7.6 million—his face took on a look of amazement that quickly morphed into anger.

"There is no way we are going to pay you this money," Icahn told Antioco.

"What do you mean," the shocked CEO said. "You approved it. You're on the compensation committee."

Under the terms of his contract, which the directors had set the previous year, if Blockbuster reached $285 million in adjusted gross income and Blockbuster Online had signed up two million subscribers by December 31, Antioco was due the additional bonus. He had earned it, and he knew it.

In 2005, Blockbuster posted a $500 million loss (although noncash charges accounted for more than half of the loss), as store revenues staggered under weak DVD releases, competition from cheap DVDs sold at Walmart and Best Buy, and the costs of eliminating unpopular late fees. Antioco had to renegotiate the debt-to-income ratios of the company's credit agreements four times in two years to keep cash flowing to Blockbuster Online. He had turned things around in 2006. The company had eked out a small profit, but its stock price had reached an all-time low of seven dollars and that was the only measure that mattered to investors.

"I didn't know it was going to be this big," Icahn said of the bonus.

"Well, you should have done the math," Antioco retorted.

At Icahn's urging, the board voted to cut Antioco's bonus in half. Had his fellow directors asked Antioco to voluntarily forfeit part of the amount to make nice with shareholders who had lost money in the costly war with Netflix, he probably would have agreed. He was, after all, a rich man, and the bonus was merely a way to put points on the board. But asking nicely was not Icahn's style.

In late February, the board cut Antioco a check for $2 million, and had Zine deliver it to the CEO.

Antioco handed it back, telling Zine, "Thank you very much; you can have it back." His attorney promptly delivered a copy of a claim for arbitration over alleged board misconduct that Antioco planned to file the following Monday to Blockbuster's outside counsel. The Blockbuster board voted to set aside $4 million in case it had to fork over the disputed funds and informed investors in a February 23 securities filing that it was officially feuding with its own chairman and chief executive.

The phone rang at Antioco's home in Dallas on the Friday night before the Monday arbitration. It was Icahn, having had a martini or two and up past midnight New York time, looking for a fight.

Antioco picked up the phone in his bedroom, where he had been watching a movie.

"Hi, Carl," Antioco said, bracing for battle when he heard the familiar voice. His wife, Lisa, hearing Icahn's name, wordlessly went downstairs to fetch him a bottle of tequila and a shot glass.

Icahn laid into him immediately. Why was Antioco dragging the company through another embarrassing chapter in this pay argument? Why couldn't he just accept the lower bonus? Didn't he care how a double bonus looked to people who had lost 40 percent of their investment in Blockbuster in just three years?

Finally, Antioco could take no more. With the tequila lighting a fire in his belly, he started shouting back at Icahn. He had never before lost his temper with Blockbuster's largest investor, but he had reached his limit, emotionally and mentally.

As the two men argued, Antioco suddenly realized that the effort—to fight Icahn, to fight for a bonus he would ultimately give to charity—was pointless. He had enjoyed a decade-long ride at Blockbuster, taking it from a failing unit of Viacom to a colossus astride the world of movie rental. Guided by his grit and instinct, Blockbuster had stolen from a technologically superior rival the title of fastest-growing online rental business. Antioco was on the verge of putting Blockbuster back on top after blows that most companies would not have survived—a technology revolution, a management crisis, credit problems, a revolt by franchisees.

He had put his reputation on the line in a risky bet that the outsized spending on online rental would eventually pay off. The market research flowing in every day proved him right—foot traffic in stores was up, as Total Access made even Netflix subscribers take a second look at Blockbuster Online.

In early 2007, Movie Gallery had had to refinance its $1.4 billion debt from its purchase of Hollywood Video, a sign that Total Access was accelerating the demise of Blockbuster's store rivals—just as Antioco had predicted. Movie Gallery CEO Malugen had been forced to retreat from his position that online movie rental was a "niche" that his rural customers did not understand. Malugen announced that Movie Gallery would provide an online rental option later in the year and would buy online download service MovieBeam from the joint venture headed by Disney.

Despite Icahn's public support for Antioco's vision and the success of Total Access, the CEO could see nothing ahead but struggle. If hard numbers couldn't convince the Blockbuster board of his worth, Antioco preferred to retire to his ranch and spend time with Lisa and his children.

"Let's negotiate my exit," he told Icahn.

Icahn agreed, and the conversation turned to the nuts and bolts of pay and benefits. Antioco would receive $8 million in severance and bonus—a fraction of what he was entitled to under his contract—plus five million stock options that vested by his last possible day on the job—December 31, 2007. Antioco could not have cared less about the pay cut—he felt like a weight that had been drowning him for two years had lifted.

On March 20, 2007, the day Blockbuster announced Antioco's departure, Icahn told the financial press that the terms of the CEO's exit "are clearly in the best interests of the shareholders."

Antioco said only that he was "pleased" to have reached a settlement and would stay on until at least July 1 to provide an orderly transition to the next CEO. In the meantime, he planned to run the Total Access promotion "pedal to the metal" to reap as much subscriber growth as possible while the Blockbuster board searched for his successor.

Antioco had convened a meeting of his top executives a day earlier, including Evangelist, and broke the news. He reminded them that they had a lot of work ahead to make the online business profitable and to keep up pressure on Hollywood Video and Movie Gallery. While the search for his successor was on, Antioco expected them all to maintain their focus on making Total Access sustainable.

The suddenness of the announcement stunned the room, but no one wondered why Antioco had made the decision. They all knew of the struggles he had faced with Icahn and the board, even if he had not explicitly discussed them. After the meeting, Evangelist returned to his office and fired up his desktop computer. It was time to update his résumé. He had been blowing off periodic calls from headhunters—maybe it was time to start returning those calls, he thought.

Antioco's goal before he left at year's end was to get Blockbuster through the transition to a smaller store base, launch an electronic movie delivery option to match Netflix's instant streaming service, and maximize online subscriber growth with an all-out push with Total Access.

In June, he had the unpleasant task of reporting to his lenders that store sales had slipped by nearly 16 percent compared to a year earlier, and he needed another waiver of the company's credit terms—its fourth since 2005—to commit the $170 million he had pledged to Total Access.

That summer, Movie Gallery signaled that it was in deep trouble and would default on its new debt terms due to poor second quarter results. Soleil Securities analyst Marla Backer cut her rating on Movie Gallery to "sell" from "hold" on its stock, saying that the number two rental chain's plight "highlights the challenges currently facing video retailers in general, as well as the competitive impact of Blockbuster Inc.'s Total Access program."

There was no getting around it: Store-based rental was on its way out, and Antioco was determined that Blockbuster would make the transition.

Blockbuster had tripled its online subscriber base in six months, to 3.6 million. By June, Blockbuster Online was signing up every new online rental subscriber, as well as customers who had defected from Netflix. Evangelist was ecstatic. He knew Hastings had to be desperate—now was a perfect time to wring a better deal out of Netflix. Antioco hesitated. He knew that Icahn was eager to replace him, and he did not want to leave such an important deal half done at his departure.

"That's for the next guy," he told Evangelist.

BLOCKBUSTER'S ENORMOUS MARKETING spend to raise awareness of Total Access had pushed average Americans off the fence about online rental. The new customers trying online rental for the first time—ten million of them—proved Hastings's theory that the market was far larger than Wall Street imagined. Unfortunately for Netflix, most of these new customers continued to sign up at Blockbuster Online as spring turned into summer.

"Our thesis that online rental would become very large appears more and more credible," Hastings said on Netflix's first quarter conference call in April. "Our thesis that most subscribers would choose Netflix seems more open to question, at least for now."

Netflix ended the first quarter at the bottom half of its forecast range for revenue, subscribers, and earnings for the first time in its twenty quarters as a public company. Worse, Hastings and McCarthy had to revise their year-end forecasts, and to renounce their long-range plan of achieving 50 percent annual earnings growth and twenty million subscribers by 2012.

On the other hand, instant streaming was performing better than expected. Hastings and Ted Sarandos and his content acquisition team in Beverly Hills worked full speed to increase the title selection and get the software embedded in enough platforms—cell phones, game consoles, DVD players—to make it a convenient alternative to both the video store and online DVD rental. With video streaming under way, Hastings took the first steps toward sacrificing a critical piece of Netflix's business model to focus the company on a superior consumer proposition.

Netflix was close to solving the problem of getting the Internet to the television with a set-top box that would be ready to roll out in 2008. The question was, would it be soon enough to save the company from another devastating meltdown of its stock price?

Kilgore started market tests to determine the effect lowering the price of the two-out plan by a dollar had on marketing costs and on subscriber growth and retention. The test showed that Netflix could lower the now record forty-seven dollars to acquire each new subscriber in the overheated atmosphere created by Total Access.

Hastings and Kilgore pushed to cut prices on all three of Netflix's subscription plans, arguing that they had to stop what by June had become an outflow of customers to Blockbuster Online. For the first time since it adopted its subscription plan in 1999, Netflix was losing its customers. Even peerless word of mouth, the most valuable marketing tool Netflix possessed, was no longer compelling enough to keep its subscribers from what looked like a better bargain.

In July, Hastings faced going to the market with Netflix's second-quarter earnings report and reporting that the company had lost 1 percent of its subscribers, and would—for the second time in six months—revise its fiscal year forecasts for subscriber growth and net income. Any hope they had of stopping Blockbuster Online through the patent infringement lawsuit they had filed in 2006 also disappeared. They would have to tell the market that the companies had settled the matter out of court for a nominal one-time payment to Netflix and no hoped-for ongoing license fees.

In the days leading up to the earnings conference call, McCarthy and Kirincich argued against making a second round of price cuts. The Netflix executives agreed as a team to table the discussion of price cuts for another month to see if McCarthy's prediction that potential losses on Total Access—$200 million or more for 2007—would spur Blockbuster Online to alter the program, either by raising its own prices or stopping the free in-store rentals, to make it profitable.

But the pressure on Hastings and his exhaustion from constant traveling worked on his mind. The next day he unilaterally decided to cut Netflix's prices across the board.

The about-face shocked some staff members, who felt that Hastings had lost his focus. Yes, they were all scared, and the stock had dropped by more than 30 percent since the beginning of the year. But they had come this far by focusing like a laser on their strategy and executing it by the numbers.

They announced the price cuts along with revised forecasts for smaller subscriber growth and profits in 2008. All the numbers were going in the wrong direction. Revenue, profit, and even the average amount of money subscribers spent on Netflix would all drop in the coming two quarters, McCarthy told investors.

"When Blockbuster decides to operate its online business profitably, our financial results will improve also. But until that time, both sub growth and earnings will remain under pressure," McCarthy told analysts on the second-quarter conference call on July 23.

The only bright spot in the earnings report: Mitch Lowe's Redbox was starting to pressure video stores with his growing army of kiosks. "They are still pretty small, so in the background, but have good significant potential over the next three years, mostly to negatively impact stores, which of course has a positive effect for us," Hastings said.

That summer, everyone at Netflix was exhausted and becoming demoralized. Hastings carried himself like a depleted man, and it was clear that Kilgore was very, very worried.

CHAPTER THIRTEEN

THE GREAT ESCAPE

(2007–2009)

LATER, CARL ICAHN WOULD REFLECT that John Antioco had, in fact, done a good job in setting up Total Access, and that if Antioco had not left the company in a huff over his bonus, things might have turned out differently.

But in the summer of 2007, Icahn could hardly wait to get rid of Antioco. In his view, Antioco never cared as much about Blockbuster as he did about making money and escaping to his ranch to drink tequila. Icahn wanted to replace him as soon as possible. During the search for Antioco's replacement, Icahn met former 7-Eleven chief executive Jim Keyes through another major Blockbuster shareholder, Michael Zimmerman, who ran Prentice Capital Management LLC. Zimmerman, who periodically called Antioco to offer advice on rehabilitating Blockbuster's stores, convinced Icahn that Keyes had both the solid retail background to shore up the stores and the know-how to take Blockbuster into digital delivery.

Keyes, then fifty, had retired after two decades at 7-Eleven when Tokyo-based Seven-Eleven Japan acquired the convenience store chain in a $1.4 billion buyout in 2005. He exited 7-Eleven with a $64 million golden parachute after presiding over a streamlining of the chain's operations and a doubling of its stock price in the year before the takeover. In retirement, Keyes intended to devote himself to his philanthropy, Education is Freedom, and to perhaps add a helicopter pilot's license to his airplane pilot's license.

As vice president of planning, Keyes had helped preside over a renaissance of 7-Eleven's U.S. stores after they lost market share to gas station minimarts in the early 1990s. Icahn was convinced that Keyes could do the same for Blockbuster's store operations, as well as guide the online operation to profitability.

Shortly before his retirement in 2005, embarrassing allegations that Keyes and other top 7-Eleven executives took improper gifts from suppliers surfaced in a lawsuit by a food broker named Milissa Boisseau. The convenience store chain ended its relationship with Boisseau, and four 7-Eleven administrative assistants, whom they alleged had taken kickbacks from her, were fired or forced into retirement. The impetus for those actions had allegedly been Keyes's relationship with another broker named Debra Miller, who subsequently attempted to pick up Boisseau's accounts with 7-Eleven.

The discovery process revealed, however, that Keyes himself had attended a fantasy baseball camp with the St. Louis Cardinals for several years, courtesy of Anheuser-Busch, and had accepted a spot on the AT&T Pebble Beach National Pro-Am tournament from AT&T, among other gifts from vendors. Other executives accepted special treatment from vendors at the same time that they decided to fire the four low-level assistants for accepting money to type up reports for Boisseau on how her products were selling in 7-Eleven stores, according to lawsuit documents.

When Antioco heard that the board was seriously considering Keyes, with whom he had worked at 7-Eleven, he was surprised but did not believe Keyes could possibly win the job over Shepherd, whom he had promoted to chief operating officer in April after his brilliant rollout of Total Access. Realizing that Blockbuster lacked the in-house talent to run a streaming service, Shepherd had spent six weeks that spring on the road learning about digital delivery from the best in the business. With Blockbuster and the entire movie rental industry headed toward digital delivery, Antioco wondered how Keyes's retail-heavy résumé was relevant.

In Keyes, Icahn, who said he was attracted by Keyes's ideas for a digital business, had found the anti-Antioco.

Before the CEO position had become available, Keyes was exploring the idea of buying a large stake in Blockbuster, as a first step toward taking the company private.

On the day that Blockbuster announced who the new CEO would be, Blockbuster board member Gary Fernandes told me that the board chose Keyes because of his success in turning around declining store sales at 7-Eleven and in forming partnerships with retailers.

"That same kind of approach is what is going to be critical for Blockbuster," Fernandes said. It seemed that the board expected Keyes to essentially carry out Antioco's agenda. Work hard to squeeze every dollar they could out of their retail locations while growing the online business and creating an electronic delivery option, Fernandes said.

But Keyes had a different idea: "We will be revisiting the entire strategy."

Keyes was a round-faced man with an affable public demeanor. He had worked for Antioco at 7-Eleven many years earlier and had seemingly come away with a chip on his shoulder. At one point Antioco sent Keyes to what the latter jokingly described as "executive charm school" to remedy a marked lack of people skills. Shortly after he took over his new post at Blockbuster, on July 2, 2007, it became clear to his new colleagues that the lessons had not held up over time. They found Keyes impatient and high-handed, unwilling to listen or entertain data that undermined his ideas, and determined to eradicate any trace of Antioco. In their first meetings with Keyes, they also learned that he could be brusque to the point of rudeness and quick to raise his voice to threaten or ridicule subordinates.

Although Blockbuster indicated in the press release announcing

Keyes's hiring that Antioco would stay and smooth the transition, he left two days before Keyes arrived.

There had been a party at Renaissance Tower, complete with tributes and tearful good-byes. Shepherd, who had to retreat to his office to hide his tears, first snapped a photo of Antioco with his cell phone camera that he used as wallpaper for months to remind him of what a happy man looked like. Afterward, Antioco waited for his last paycheck to be cut and gave it to his assistant to deposit in his bank account. He later donated the disputed bonus amount to the Boys & Girls Clubs of America.

Then he drove to Love Field in Dallas and hopped a private jet to the Hamptons, where he and Lisa and his three children planned to spend a month relaxing and visiting with his sister and his friends from 7-Eleven, and the old neighborhood. It was time for him to leave Blockbuster, and he was at peace with his decision to go; he was confident he had left the company on the right trajectory.

As the jet surged down the runway, Antioco felt liberated.

NICK SHEPHERD HAD at least as hard a time as Antioco with Blockbuster's board of directors. He had been run through the ringer when Icahn's dissident directors joined the board and demanded to know why the stores kept losing money. Ed Bleier, in particular, seemed fond of strange ideas. "Nick, do people coming into your stores wear jeans?" the eighty-year-old Bleier asked, as a prelude to suggesting that Blockbuster clear room on its new-release wall for racks of blue jeans.

"They also wear sneakers. Should we put those on the wall as well?" Shepherd replied. The tense exchanges crystallized the board's sense that management was intransigent and the managers' conviction that the board was completely dysfunctional. Finally, Shepherd invited the board to a daylong retreat to explain why many of the approaches they had suggested to revive the stores would not work. Working through a half dozen boxes of research on dozens of initiatives that had been tested over the previous four years, Shepherd explained the purpose of the initiative, how they had executed it, and the results.

It all added up to the same conclusion: Nothing was going to bring the stores back. Store-based rental was on its way out. Digital delivery was the rental business of the future.

Finally, Strauss Zelnick stopped the presentation. "I get it," he said. Most of the board agreed and seemed to accept the managers' strategy, although that did not stop Bleier from occasionally suggesting initiatives like hooking up with Hallmark cards or Barnes & Noble or selling pizza at the stores.

Adding to his disappointment in not becoming Blockbuster's chief executive, Shepherd now had to go through the same routine with Keyes, who was reaching into his 7-Eleven playbook to revive the stores with a new mix of food and merchandise similar to the plan Antioco's predecessor Bill Fields had tried. Shepherd planned to depart Blockbuster in October after helping Keyes transition to his new role, and he was determined to maintain a professional demeanor.

Shepherd and Bryan Bevin offered to show Keyes the results of Field's failed initiatives and other market research, but the new CEO demurred. He returned the reports they sent to him unopened.

It was frustrating to watch Keyes make the same mistake that Fields had made in treating Blockbuster like a convenience store chain and assuming that its customers would simply shift their buying habits to purchase whatever merchandise it stocked. In consumers' minds, Shepherd knew, the Blockbuster brand stood for one thing only: a place to rent the latest DVD releases.

Blockbuster had to close nonperforming stores and use the remaining stores to support the move to online rental and digital distribution, Shepherd said.

"We're retailers—we open stores. We don't close them," Keyes retorted.

Less than a week later, Bevin walked out of a staff meeting with Keyes and quit the company. He could not bear to hear the new chief executive's plans, which would inevitably send Blockbuster straight into an iceberg.

IT WAS CLEAR to Evangelist from their first meeting that Keyes had a personal animus against the online business.

"Total Access is killing the business," he told Evangelist. "You're bankrupting the business. You can't continue to operate at a deficit."

While conceding that online rental would cause big losses in 2007, Evangelist and Antioco had planned to run the service profitably the following year through price increases and simple economies of scale once the subscriber base got large enough. Evangelist explained that he would split DVD by mail off from Total Access and price it just below similar Netflix plans. The heaviest Total Access users and new subscribers would see a 25 percent increase in rates starting in the third quarter of 2007.

Evangelist soon learned that Keyes's ideas for online rental meant essentially abandoning Total Access, raising subscription prices across the board, and diverting the money Antioco had pledged to the online service to Blockbuster stores.

"Jim, you're missing this thing," Evangelist said. "This is a singular program that attacks both Hollywood Video and Netflix. You don't have another deal for that."

He knew, from the times Antioco had briefly cut funding to Blockbuster Online to renegotiate the parent company's debt, that a strong marketing program was essential to constantly replacing customers who canceled their subscriptions Evangelist predicted that without ads to attract new subscribers, Blockbuster Online would wither from the 3.7 million when Keyes took over in July to 1.5 million by the end of the year.

Keyes laid out his store-focused strategy to Blockbuster's top management at a company retreat on July 30, 2007, at the luxurious Rough Creek Lodge & Resort about ninety miles south of Dallas. Blockbuster stores would become "great" again as entertainment destinations that would sell a new mix of prepared foods, such as pizza and fountain sodas, as well as electronics, such as iPods and DVD players. The presentation horrified old hands, who had watched nearly identical promotions crash and burn under Fields and Antioco.

More shocking—because it displayed a lack of understanding of digital video technology—was Keyes's contention that someday consumers would make it a habit to drop by Blockbuster stores to load movies and games onto flash drives or video-enabled devices at in-store kiosks, instead of simply using their home broadband lines.

Store revenues would never recover from the swoon that began in 2005, and everyone in the room but Keyes knew it.

The retreat was so disastrous that a number of senior-level executives—among them Evangelist, Shepherd, and Zine, who had announced his retirement—phoned in sell orders on most or all of their Blockbuster shares during the next "open" period when they could legally do so. Several, including Evangelist, Zine, and Antioco, when he heard of Keyes's plan, plowed the proceeds into Netflix stock. They didn't need inside information on Netflix—they knew exactly what was about to happen to Blockbuster.

Keyes was furious when he saw the securities filings disclosing the stock sales. Because his new employment contract allowed him to hold up to a 4 percent stake in Blockbuster, he ended up buying back their stock himself. "You can sell your shares, but you should tell me first," he told them.

Despite the unspoken yet pointed warning from his staff, Keyes stuck to his plan.

THE BLOCKBUSTER BOARD took its cue from Icahn and let Keyes go forward with his plans to defund Total Access and sell merchandise on consignment in the stores. Keyes's plan to make a bid for the ailing

Circuit City electronics chain also won board approval, even after Wall Street analysts roundly panned the idea.

As promised, Keyes raised subscription prices on all Blockbuster Online subscribers and diverted the millions that Antioco had pledged to Total Access to the stores. He also refused to consider Evangelist's repeated pleas to sell Blockbuster Online—now worth close to $1 billion at Netflix's original offering price—saying he needed the online service as a bridge to digital delivery. Later, he refused to consider a second offer Hastings made to buy the subscriber base.

Wall Street reacted negatively to Keyes's price increases for Total Access, which raised the cost of the premium plan by $10 a month, to $34.99. In a note to clients, Citigroup analyst Tony Wible upgraded his rating on Netflix, predicting that the price hikes could drive away as many as half of Blockbuster Online's subscribers.

NETFLIX GREETED ANTIOCO'S departure and Keyes's plan to run Blockbuster for profit with relief. Keyes's public revelation that Total Access had been killing Blockbuster validated everything that McCarthy and Hastings had been telling analysts and journalists for months. Finally Blockbuster would be forced to run a sustainable business strategy, and they believed Netflix could compete against that approach, and win.

A group of Netflix executives, including Ross and Kirincich and David Wells, listened to one of Keyes's first presentations to Wall Street, in which he rolled out plans for rejuvenating the stores with a concept called Rock the Block. He presented drawings for the elaborate new stores that Ross admired, but that he thought looked a lot like the multilevel glass Toys Я Us store in Times Square

Like the Blockbuster veterans, Ross and the others knew that Keyes could do nothing to save the stores, no matter how he rebuilt them. But if Keyes wanted to expend manpower and resources on the fruitless project, they welcomed his mistake. Publicly Hastings praised the store concepts but behind closed doors the Netflix staff were thrilled that Blockbuster had taken its eye off online rental.

As Evangelist predicted, Blockbuster Online began losing subscribers as soon as Keyes cut its marketing budget. Analysts were correct in assuming that the price hike, planned for December, could cut the subscriber base by half, he warned.

During a series of tense strategy sessions with Keyes and Blockbuster chief financial officer Tom Casey in the autumn of 2007, Evangelist again raised the subject of selling the online service to Netflix. "Sell it for what you can get for it," he said. "Guarantee our subscribers in-store exchanges for about a year—just price in what it's going to cost us to service them. Open it up to Netflix customers and tell them they can exchange their DVDs in our stores for two dollars."

Again, Keyes turned him down. "Who is going to buy it, Shane?" he asked mockingly.

"I don't know, Jim. Why don't we start with that guy in California who offered us two hundred dollars a sub?" Evangelist said. "Just let me go on the road for six months and I'll get it sold."

Evangelist's increasingly desperate attempts to prevent Keyes from gutting Blockbuster Online went nowhere. Finally, Keyes reiterated his plan to cut funding to the online service at the end of one meeting. He turned to Evangelist and said, "If you don't like it, get the hell out." Although Keyes had offered him several jobs in Blockbuster's upper management, Evangelist got a call from Blockbuster's Human Resources department as he drove home that night, asking about Keyes's ultimatum. "Just trigger my contract," he said. "I don't want to work for him."

As he sat on his back porch that evening, watching the Texas sun sink, Evangelist began sobbing. It suddenly occurred to him that four years of his life had just evaporated.

When she learned that Evangelist had resigned, the controlled Hessel locked the door, sat in her office, and cried. She resigned a few weeks later.

EVANGELIST ATTENDED A dinner at the San Francisco home of Silicon Valley investors Ellen and David Siminoff about three weeks later. Ellen Siminoff sat on the board of the online auto parts store U.S. Auto Parts Network, which had just hired Evangelist as its chief executive. And David Siminoff had invited his friend Reed Hastings to join them for dinner.

It was the first time the two men had met. They sat across the table from one another making polite conversation until dessert, when curiosity won out.

In the spirited discussion that followed, Evangelist learned that Hastings had been prepared to pay Blockbuster Online as much as three hundred dollars per subscriber to put Evangelist and his team out of business.

"You had us in checkmate," Hastings said, conceding that while Netflix knew that Blockbuster Online was burning through money, Total Access was a value proposition they could not match.

The talk turned to Keyes's new initiatives, especially the Blockbuster chief executive's preoccupation with rebuilding the store base. Both knew that Keyes would fail, and it would be a matter of time before the board replaced him, possibly with a more tech-savvy executive.

"How long do you think I have?" Hastings asked.

"Two years, tops," Evangelist said.

At the end of the evening, Hastings invited Evangelist to come speak to his team. A few months later, in early 2008, they re-created their dinner conversation. Sitting on the stage together at the Los Gatos Theater, they took turns asking each other the questions each had been dying to pose during the price war's long years.

AS EVANGELIST HAD predicted, Netflix suddenly began growing again in 2008. It was as if a spigot had been turned on as soon as Keyes shut off the Total Access marketing program. The renewed growth returned Netflix's subscriber additions, revenue, and earnings back to the previous year's level, but Hastings reported: "We are much happier today than ninety days ago, but we are still not where we would like to be in terms of subscriber growth."

Movie Gallery had filed for bankruptcy over the summer, besieged on all sides by Redbox, Total Access, and Netflix. Netflix's instant streaming feature was growing faster and proving more popular than Hastings had expected. In all, the online rental playing field looked a lot more advantageous for Netflix than at any time in the previous four years.

Hastings reminded investors that online delivery would now manifest as three distinct and only partially overlapping market segments: Netflix's subscription streaming, Apple iTunes's file download, and free streaming, in which YouTube was the innovator. Netflix intended to own the subscription streaming piece, putting the company on a collision course with the $81 billion cable industry.

Netflix's now unquestioned domination of the online rental space gave it growing subscriber and cash bases to leverage in negotiations over movie rights.

"We now have more resources, bigger competitors, and a much bigger prize to earn," he said.

But it would be a decade or more for a streaming-only offering to win with consumers, simply because it would take at least that long to obtain streaming rights for all seventy-five thousand titles in Netflix's DVD library. Studios got 41 percent of their revenue from DVD sales in 2006, and they would protect that source of cash as long as possible.

The format war between Blu-ray and HD DVD to win the high-definition video space would add another few years to DVD's life span, and Netflix was content to let DVD wind down at its own pace, Hastings said.

In early 2008, Netflix announced its first consumer electronics partnership incorporating its streaming software into a set-top box by LG Electronics. The goal was to bring a smooth streaming signal straight from the Internet to users' big-screen televisions for an experience that was as good as cable or satellite. A few months later, Roku, the streaming technology company that Hastings and Anthony Wood had incubated at Netflix's Los Gatos headquarters, was ready with its own Netflix-powered set-top box.

The ninety-nine-dollar Roku box, about the size and shape of a square hockey puck, was an instant hit with tech writers and consumers alike for its instinctive user interface and ready-out-of-the-box installation. Consumers and critics responded to the luxurious experience of selecting from the relatively enormous (by pay-per-view standards) catalog of twelve thousand streaming titles and waiting only about twenty seconds for the DVD-quality picture to appear and play without a hitch.

The first shipment of Roku boxes sold out within a few weeks of the product's launch, and the critical and popular reception opened the door to other partnerships.

The timing of the Roku launch in May 2008 brought the first big disagreement over public relations strategy between Hastings and Ross, who believed they should introduce the little box after announcing a big streaming partnership with a major platform like Sony's PlayStation or Microsoft's Xbox, so it would not appear as if Netflix had been unsuccessful in finding other platforms for instant streaming. In fact, the nearly unanimous praise for Roku provided an enormous publicity boon for Netflix, as it showed the world its ability to create beautiful, elegant, and user-friendly hardware.

The blogosphere buzzed with excitement about a potential tie-up between Netflix and Xbox, after Netflix began surveying subscribers about their interest in streaming movies through the popular game console. Getting in the Xbox did much more than give Netflix access to ten million Xbox owners. Microsoft taking on the likes of Netflix—even though Hastings had joined the software giant's board of directors a year earlier—gave the fledgling streaming service the imprimatur of the mighty, ubiquitous Microsoft brand.

The companies announced at the E3 Media and Business Summit

in Los Angeles that Microsoft would launch the Netflix service—by subscription—in an upgrade to its Xbox 360 right before the holiday season. Ross was disappointed that Microsoft Interactive's John Schappert had sandwiched the Netflix news into a number of other announcements, but the media and consumer reaction was gratifying.

The successful launches of Roku and Xbox opened a floodgate to similar deals. A steady flow of new streaming partners followed: Blu-ray players, set-top boxes, televisions, laptops, and mobile devices all equipped with Netflix software. Netflix implanted its streaming software in more than two hundred types of Internet- and video-enabled devices over the ensuing three years.

Ross and Swasey worked multiple deals simultaneously, feverishly slotting the announcements into Netflix's calendar as each deal closed and the software was finalized. The impression Netflix created with its constant drumbeat of partnership announcements was that of the inevitability of digital delivery over physical media.

On the content side, Sarandos cut deals with CBS and Disney to stream TV shows on Netflix, and pay-television channel Starz Entertainment signed a three-year deal to let Netflix stream twenty-five hundred movies, TV shows, and concerts that had been destined for Starz's defunct online movie service, Vongo.

Success bred success, and partnerships bred more partnerships, Ross believed. If Netflix built momentum with a steady stream of deals, electronics manufacturers and movie studios would fear being left behind as video streaming took off.

Walmart shuttered its movie download service at the end of 2008, less than a year after it launched, emphasizing with its second failure that size and money alone did not guarantee success in the new world of digital delivery.

AT BLOCKBUSTER, KEYES was also pursuing a deal to make consumer electronics an integral part of his movie rental scheme. In April

2008, he made an unsolicited $1 billion offer to buy Circuit City Stores to accelerate Blockbuster's transformation into an electronics retailer. The proposed deal became public a couple of months after Keyes saw his private offer rejected, because the Circuit City board did not think Blockbuster could find financing for the deal.

CNET's Jim Kerstetter captured Wall Street's reaction to the proposed merger the day it became public: "Like most other people who learned about this deal Monday morning, I'm baffled. And I smell desperation."

The Circuit City board was equally perplexed, and at first refused to open its books to Blockbuster, until Icahn said he and other investors would purchase the chain if Blockbuster could not find financing. Three months later Blockbuster bowed to resistance from Circuit City and public ridicule of the idea and withdrew its offer.

"Although we withdrew our offer for the company, and have no plans to continue that course of action, we remain confident that consumer electronics, especially portable video-enabled devices, represents an opportunity for Blockbuster stores to remain relevant and viable well into the future," Keyes told investors.

Finally Keyes turned to looking for a viable streaming plan after publicly downplaying the importance of both online DVD rental and digital delivery for more than a year. In an interview with technology blog PaidContent.org, Keyes defended his strategy of cutting marketing for online DVD rental by insisting that Blockbuster had been "taking people out of the $24 billion in-store segment, and we're forcing them into this smaller by-mail segment."

"Really, where all the money is, is in stores," Keyes said. To that end Blockbuster had invested in in-store kiosks that would someday be transformed from movie vending to digital download machines. "Imagine in the future the ability to have the entire library captured on a kiosk," he enthused.

Before Evangelist left he convinced Keyes to pay $6.6 million to acquire Movielink, the movie downloading service founded by the major Hollywood studios, mainly because of the content deals that came with the deal. Nearly a year after Netflix rolled out its first streaming partnership, Blockbuster announced that it, too, would get into the set-top box business. In November 2008, Blockbuster introduced a ninety-nine-dollar digital media player that downloaded high-definition quality movies to customers' televisions via broadband lines.

Although the title selection was smaller than Netflix's instant streaming service, Blockbuster OnDemand boasted newer titles as a result of the movie rights granted to Movielink by its studio founders. But Keyes still had not caught on to consumers' impatience with being told how and when to watch movies: Blockbuster OnDemand charged $1.99 for movie rentals and gave renters twenty-four hours to watch the movie once they pressed play. The rental expired after thirty days even if the customer never watched it.

WHEN THE RECESSION derailed the U.S. economy in late 2008, Netflix found itself well-positioned to take advantage of new trends in collaborative consumption. Customers stayed home and turned to Netflix for cheap entertainment and got hooked on a growing number of devices that could suddenly stream videos—game consoles, cell phones, DVD players. The Netflix application was everywhere, and consumers signed up at a rate of ten thousand per day in late 2008 and early 2009.

The DVD-by-mail operation also reached its pinnacle of efficiency, delivering 97 percent of its deliveries in one business day from sixty distribution centers and scoring at the top of e-commerce customer satisfaction surveys.

About a month after Netflix surpassed ten million subscribers, in spring 2009, I interviewed Hastings at Netflix's offices in Beverly Hills. During our forty-five-minute conversation he seemed relaxed and thoughtful, fluently answering questions ranging from the effect of the recession on subscriber growth (there had been none: They posted record subscriber additions that quarter), to why Blu-ray DVD penetration was growing so slowly, to how long it would take for Netflix to get the rights to stream new releases (at least ten years).

When we got around to discussing the competitive landscape, I could tell something had shifted profoundly. Rumors had been swirling that week that Blockbuster was exploring a prepackaged bankruptcy filing—a rumor it would later deny. Hastings was always quite circumspect in talking about Blockbuster during the thick of their battles. I was never sure whether he wanted to avoid telegraphing anything to investors or to Blockbuster about his state of mind with regard to their competition.

"Now let's talk about your archrival—Blockbuster," I said.

"Who?" he asked, feigning ignorance. "Our archrival is Redbox. Blockbuster is heading down."

I laughed in surprise. I couldn't help it. He was making a rare joke about Blockbuster—something I had not heard him do since first dismissing Blockbuster Online five years earlier.

If Viacom had let Blockbuster spend the money to attack Netflix earlier, or had not extracted a $1 billion dividend, or the "good-bye kiss," as Hastings put it, "things might have been different today."

"How do you feel about the rumors that Blockbuster is exploring bankruptcy?" I asked.

"A mix of sadness and elation," he said. "Sadness because they are decent people, and they have been working hard, and elation because the company that has been trying to kill us for so long is dying."

"That's a sad thing to see all those stores close and the jobs lost and we are doing fine," he added. "I felt more aggressive toward them when they were killing us, but now I wish them the best. We have our next round of foes."

He mentioned that exit surveys Netflix conducted on subscribers who canceled revealed that a growing number were transferring their movie renting habit to Redbox kiosks. By the end of 2009 Redbox had deployed twenty thousand kiosks and were disrupting the market enough for Movie Gallery to cite the kiosk company as the primary reason it failed again after emerging from its 2007 bankruptcy.

Redbox would be a tough competitor, he said.

AT THE PARTY in Los Gatos the night after our interview, Netflix staffers flowed out through the ground-floor kitchen, through a lovely tented area in the courtyard of the faux Mediterranean villa, and enjoyed hors d'oeuvres and wine. Hastings had a fake tattoo with the number ten million inscribed inside a heart on his face for the evening. It was perfect moment—an idyllic if brief resting point.

Mixed with the satisfaction and pride in reaching a benchmark that many experts once believed did not exist in online rental was a sense of a job left undone. Another unlikely prize waited unclaimed—twenty million subscribers by 2012. The forecast, made nearly a decade earlier, was suddenly feasible again. They had three years to double their subscriber base.

How far and how fast could they take the company? No one wanted to waste a second, and despite the grueling hours they had already put in, no one wanted to miss what happened next.

CHAPTER FOURTEEN

TRUE GRIT

(2009–2010)

THE TIGHTENING OF THE CREDIT market in late 2008 made it tough for Jim Keyes to amend and extend Blockbuster's credit lines for a fifth time in three years to carry out his store expansion plan. A year into his tenure, Keyes was consumed with revamping Blockbuster's stores into "full-service entertainment destinations" where, he envisioned, customers would drop in for pizza and a Coke, or buy a book or a flat-screen television or hang out with their kids on weekends while waiting for a movie to download.

Blockbuster Online dropped below 1.6 million subscribers before Keyes stopped reporting subscriber numbers, telling investors the metric was not material to Blockbuster's financial results since digital downloads and streaming made up only $1.5 billion of the $25 billion universe of DVD rental and sales in the United States. "So the bottom line is, the focus on subscription service, we don't think is a relevant measure for the Blockbuster business. It's a data point, an interesting one, but it is not one that we think is of great meaning to our future," he said.

Unfortunately for Keyes, as year-over-year store revenue comparisons continued their steady march into negative territory, the rest of the world had stopped debating whether digital media would be significant. *Variety* lauded 2008 as "the year when global revenues from digital media exceeded revenue generated by movie theaters and home video combined." The entertainment trade magazine cited a study by the London research firm Strategy Analytics in early 2009 that showed that online and mobile channels accounted for $90 billion in worldwide revenues, while global filmed entertainment generated $83.1 billion.

"We're starting to see now that digital media is becoming a significant part of revenue for a lot of companies, Martin Olausson of Strategy Analytics told *Variety*. "A few years back, everyone was still discussing whether movies would be distributed online. That's not a discussion any more."

Still Keyes remained resolute in focusing what little capital Blockbuster had on the stores and on publicly assuring Netflix that he had no designs on its subscribers. "We don't want to try to aggressively steal share from Netflix. We think that would be an expensive proposition," Keyes said.

Nor would Blockbuster compete head-to-head with Redbox. Keyes weighed a vending operation for two years while wondering how to keep the machines' one-dollar-per-day rentals from cannibalizing the stores' sales. He approached Lowe with an idea for an in-store–kiosk partnership that the latter turned down as ludicrous. They were competitors fighting over the same turf.

By the time Keyes licensed Blockbuster's brand to NCR in 2009 for kiosks that he planned to park mainly outside Blockbuster stores Redbox had deployed more than twelve thousand kiosks in major grocery and convenience store chains. "Our vending approach would be more a satellite operation for the store," Keyes told investors.

The Blockbuster store was still an important part of the entertainment lifestyle of mainstream America, especially since digital rental was too complicated and confusing for most customers, Keyes insisted. "As long as we change the product assortment to meet the changing needs of the customer, our stores will remain relevant."

Blockbuster was a relic, and Keyes's strategy was doing little to change that impression. A popular YouTube video posted in 2008 by *The Onion* poked fun at the chain's stubborn refusal to embrace the digital age. The video purported to show a Living Blockbuster Museum in Auburn Hills, Michigan, where tourists learned about the "hardships" that Americans faced before the advent of Netflix and iTunes.

I never learned whether Keyes saw the video, but it seemed clear that he never got the message about Blockbuster's slide into obsolescence, even after a couple of his major initiatives failed.

Stocking Blockbuster stores with games proved too expensive in light of the company's strained cash situation, and the download kiosks that had appeared in a few stores had few movies to rent, because the studios had not worked out how to encrypt them. None of the content was available in high definition.

As soon as the content started rolling in, however, Keyes predicted confidently that customers would line up to load movies onto their thumb drives and "take them home and put them in their set-top boxes, or whatever."

When the economy fell off a cliff in late 2008 it took Blockbuster's fragile store revenues with it. Netflix's subscriber growth chugged along nearly unchanged, inciting analysts to make unwelcome comments about Blockbuster's poor performance. Keyes first blamed lower store sales and rentals on a poor slate of DVD releases, and then on a slate of hot theatrical releases that stole business from Blockbuster when consumers spent money at the box office instead. In early 2009, Blockbuster notified the Street that it had hired a law firm and an investment bank to explore restructuring options, including a potential bankruptcy, a source said.

Instead of accepting a second overture from Netflix to sell its subscribers, Blockbuster looked to the past for answers. Keyes raised prices for in-store rentals and reinstituted late fees, which he called "a daily rate. . . . We're very careful not to call it a late fee," he told analysts. The one-dollar daily rate started accruing after five days and resulted in consumers purchasing a DVD if they kept it longer than fifteen days.

Keyes launched a rental plan called Direct Access that allowed customers to order back catalog titles from the stores and have them shipped to their homes for a five-day rental, in an unconscious resurrection of Netflix's first business model from more than a decade earlier. Blockbuster had no money to promote the program, and it sank.

Keyes advocated instituting the "vending rental window" proposed by the movie studios: Kiosks, including those of Redbox and Blockbuster, would not be able to buy and rent new titles for at least a month after their release. He aimed to rely on the studios to enforce the windows against his competitors and loaded up on new Christmas releases; then he waited for consumers to stream into Blockbuster stores.

"Certainly the windows, to the extent that they do stick, they help the stores, because it gives the store yet another reason to be and makes them more relevant for the consumer. Frankly, the consumer's awareness of movies that are one week old, two weeks old, I challenge most of the people on the call to tell me what movies were released last week," Keyes said.

But the windows did not stick, and Keyes's plan to profit from new DVD releases that Netflix and Redbox could not obtain in bulk from the studios or wholesalers backfired. Predictably, Redbox and Netflix flouted the studios' rules and bought the disks from big-box retailers like Walmart, which discounted them heavily over the holidays.

The outlay of money for the unsold Christmas inventory left Blockbuster with a huge earnings shortfall. "We had every reason to believe that December, especially the holiday season, would provide its historic contribution . . . with newly announced studio windows," Keyes explained.

Kiosk deployment was far behind schedule, with just two thousand units rolled out compared with nearly twenty thousand for Redbox, whose revenue had shot up to $1.1 billion and was growing at 26 percent per kiosk in 2009—far from the "oversaturated" market Keyes had described.

Movie Gallery filed for bankruptcy protection for the second time in February 2010, less than two years after emerging from its 2007 bankruptcy. This time it would be forced to close its remaining twenty-four hundred Movie Gallery and Hollywood Video stores for good. The company's chief restructuring officer, Steve Moore, told the bankruptcy court the beleaguered chain could not compete in the changing rental landscape. "One of the most significant industrywide factors affecting the company's performance since the 2007 bankruptcy cases has been the cannibalization of rentals by DVD-dispensing kiosks operated by Redbox, which offer low-priced rentals and convenience," Moore said.

The following month, Blockbuster, too, began its descent into bankruptcy. It had $1 billion in debt on its books and reported a half-billion dollars in losses. Icahn sold off his nearly 17 percent stake in Blockbuster and left the board. On a conference call with investors, Keyes pleaded with shareholders, bondholders, and creditors to stay the course as Blockbuster tried to recapitalize again in May 2010.

"Netflix is growing really well in a bad economy—the same economy Blockbuster is facing," Wedbush Morgan Securities analyst Edward Woo said. "You have to wonder how much more patience investors have."

When Blockbuster's stock price fell below one dollar, it faced delisting on the New York Stock Exchange. The once-mighty rental chain now consisted of just thirty-five hundred U.S. stores and four thousand kiosks.

REDBOX OCCUPIED SIX floors in a sleek glass tower in suburban Chicago. A huge electronic ticker board in the lobby showed the number of rentals that customers made each day—usually in the millions—as well as the number of first-time visitors to the DVD vending machines. An electronic map mounted on the wall below displayed a rash of red dots where Redboxes were springing up at supermarkets, airports, and convenience stores across the country at a rate of one an hour by 2010. Parked near the elevators on each floor stood iterations of Lowe's beloved kiosks, including the one he designed in 1984 and had a Connecticut robotics company build for fourteen thousand dollars.

Shortly after he left Netflix, Lowe went to work as a consultant for a venture that McDonald's was testing in-house to drive traffic to its fast-food restaurants: a DVD rental kiosk called Tik Tok DVD Shop and an enormous convenience store–type vending machine called the Tik Tok Easy Shop that sold everything from soup and sandwiches to diapers. The twenty feet by ten feet by ten feet convenience-store machines drew crowds when they appeared in six McDonald's parking lots in the Washington, D.C., area in 2003, but the fast-food giant quickly pulled the plug on the rather ungainly, glitch-prone machines to concentrate on the DVD kiosks. The DVD machines were bright red, and after fruitlessly hiring a branding company to come up with a name, the Tik Tok team decided to call the business Redbox.

Lowe had been almost certain that consumers' discomfort with being locked into a subscription would hold Netflix's growth to no more than two million subscribers. He thought there was more opportunity in challenging store chains, which had not lowered their prices even after their inventory costs dropped from sixty dollars per VHS title to sixteen dollars for DVDs.

Most importantly, however, it irritated Lowe that the people at Netflix said no one would rent movies from a machine, and he planned to prove them wrong.

It made perfect sense: Shrink down the bloated real estate costs that Blockbuster and Movie Gallery were shouldering and concentrate on the big new releases that would attract impulse rentals as consumers walked past the machines on their way home from the grocery store or fast-food restaurant.

Redbox's first test market for McDonald's was Denver, and Lowe was shocked to see Blockbuster make the same mistake it made with Netflix. It ignored the kiosks that sprang up in 140 McDonald's restaurants across the city. That neglect allowed Lowe to tinker with his pricing and product mix completely unchallenged by Blockbuster throughout 2004 and into 2005.

In early 2005, McDonald's decided to exit the kiosk business, realizing, as one executive told Lowe, that late founder Ray Kroc would roll over in his grave at the revelation that McDonald's was peddling R-rated movies at its restaurants. Redbox convinced McDonald's to let it keep the revenue from its eight hundred or so kiosks in a half-dozen markets. Then Lowe and McDonald's' strategy executive Gregg Kaplan went to seek $30 million in funding from another big investor. Lowe's first two stops: Netflix and Blockbuster.

Blockbuster stores had belatedly pushed back against Redbox's Denver test by offering a ninety-nine-cent one-day rental that turned into a four-dollar rental if customers didn't return the DVD the next day. So Lowe figured Blockbuster executives considered the kiosks a competitive threat. He called Shepherd at Blockbuster and explained that Redbox wanted to sell half the kiosk company for $30 million. Was Blockbuster interested?

Shepherd turned him down flat.

Lowe tried again: "This is the second time I've talked to you guys about an investment," Lowe said. That was as far as he got. Shepherd had hung up the phone.

(Shepherd does not recall this conversation with Lowe, but he says he participated in 2006 talks with Redbox over a joint venture that never materialized, because of Redbox's apparent lack of interest.)

Lowe had kept Hastings apprised of his new business, and he and Kaplan met with the Netflix CEO several times about investing in Redbox. While Hastings seemed increasingly interested—especially after Redbox expanded nationwide—he hinted that McCarthy and Kilgore disliked the idea and preferred to spend their capital on streaming.

When Blockbuster's Total Access program surfaced a year or so later, the two companies again discussed teaming up on a hybrid Redbox-Netflix offering but could not agree on how it should be structured.

The rejections by both rental companies and the venture capital community in 2005 stung, because Lowe and Kaplan knew there was a waiting market for Redbox. Lowe remembered a guy he had met during his Netflix days who worked at a vending machine company named Coinstar. The Bellevue, Washington–based company, which took its name from the army of coin-counting machines it installed in supermarket lobbies, had since expanded its reach into other types of vending machines. It purchased about half of Redbox for $32 million in 2005 and bought the remaining stake from McDonald's four years later for around $175 million.

AT FIRST LOWE and Kaplan assumed Redbox would attract the young affluent males who were Netflix's early adopters, because customers had to have a credit card to use the kiosks. But the fluke placement of a kiosk at a Smith's grocery store in a low-income Las Vegas suburb showed them otherwise. The machine unexpectedly rented two or three times the number of disks of any other Redbox kiosk. Lowe stationed staff members in front of the machine, and others in well-to-do areas, to interview customers to find out what was going on.

Those surveys revealed that affluent grocery store customers were nervous about putting their credit cards into the machines and viewed the one dollar price with suspicion—it was too low. But for the poorer patrons the one dollar rental was so compelling that they were less concerned about credit card security.

As a result, Redbox reconfigured its kiosk placement to low-income areas, and as the brand became better known, more prosperous customers came along as well. Redbox fended off challenges from other small vending competitors with the help of Coinstar, whose relationships with grocery store chains opened doors that Lowe and Kaplan had been pounding on without success. Once they had taken out rival kiosk chains, Redbox set its sights on Blockbuster, and by 2007, Redbox kiosks outnumbered Blockbuster stores.

The store chains were not the only companies affected by the rise of rental kiosks. Netflix and Hollywood studios had both started seeing an alarming dent in revenues as a result of Lowe and Kaplan's creation.

"The long-term effects of ubiquitous one-dollar new release DVD rental are not positive for us or the industry as a whole," Hastings told investors in 2009.

The studios had been clamoring for a window of twenty-eight days or more to let them sell new DVD releases before rental outlets began offering the titles. In exchange, the studios would not try to block sales of the new titles, and would offer incentives to the rental companies, in the form of lower costs on bulk purchases of new titles.

New releases comprised Redbox's entire business, and Lowe fought the proposal strongly, but more than 70 percent of Netflix rentals were older titles. Hastings was all for the windowing deal.

"The advantage to taking the windowing deals is cost savings. Warner has given us a huge number of copies up to the twenty-ninth day at a very attractive price, so we are able to fulfill all of the consumer demand, and then we are able to use those savings to pour that into more streaming," Hastings said in late 2009.

Consumers had embraced instant streaming; within eighteen months of its launch, half of Netflix's subscribers were using the feature to watch movies and TV shows, and Hulu, YouTube, Amazon, and Apple's iTunes were quickly filling in gaps in Netflix's catalog by offering newly released titles for sale and rental as downloadable video files.

The online video services provided "drops of water in an ocean of viewing," but they were competing for the five hours a day of U.S. householder viewing time alongside cable, satellite, and telecoms, Hastings said. One day Netflix would become one of the studios' and networks' largest customers—a fourth option, representing Internet television, he said.

Netflix, Facebook, and YouTube were forerunners of television for the Internet generation, as Hastings saw it. He envisioned personalized and portable applications featuring content shared and promoted through social networks replacing the standard channel grids with the scheduled programming that populated cable, satellite, and telecoms' video products. Hastings and his team viewed the cable bundle as a sort of latter-day record album that would be torn apart and shopped to consumers as pieces of programming by the video equivalent of iTunes.

While Netflix reached for bigger content deals and a slice of online video profits, Hastings publicly tried to mollify threatened cable and satellite operators and telecoms by linking the rise in online streaming to a corresponding bonanza in higher-margin broadband services. "As we see it, the growth of Internet video is likely to boost overall cable profit," he said, on a conference call with investors.

Netflix had to work hard, as a new player in the content game, to amass its streaming library, at first picking up shows piecemeal, as it did with Comedy Central's *South Park*, and then striking deals for bundles of shows, such as the Disney–ABC Television Group's prime time hit shows *Lost*, *Grey's Anatomy*, and *Desperate Housewives*, as well as popular Disney Channel kids' shows.

Every year the deals got a little better, although Netflix still was not part of the decade-long distribution agreements for home entertainment. Doubts about the long-term growth of online video were so pervasive that Netflix was able to strike a deal with pay-TV channel Starz for streaming rights to its films for two years for a paltry $25 million. The licensing agreement for Starz's roster of top-tier movie titles gave the instant streaming service legitimacy as a content provider equal to cable but at a fraction of the price. A similar deal with NBC Universal, for a deep selection of hit and classic television shows, including making *Saturday Night Live* available the day after it aired, came just as cheaply.

Hastings made it known that Netflix had cash to spend for TV shows, movies, and straight-to-video content, but the overtures to studios and other content owners went unnoticed.

The dam finally broke with the signing of an $800 million, five-year licensing agreement for new releases and library titles owned by EPIX, a pay-television service owned by Paramount Pictures, Lionsgate, and Metro-Goldwyn-Mayer. The remarkable price tag—reported as "close to $1 billion" in the trades—had potential licensors flowing into Netflix's Beverly Hills offices to talk about their online video strategies. Those in the movie industry—directors, actors, writers, and other artists—wanted to discuss their share of online video revenues. Suddenly, everybody was paying attention.

By 2010, the studios and cable operators realized they had invited a Trojan horse into their midst. Netflix was hardly the size of a regional cable carrier when it obtained the Starz and NBC Universal deals. Two years later its subscriber base rivaled that of Comcast, the largest U.S. cable operator.

"The problem is that Netflix is not the company we thought it was when we started doing these deals a few years ago, it has changed," a studio executive told Reuters anonymously in late 2010.

To make matters worse, the first-ever decline in pay TV subscriptions ignited a debate about whether recession-weary consumers were canceling their pay TV services to watch videos online via Netflix and other Web-based sources.

Ted Sarandos maintained, however, that Netflix was "absolutely complementary" to cable.

When the Starz and NBC Universal contract came up for renewal, the price tags had ballooned to hundreds of millions of dollars, and studios were adding restrictive conditions, in an effort to protect eroding DVD revenues. Sony and Disney yanked popular movies from Netflix's streaming lineups unexpectedly, after the titles reached caps on the number of subscribers that could view them.

Analysts began worrying about the overhead associated with

multiyear content deals and noted that larger competitors entering online video delivery, such as Amazon and Google, had much deeper pockets for buying content. "Netflix is merely a conduit," Wedbush Morgan analyst Pachter said. "The big boys will take a share of subscribers or bid up the cost of content. Either way, Netflix loses."

At Marathon Partners, Cibelli knew it was time to sell his Netflix stock. With its stock price at two hundred dollars, and cable outlets treating Netflix like a real threat, it was clear to Cibelli that the online rental company had taken its place in the entertainment industry establishment. He made his money on contrarian bets, and Netflix was no longer an outsider. The risky little company he had backed six years earlier had become a sure thing.

Data showing that Netflix originated six out of every ten digital movies streamed, and accounted for 20 percent of U.S. broadband traffic, brought the service unwelcome attention from broadband providers and cable operators, who downplayed the rental company's influence. "It's a little bit like, Is the Albanian army going to take over the world? I don't think so," Time Warner chief executive Jeffrey Bewkes told a media industry conference hosted by financial services group UBS that turned into a gripe-fest about Netflix. In another interview, Bewkes denied that the subscription streaming service was a threat to Time Warner's HBO movie channel. "I would say it (Netflix) is like a two-hundred-pound chimp. It's not an eight-hundred-pound gorilla," Bewkes told CNBC's Julia Boorstin.

Netflix executives took the criticism in stride, joking among themselves that Bewkes probably suffered from traumatic flashbacks to Time Warner's disastrous 2000 merger with AOL whenever the media asked him about his company's online strategy.

When *Huffington Post* publisher Arianna Huffington asked about the comment during the 2011 Consumer Electronics Show in Las Vegas, Hastings pulled a chain from beneath his shirt and joked that he was proud to wear the dog tags of the Albanian army. He later issued "Albanian Army" berets to executives for a two-day retreat at a Silicon Valley convention center. Many of the ninety-plus executives wore the berets throughout the two-day event.

The chimp comment also provoked much mirth at Netflix, especially after David Wells mocked up a PowerPoint presentation for an all-staff meeting to show why chimps are smarter than gorillas. The final slide showed a photo-shopped picture of a chimp wearing an Albanian army beret and waving a Netflix flag.

At the same time, the Internet service providers acted to curb Netflix's growing might—first by threatening to stop offering unlimited bandwidth access and then by charging customers per gigabyte of bandwidth they consumed.

Comcast, in the midst of acquiring NBC Universal, provoked public outrage by charging extra fees to Internet service provider Level 3 Communications for carrying Netflix streaming movies over Comcast's broadband fiber. Hastings called the Comcast fee "inappropriate." The incident set off a feud between Netflix and Comcast.

Netflix hit back in a blog posting that ranked the speeds of U.S. and Canadian ISPs in delivering Netflix streaming videos to consumers' homes. The threat of bandwidth caps propelled Hastings back into national politics for the first time since he lost his seat on the California board of education.

He called on Netflix subscribers and public interest groups to demand greater U.S. government oversight of Internet neutrality rules to ensure that Internet service providers could not tamper with Web traffic to favor their own programming and slow down that of rivals like Netflix.

To bolster Netflix's spending on federal lobbying, which grew from $20,000 in 2009 to $500,000 in 2011, Hastings formed a political action committee called FLIXPAC to get his two cents on a raft of internet-related legislation governing Internet neutrality, offshore movie piracy, and the sharing of consumers' video rental records.

Federal Communications Commission rules approved in late 2010 barring ISPs and wireless providers from blocking any content or applications from customers won guarded praise from Hastings. By then the Netflix chief was riding high—and using his newfound stature as *Fortune* magazine's Businessperson of the Year to influence the debate over Internet openness.

THE MAGAZINE COVER had been a sort of parting gift to Hastings by Ken Ross, the first of Hastings's hand-picked senior executive team to leave since Tom Dillon retired in 2006.

The *Fortune* cover had been a personal goal Ross had set several years earlier, when Netflix was trying to buck Wall Street's perception that the company would be lucky to last a year against its store-based foes. For Ross a *Fortune* cover represented a distant peak in Netflix's climb to legitimacy—a sign that it had achieved the well-deserved status of an iconic American brand.

Once or twice a year, he would bring Hastings to the Time-Life Building in Manhattan to meet with *Fortune*'s editors, including editor-at-large Pattie Sellers, for extended chats about the business of rental. Hastings was at his best in these off-the-record conversations— provocative, candid, and smart.

Swasey took up the cause as well, meeting with *Fortune* senior writer Micheal Copeland and with managing editor Andy Serwer and Sellers while Ross was out of the office after a serious health scare. Their careful, patient tending of Netflix's image paid off in mid-2010, just as Ross returned to work. *Fortune* wanted to do a major story on Hastings but would not discuss the story's placement within the magazine. Hastings sat for the interview. The story was delayed by two weeks, and then by two more weeks. When Ross learned that the piece would run in the Businessperson of the Year article, he felt deflated. The conservative magazine would never give the CEO of a tech company like Netflix that cover.

We're fucked, he told Swasey. The dream is dead.

Swasey arranged for Hastings to be photographed for the article at the Los Gatos headquarters. When the *Fortune* crew headed by the magazine's associate photo editor arrived with an enormous lighting kit and backdrops, and a make-up artist and wardrobe consultant, Swasey and Ross knew the portrait was destined for the cover. They could hardly believe it.

The cover story lauded Hastings as "a guru to a new generation of Silicon Valley entrepreneurs" and noted that Netflix was "killing it," even by the standards of the Valley's number one export: Apple. The exposure and praise in one of America's most conservative business magazines had an odd effect—it made Hastings and Netflix's spectacular rise in a fast-evolving competitive landscape—and its frothy share price, which was approaching three hundred dollars—seem bulletproof. It soon appeared that Hastings thought so, too.

Ross left six weeks later, satisfied that his ride at Netflix had ended at the right time but never knowing whether the *Fortune* cover had impressed Hastings.

The close-knit senior team—Hastings, McCarthy, McCord, Hunt, Kilgore, and Ross—had imbued Netflix with a continuity that had comforted investors during the long and grueling war with Blockbuster. But absent the challenges that had focused them outward, the strong-willed executives had become more siloed and territorial. Hastings seemed less receptive to challenge and criticism. Blame for mistakes was assigned far down the chain of command, and in the opinions of their underlings, a culture of fear and inaction set in.

McCarthy had been wrestling for the better part of a year with the idea of leaving Netflix, too, when he met with Hastings shortly after the *Fortune* cover debuted to talk about compensation, as he and every executive team member did at that time of year. He had seen the company through its knife fight against Blockbuster and Amazon, and there was no broader role for him at Netflix.

Hastings was surprised but would not agree to give McCarthy the expanded responsibility and influence he required to remain at

Netflix. McCarthy, perhaps anticipating Hastings's answer to his demands, had cashed out $40 million, or 51 percent, of his Netflix holdings in previous months. He walked out of the office that day and never returned. A press release issued later that afternoon related simply that he had left Netflix to "pursue broader executive opportunities outside the company."

McCarthy declined to comment about his departure but attended a previously scheduled appearance at an investor conference with Hastings at his side in a show of mutual support. Hastings promoted David Wells, vice president of financial planning and analysis, to his place, a bright and capable man who some nevertheless saw as an executive that the Netflix chief could control more easily than the outspoken McCarthy.

Others noticed that Hastings, seemed to take the star status conferred by the *Fortune* cover as a validation of his opinions above those of his executive team—or anyone else—and he became increasingly resentful of dissension. Investors and subscribers alike would soon have cause to lament the departures of Ross and McCarthy, and the reality check they might have provided, as Hastings retreated into an echo chamber of his own making.

CHAPTER FIFTEEN

CINEMA PARADISO

(2011)

THE COLLAPSE OF BLOCKBUSTER TOOK down its Canadian operations, which left an opening for Netflix to fulfill the international expansion dreams Hastings had had to abandon six years earlier. Blockbuster filed for bankruptcy just as Netflix launched its streaming-only service in Canada with great fanfare and a couple of embarrassing gaffes.

A public relations firm that assisted with the launch hired actors to fill out a street party in downtown Toronto, and it passed around a written instruction sheet to "look really excited, particularly if asked by media to do any interviews." The paper immediately fell into press hands and was widely ridiculed. Swasey went into action—meeting personally with reporters from the major outlets the following day to assure them that this was not how Netflix did business. The furor over the actors died quickly but Hastings's remark in an interview that Americans were too "self-absorbed" to pay attention to world events required an apology, another intensive mop-up by Swasey, and still subscribers canceled.

The bad press did not have a lingering effect. In less than a year, Netflix in Canada surpassed one million subscribers. A year after the Canada launch, Hastings personally rolled out Portuguese and Spanish-language streaming-only services in forty-three countries in Latin America and the Caribbean.

One of the factors that helped Ross decide to leave Netflix was the prospect of spending what he estimated would be nearly two years on the road rolling out the service internationally. When he made up his mind to depart he jotted down a few names of potential successors on a napkin during a plane ride from Los Gatos to his home in Los Angeles. Heading the list was a former *Wall Street Journal* editor named Jonathan Friedland, who worked in the communications department of the Walt Disney Company.

Friedland was a laid-back California native who had built an impressive career at the *Journal*'s bureaus in Latin America and Asia. Along the way he had earned a master's degree from the London School of Economics. He arrived at Disney in 2006 after starting a chain of Spanish-language newspapers in Texas. With his business and media backgrounds, and ties to Latin America, Friedland looked like the perfect PR executive to take Netflix through its international expansion. He started in early 2011, in time to plan and execute the Latin American launch nine months later. It would be a rough year.

Friedland and Swasey spent an exhausting eight days in South America and Mexico in September 2011 doing press for Netflix's first launch of its streaming service in a non-English-speaking country. They put Hastings in front of four hundred journalists in São Paulo, Buenos Aires, and Mexico City on a junket that resulted in overwhelmingly positive coverage. Back home, however, Netflix was taking a drubbing in the press and on social networks for the lingering effects of a price hike it had introduced in its home market—it raised the price of its popular hybrid streaming and DVD subscription to a painful sixteen dollars during the worst economic downturn in a century.

The media team was caught flat-footed by untimely—and inaccurate—reports that Netflix would levy a 60 percent across-the-board price hike on its U.S. subscriber base. In fact, just half of

Netflix's twenty-five million subscribers would see the steep rate increase, and another third—subscribers who wanted streaming only or DVD by mail only—would have a rate cut of up to 20 percent, as part of a new rate scheme. The news had leaked from a confidential briefing Netflix had done that summer, and the media team had no chance to stop the story from spreading throughout social networks and spilling into the media.

The news reverberated through the burgeoning social networks—Facebook, Twitter, and the blogosphere—and simply would not die down. Consumers could not be talked down from their outrage. The stock price plunged, and one million subscribers eventually canceled their service.

Lost in the maelstrom was the news that the DVD by mail operation would be spun off to a separate location and have its own workforce that would be headed by Andy Rendich, who had been Tom Dillon's protégé and successor in operations.

Hastings had often joked in years past that he would deliver the last DVD Netflix mailed out, sometime around 2030. That time frame seemed long to some, but Hastings insisted that Netflix could not retire the format until instant streaming could offer customers an equally satisfying experience, with a complete library of movies and television. It was not clear what changed his mind about waiting patiently until DVD rental died naturally as subscribers migrated into streaming—Hastings later blamed a "slide into arrogance" born of his previous successes.

"The size and timing of that price leap still doesn't make sense to me. Especially when Netflix used to be considered such a good-hearted, consumer-focused company," *New York Times* tech blogger David Pogue wrote. "The way it handled this shift feels extraordinarily blunt, ham-handed and emotionally tone-deaf."

Swasey had had the unenviable task of downplaying the price difference to angry consumers as the size of "a latte a month," rather than making the common sense explanation he had pushed Hastings to make: Netflix was losing money on DVD by mail as a result of the escalating costs of postage and shipping. The "latte" remark infuriated recession-weary subscribers, one of whom posted Swasey's cell phone number in the comments section of Netflix's blog. He patiently responded to the hundreds of calls and vitriolic voicemails by returning them personally and admitting to the surprised callers that the comment had been thoughtless and insensitive.

Hastings summoned Swasey and Friedland to Netflix's headquarters the Sunday after they returned from Latin America and informed them of his plan to try to refocus consumers and the press on the part of the announcement that they had overlooked—Netflix's plan to split off its DVD by mail service as a new business called Qwikster. He thought that if consumers understood Netflix's need to use its resources on streaming to create a better experience—a sleeker interface with more and better titles—perhaps he could stem the mounting subscriber losses.

He wanted to avoid the mistake of protecting the still-strong but ultimately doomed DVD business—as he had seen Blockbuster try to protect its store base from online rental. Businesses that failed to evolve along with technology died—this was a central tenet of Hastings's and Netflix was the manifestation of that belief. The death of DVD was inevitable, and Hastings was simply prodding it along—for the good of Netflix and its customers.

The PR team was horrified at his idea: make a major product announcement in a homegrown video that would be posted on YouTube at midnight East Coast time on a Sunday. The financial press would be livid. And the script he intended to read buried the news of the split off of the DVD by mail service deep in the ninth paragraph. The makeshift message had every mark of another PR disaster, but Hastings would not be dissuaded.

Hastings arrived at Netflix's headquarters wearing a rumpled, teal beach shirt. He had recruited a reluctant Rendich to star in the video with him. He had liked the idea of using a handheld, homemade-looking video camera to make what he expected would be an unvarnished apology and explanation. He refused to rehearse his message, but Swasey insisted on ordering a professional camera crew to the makeshift set.

"We're making this video today to apologize in person, or at least on camera, for something that we did recently," Hastings began, as Rendich looked on uncomfortably.

Reaction to the video, posted on YouTube, was swift and almost universally negative. Intellectually, the tech and financial press supported the idea of splitting up two different businesses—one growing rapidly and the other slowly fading. But they concluded that requiring subscribers to the hybrid plan to maintain separate accounts, billing, and queues was a customer service disaster.

Consumers agreed, and Hastings's blog quickly accumulated more than thirty thousand mostly angry posts.

"Reed, you may have an amazing vision of the future but you are suffering from major George Lucas syndrome—a visionary with a bunch of yes-men working for him," wrote one poster.

"Terrible idea. Bad after bad decision. What's next, only offering movies made in the eighties? I'm getting tired of this. And you," another wrote.

When it seemed as if the opprobrium could not get worse, late-night television and professional comics piled it on: *Saturday Night Live* comedians Jason Sudeikis as Hastings and Fred Armisen as Rendich appeared in a Web video to poke fun at the apology and strategy changes, and *Seinfeld* actor Jason Alexander begged for donations for the Netflix Relief Fund on the Funny or Die Web site, calling the price increase "the worst thing that has ever happened to white people." One cartoonist compared splitting the streaming and DVD services to having to get a sandwich's bread at one restaurant and the meat at another.

The public ridicule appeared to humiliate Hastings, and finally he seemed to realize the gravity of his mistake.

A few days before the videotaped announcement, Kaltschnee at HackingNetflix got word of something a Netflix insider had called

"Quickster" in a hurriedly dashed off e-mail. "That is a really silly name," he thought.

When he heard the details of the Qwikster split off—during a party at the home of a neighbor who was also a subscriber—he was dumbfounded. Kaltschnee shot a couple of e-mails to Swasey while fielding a barrage of messages from HackingNetflix readers asking, "Is this for real?"

From Swasey's tight-lipped response, it was clear the communications executive had "been caught in the middle between what they did and what they should have done," Kaltschnee reflected later.

As a programmer, he knew Hastings had to split the two very different services. But it shocked him that the lessons of the Profiles and Friends debacles years earlier apparently had taught the Netflix CEO little about how to communicate with his customers.

The concept of making subscribers maintain two queues and search two separate databases for movies was ridiculous. If they could not find the movie they wanted on the streaming site, Kaltschnee thought, people obviously would just go to iTunes or Amazon instead of ordering it on Qwikster.

It frustrated Kaltschnee that Hastings still seemed to think that he could write a blog post or slap a video together and all would be forgiven.

RENDICH KEPT HIS head down and proceeded with the spin-off plans. The Qwikster staff of about two hundred people had moved into a small satellite office down the street from Netflix's campus, so as not to distract the streaming operation. Hastings barred Swasey and Friedland, who had their hands full with the continuing international rollout, from helping Rendich with the public relations disaster he had handed Qwikster.

Following close on the price hike fiasco, Swasey set up a round of interviews with high-profile financial news outlets to try to do damage control but Hastings, backed by Friedland, refused at the last minute to do them, leaving Swasey to mop up once again.

So Rendich reached out to someone who had plenty of experience pulling Netflix out of PR messes—Ken Ross. When Rendich called about two weeks after the YouTube video debacle, Ross advised the Qwikster CEO to lob the problem back to where it originated.

"This is Reed's and Leslie's headache," Ross told him. "This is Jonathan's and Steve's problem. This is Netflix they are angry at."

The ridicule had started to taint Qwikster before it even got off the ground. No launch date had been set. Netflix had failed to secure the @qwikster Twitter handle from a profane, pot-smoking soccer fan named Jason Castillo, whose plans to profit from Netflix's mistake were provoking much mirth in the media.

Even the name Qwikster evoked derision—as though Netflix had chosen the terminally uncool moniker to drive customers away from DVD by mail in shame. But under Rendich and Ross's direction the Qwikster team did what they learned to do at Netflix—focus and perform. They forged a plan to position Qwikster as a reliable bridge to an online rental future of unlimited movie choice.

Slowly the vitriol began to ease, but it was simply too late for Qwikster. Netflix's stock price had been hammered from an all-time high of $305 per share before the price increase to $65 after the debacle. Hastings, the author of both mistakes, canceled Qwikster's launch and took the DVD by mail service back under Netflix's umbrella—at least temporarily.

Rendich, a twelve-year Netflix veteran, resigned. About one hundred others lost their jobs, including many who left senior posts at Netflix under the assumption that Hastings was committed to Qwikster. Kilgore announced a short time later that she would cede her post as chief of marketing to her loyal lieutenant, Jessie Becker, on an interim basis. Kilgore took a seat on the company's board.

In a curious move, Hastings reorganized Kilgore's marketing department in what some said was a long-held desire to increase his own power over the one function at Netflix that he understood the least—customer and public relations.

It was never clear whether Hastings realized that the Qwikster debacle was as much a betrayal of the people who had zealously built and protected Netflix's brand over the years as it was a slap to subscribers who had invested their loyalty in the company.

When Rendich and his team first asked how they should think about what had happened to the brand, Ross was hard-pressed to find an equivalent situation. He thought for a moment, and then it came to him—Tiger Woods. The champion golfer had seemed almost godlike until a sordid infidelity scandal destroyed his marriage and marred his career. Woods fell harder and faster than a regular celebrity, because he had been so esteemed.

That's how you have to think about Netflix, Ross told them. That's not to say the company won't regain its footing. But the damage is irreparable. Now it's just another brand.

MARC RANDOLPH WATCHED the furor unfolding around Qwikster, paged through the tens of thousands of angry comments that appeared on the Netflix Web site, thought about what it all meant. There was no question that Hastings had damaged the brand with his tone-deaf launch of the price increase and Qwikster, but Randolph thought the decision to split the DVD and online services had been correct—just as it had been right for Netflix to give up DVD sales more than a decade earlier to focus on becoming the superlative in online rental.

"[W]hat is truly mindblowing is that when I was CEO trying to screw up my nerve to walk away from selling DVDs, I risked alienating tens of thousands of customers. Reed is showing that he has courage and conviction to do the right thing despite having tens [of] millions of them," Randolph wrote on his blog, Kibble, in September 2011.

In the years since he left Netflix, Randolph had traveled a little and returned to work in Silicon Valley advising tech start-ups. It still amazed him how often he was approached by young entrepreneurs who wanted to start the Netflix of—something—just as he had wanted to start the Amazon of something. But to his young protégés, "the Netflix of" seemed to involve simply ordering something on the Web and round-tripping it to customers' homes and back. Was perfecting a way to ship plastic disks around the country all they had accomplished at Netflix?

The depth of public fury surrounding Qwikster surprised Randolph as much as it revealed that consumers felt that they had really lost something irretrievable in Netflix's steep fall from grace. Although it existed to its subscribers as little more than a red envelope in the mailbox or a flickering image on a screen, Netflix was as real to them as the groovy little video store on the corner where the clerks knew what they liked and the movies were always in stock.

To them, Netflix was not just a movie delivery service—it was the very best way to find something they wanted to watch, a friend with whom they shared their deepest secrets about what truly delighted them, and someone they trusted to provide an even better experience the next time they met. To think that it was all just a bunch of algorithms was simply too heartbreaking to bear.

Then it occurred to Randolph, in a rush of feeling: "Holy shit, we did it."

EPILOGUE

GO TO THE MAILROOM OF almost any American workplace on a Monday morning, and in the plastic U.S. Postal Service bins you are sure to find a litter of red envelopes waiting to be collected with the outgoing mail. Nearly every U.S. mail truck carries a separate bin for red Netflix envelopes, because the Los Gatos, California, company is the postal service's biggest customer. Now Netflix is even larger than the number one U.S. cable company, Comcast. Its subscribers claim 35 percent of U.S. Internet bandwidth by streaming movies during evening hours—the largest source of Internet traffic overall. In 2011, Netflix replaced Apple's ubiquitous iTunes store as the top U.S. online seller of movies and TV shows—its signature subscription service claiming 44 percent of total online movie business to 32 percent for Apple.

It is the world's largest Internet movie subscription service, with growing influence in how movie distribution deals and laws pertaining to online bandwidth usage and traffic are made. The service has even prompted international political action; Canadian subscribers called for an end to national bandwidth caps in 2011, in part to better watch Netflix movies in high definition.

The Netflix mailer has featured prominently in American pop culture: as a prop; as a mention on prime-time television shows; twice as a clue in the *New York Times* crossword puzzle; as a punch line on late-night talk shows; and even as a verb ("We can Netflix *Prison Break*, can't we?"). So powerful was the illusion that Netflix could be a trusted member of consumers' households that the clumsily executed 2011 price hike and split-off of the company's DVD by mail service as Qwikster provoked a remarkable sense of anger and betrayal. Subscribers took what Hastings did very personally, because Netflix had encouraged them to participate in creating a flawless interface between consumers and commerce, and people and technology. The fact that the company once listened set it apart from its rivals and accounted for much of its success against them.

The ongoing dialogue between the consumer and the business is a development of the modern age that Randolph and Ross understood well but Hastings does not seem to want to acknowledge. This is evident in his recent moves to purge Netflix of dissenters and push ahead with his plan to split the company in a manner that advances his scientific aims but alienates consumers.

As Randolph's great-uncle, Edward Bernays, wrote in 1928 in his book *Propaganda*: "The public has its own standards and demands and habits. You may modify them, but you dare not run counter to them. The public is not an amorphous mass which can be molded at will, or dictated to."

No matter what happens to Netflix, consumers have adapted to a new type of movie watching, courtesy of Reed Hastings and Marc Randolph. Randolph gave Netflix an extraordinary start, and Hastings turned it into a force that changed the world.

In its fifteen-year run Netflix has grown from an innovative yet struggling start-up with a big target on its back into a disciplined $5 billion corporation with international reach and a huge margin for growth, as worldwide broadband penetration cruises past 50 percent. Its DVD library is the world's largest, with two hundred thousand titles that reach into every country and every genre, opening to subscribers—as only film can—lives and points of view we otherwise might never know. Its streaming service has grown from one thousand titles at its launch in January 2007 to forty-five thousand that can be streamed on more than seven hundred devices. The company signed a paradigm-shattering deal in late 2011 to stream DreamWorks Animation SKG's popular films in the pay-per-view window starting in 2013.

By using the goodwill accrued over years of peerless customer service, Netflix persuaded subscribers to have patience with a limited selection of streaming titles, and to see the future of home entertainment in the elegant technology of instant streaming and the Cinematch algorithm. Hastings's ruthless and unwavering focus on the top prize—getting the largest selection of content possible straight from the Internet to any video-capable device—prevented Netflix from becoming bogged down in the intermediate stages of physical media distribution.

Had Hastings bowed to shareholder pressure in 2005—when he vowed to sacrifice profits for as long as it took to run off Blockbuster, Amazon, and Walmart and reach a decisive but then unlikely twenty million subscribers—it is likely that the journey between the Internet and the television would have taken years longer.

While Hastings has insisted that Netflix has no intention of turning cable customers into cord cutters, the cable industry should take heed. Consumer dissatisfaction with being tied to tiered cable plans—with hundreds of channels they did not choose and aren't interested in watching—bears a suspicious resemblance to Blockbuster's toleration of managed dissatisfaction. The cable industry, which has carved up the country into minimonopolies, is ripe for a Netflix-led insurrection over high prices and poor service.

But this is how the free market is supposed to work: A better product, a clean balance sheet, and a near flawless execution of a business plan should be enough to win the customer and vanquish an outdated rival.

AFTERWORD TO THE PAPERBACK EDITION

FOR NEARLY TWO YEARS AFTER the Qwikster debacle, Reed Hastings disappeared from public view—and went to work fixing his mistakes.

Those who had borne the brunt of Hastings's sloppy attempts to bury his wrongdoings—the mass firings of loyal longtime executives and the attempts to deprive the story of oxygen by refusing to discuss it with reporters—wondered if Hastings had lost his vision, and Netflix, its relevance.

"It was arrogant and it spent every last cent of goodwill Netflix had deposited in the bank and was well into deficit spending mode," Ken Ross later reflected.

The financial press and bloggers vented their frustration at Netflix's silence in a raft of negative stories about the company's struggles to renew important streaming deals that expired in 2011. As its share price dipped below $60, Wall Street joined the chorus of doom with talk of a takeover, possibly by Amazon or Microsoft.

Financier Carl Icahn circled the company like a shark, biting off chunks of stock here and there until he had accumulated a 10 percent stake. As he had done years earlier with another home entertainment giant, Icahn spoke of management changes.

What appeared to be the apocryphal demise of another pioneering tech company, whose model was adopted by rivals and perfected beyond its ability to compete, turned out to be another painful but necessary transformation for Netflix.

Gone was the scrappy, iconoclastic underdog beloved for its meticulous attention to a highly personalized "customer as hero" experience—DNA that Netflix inherited from Marc Randolph.

In its place, Hastings and his team erected a monolithic, mainstream corporation whose mission was to offer the best online movie watching experience at the best price. Period. And, so far, that's enough for consumers.

"The brand lost a lot of its luster because of all of it . . . but we are sort of a bottom-line culture," Ross said. "We don't have to be the darling. We are the way you watch movies."

The "customer as hero" approach won Netflix tremendous loyalty early in its struggle to reach mainstream users. The post-Qwikster shift to a "product as hero" approach—showcasing Netflix's seamless and ubiquitous streaming technology and expanding content library— plays to Hastings's strengths as an engineer and downplays his chronic lack of understanding of consumer sentiment.

To resurrect his company, Hastings aimed his team's considerable computer engineering and marketing skills, as well as the Netflix Web site's data-collection capabilities, at improving the product—both the content and the technology—as a means of reconnecting with consumers.

Certain that a better content selection could win back his customers, Hastings created a new marketing team headed by former Warner Bros. home video chief Kelly Bennett to cut deals for the movies and TV shows that Cinematch told them subscribers wanted.

The fifteen years' worth of data that the Web site had collected not only told the story of how the online movie rental business had developed, it also allowed Netflix to predict with a great degree of accuracy where the industry was going.

By watching those whorls and patterns develop over time, Netflix's content acquisition team was far better prepared than competing services to identify trends in consumer tastes, and it tailored the catalog accordingly. For example, the data revealed an emerging trend—"binge viewing," or watching multiple episodes of a TV series in one sitting. It also caught a rising demand by subscribers for children's programming, and Ted Sarandos stocked up accordingly, cutting deals with Nickelodeon, DreamWorks Animation, and the Walt Disney Co.

Increasingly, those algorithmic insights conflicted with conventional wisdom about consumer behavior.

Cinematch showed the Netflix team that while subscribers expected a healthy movie selection, they actually watched TV series more. Despite taking a hammering in the media for failing to renew a deal with Starz for new-on-cable movies, Netflix found that TV shows aged better, with "water cooler talk" fueling demand for old shows and little-known gems that were still airing.

Following the data made good economic sense, too: Each TV series produced tens of hours of viewing compared to the two or three hours for each film—resulting in greater rates of subscriber usage and satisfaction.

As a result of this demand, Netflix reassembled the cast of *Arrested Development* for a fourth season and used it to lure viewers who had loudly complained when the FOX network canceled it in 2006.

As streaming grew, movie studios began dropping exclusive deals and demanding that Netflix and other services buy titles in bulk rather than choosing what they knew would resonate with viewers.

These factors played into a massive reshaping of Netflix's catalog in 2011 that made Sarandos, Bennett, and Hastings take another look at a business the company had tried and abandoned years earlier—producing exclusive content.

Netflix's Red Envelope Productions, formed in 2004, had backed small independent filmmakers and had purchased a number of inexpensive titles from film festivals that it had promoted to audiences selected by Cinematch. The business was shuttered in 2009 after Hastings determined it was distracting his team from their primary goal of acquiring subscribers. The company had ventured into content creation two years later with *The Sopranos* clone *Lilyhammer,* but the next project had to be of a different magnitude.

Netflix's competitive landscape now included cable companies that rightly considered the online rental company as a dangerous rival. While Netflix still could not match the cable companies' access to first-run movies; its cheap, all-you-can-eat subscription plan, growing content catalog, and "watch anywhere" capability was encouraging "cord cutting" among cable customers frustrated with their tiered channel plans.

But in the battle to convince subscribers to return to Netflix, the competitive environment and Cinematch data showed the company had to take a big risk and produce its own exclusive content.

To Hastings, this fulfilled a "virtuous circle" for Netflix: better content meant more subscribers; more subscribers meant more money for better content.

Netflix had to reach into the ranks of cable subscribers and take on aspects of premium cable channels like HBO and Showtime to tip their subscribers into Netflix's camp. To achieve this, the productions had to be first class.

Among the projects under consideration was a remake of a British TV series called *House of Cards* set in the U.S. Congress, brought to Netflix by director David Fincher and actor Kevin Spacey.

Data showed that while Netflix subscribers did not often go looking for Spacey's films, once they discovered the actor they often went on to watch all his work. Fincher's films, including *The Curious Case of Benjamin Button, The Social Network,* and *The Girl with the Dragon*

Tattoo, shared the same attribute. The original British series had also captured a healthy share of Netflix users.

Armed with data that showed a wide potential audience, Netflix committed $100 million for two seasons of the show, which debuted to critical acclaim and popular buzz on February 1, 2013.

In a move that defied television industry wisdom of building audiences—and ratings—through "appointment television," Netflix released all thirteen first-season episodes at once, believing more in data that showed subscribers would excitedly "binge" on the show and evangelize it to their friends.

While the data did not guarantee the show would succeed, the fact that a ready audience awaited mitigated the risks associated with its high cost.

Less than a month after its release, *House of Cards* became the most-watched series on Netflix. The same month, Netflix reported higher-than-expected subscriber growth in the United States and new international markets—more than regaining the losses it suffered in 2011. Its share price soared past $200 per share, and Hastings set 90 million subscribers worldwide as the company's next goal.

"The real advantage we have is not in picking the perfect content, it is in marketing it more efficiently," Netflix spokesman Jonathan Friedland said. "It's just like any other artistic risk. [The data] helps you create a package that is likely to be more attractive and gives you the ability to merchandise and market it. Math won't help you make a great show."

Netflix has teed up a roster of original series designed to change, perhaps forever, the way television is made and marketed. Its next shows, including horror-thriller *Hemlock Grove*, prison dramedy *Orange Is the New Black*, and *Derek*, with comedian Ricky Gervais, provide a glimpse into the future of television—as viewers would like it to be.

Hastings has predicted that the linear TV schedule will be relevant for about five more years, when the bulk of mainstream consumers find more of what they want, when and where they want it, online.

But Netflix isn't out of the weeds yet.

The latest American Customer Satisfaction Index shows that the company still hasn't recouped the fourteen points it dropped in that survey in 2011—one of the largest-ever single-year drops in the ACSI survey's history. It remains at 75 percent, well below the average customer satisfaction rating of 85 percent among its e-commerce peers.

Hastings has now remade Netflix in his own image—a sleek, visionary corporation with confidence born of simply being the best way to watch television. Netflix has bet its future, and perhaps that of home entertainment itself, on this dream of a better world, where viewers are served just what they want before they even know they want it. Along the way it is changing the industry, and the world is watching.

ACKNOWLEDGMENTS

NETFLIXED IS MY FIRST BOOK. I may have performed all the tasks associated with producing the manuscript alone, but I had a mighty team backing me up, and turning what could have been a mysterious, fraught process into one of all-consuming joy and absorption.

My agent, David Fugate, was consistently patient (and tough when necessary) in molding a rather nebulous concept into a compelling proposal that sold its first day on the market. I am grateful to him for being ever accessible, practical, and honest throughout this journey.

The support and feedback I received from my team at Portfolio, Courtney Young, Emily Angell, and Bria Sandford encouraged me to find the best possible rendition of this remarkable story. I thank them for their gentle care of my initially less than wonderful manuscript. My publicity team, led by Penguin's Jacquelynn Burke and my own publicist, Carla Sameth, declawed a process that I initially feared with their enthusiasm for this book and their diligence in finding the right audience for it.

My writing coach, Stacie Chaiken, helped me define the story's structure and define its characters through her "wild brain" exercises, which freed me from my mental cul de sacs and allowed me to turn out a remarkably clean first draft. Her husband and my good friend, Martin Berg, provided the same excellent journalistic guidance I enjoyed when we worked together as reporter and editor.

I am deeply indebted to Marc Randolph, cofounder of Netflix, and to Shane Evangelist and John Antioco, formerly of Blockbuster, who were extremely generous in agreeing to meet with me, in encouraging others to speak frankly with me, and in answering many sometimes uncomfortable questions even before I had a book deal.

Netflix's Steve Swasey and Ken Ross were indispensable—Swasey was in the strange position of constantly denying my requests for access while agreeing to help fact check the manuscript, and Ross by also checking it over for accuracy and fairness. Although Netflix's former chief financial officer Barry McCarthy had no intention of becoming a source, he was kind enough to correct several misapprehensions I had about crucial events after I pestered him for more than a year, and for this I thank him. I would also like to acknowledge the others, named and not, at Netflix and Blockbuster, and in the financial and entertainment communities who gave me their time and perspectives.

There were a number of dark nights of the soul on this project—when I was not sure whether I could deliver the story I had witnessed and that I wanted to tell—and I have my family and friends to thank for slapping me back into reality.

My father, John Sopuch, provided critical support and encouragement, as did my brother Michael Sopuch and my sisters Amy Gonzalez and Maggie Marcrander and their families. My sister and brother-in-law Alicia Romero and Mike Spence put me up at their home in San Francisco and fed me in the city's finest restaurants more times than I can count or could have afforded on my meager budget. My uncle Harry Shapiro also deserves more thanks than I can express for moving me and two dogs halfway across the country by himself, as I faced my manuscript deadline.

My dear friend Carmela Wise and her husband, Rick, put their homes in Boston and New York at my disposal to facilitate my research and interviews in those cities.

This book is dedicated to my brother, John A. Sopuch III, for correctly advising me that the terror induced by quitting my job to write a book would carry me safely through the process, and to my mother, Margaret Romero, for keeping me on course. She and my stepfather, Richard Romero, saw to my every need and provided a haven for me during the unfamiliar process of writing so long a work. I will never be able to repay their care of me.

A NOTE ON SOURCES

THIS BOOK IS BASED PRIMARILY on my own reporting on U.S. entertainment companies for Reuters between 2004 and 2010 and on more than one hundred interviews with as many of the players in this drama as would agree to speak with me. All but a handful of the interviews were conducted on the record, and these were audiotaped with the interviewees' consent and transcribed by a professional transcription service. I also conducted a few interviews and asked many follow-up questions via e-mail.

I traveled extensively over two years of research and writing to meet with my subjects in person and to familiarize myself with the settings they described. I knew or had met most of my subjects in the course of my work for Reuters, so many of the character descriptions consist of my own impressions and nuances gleaned from my research.

Much of the financial and strategy information comes from: my review of a couple of thousand pages of transcripts from quarterly investor conference calls; from investor presentations by Blockbuster, Netflix, Movie Gallery, and Hollywood Video; and from lawsuits and regulatory filings by these companies and others. I filled in gaps in my rather utilitarian wire service copy with well-sourced stories from a number of reputable news outlets and blogs. I have endeavored to include attributions along with the material I used wherever possible. A list of the articles I referred to follows.

I came across Hastings's connection to millionaire-scientist Alfred Lee Loomis in the *New York Times* society pages in the course of researching his family. I owe a debt to Jennet Conant's excellent book *Tuxedo Park: A Wall Street Tycoon and the Secret Palace of Science that Changed the Course of World War II*, for her meticulous descriptions of Loomis, and for prompting me to consider the wider implications of the marriage of science and marketing that is Netflix.

I learned about Marc Randolph's great-uncle Edward L. Bernays primarily from Bernays's books, and about Bernays's profound impact on American culture from Larry Tye's *The Father of Spin: Edward L. Bernays & the Birth of Public Relations.*

I could not have written the early chapters about Netflix's nonpublic years without generous and enthusiastic support from the company's founding team—Marc Randolph, Mitch Lowe, Christina Kish, Te Smith, Jim Cook, Corey Bridges, Boris and Vita Droutman, and others—and the documents, screen shots, photos, and mementos they shared with me.

Although Reed Hastings did not consent to an interview or otherwise cooperate for the purposes of this book, I gleaned much essential information from the more than two dozen interviews I conducted with him over my nearly seven years covering Netflix's quarterly earnings reports, product rollouts, and other company events.

In addition, while Hastings did not allow any of Netflix's current executives or employees to participate, he did not—as I know—dissuade former executives or employees from speaking with me. Silicon Valley is, in many ways, a small town; Hastings's star was on the rise for most of the time I was collecting information and doing interviews, and many people feared offending him.

As a result, some sources asked not to be identified by name when revealing information that could have been interpreted as unfavorable or damaging to him. I agreed to these terms in cases in which I could verify the same information with at least one other reliable source who had direct knowledge of it. I was easily able to verify these facts with two or more other sources in nearly all of these cases.

I used direct quotes to re-create several conversations that were told to me in most cases by participants. I have also either confirmed the framing of these conversations with both parties to it, or with people who were present, or who were informed about it contemporaneously.

In re-created conversations that do not use direct quotes I was able to verify the gist of them, but not the wording, with at least two people who were present or who were told what was said by a participant.

When I first approached the Netflix and Blockbuster executives about writing an account of the battle between the two companies and how it transformed American home entertainment, both sides agreed it would be a great story. I found it relatively easy to persuade the former Blockbuster executives to speak to me about their battle with Netflix. Those who had left the company shortly after Jim Keyes changed the company's direction from online back to store-based rental went on to high-ranking corporate jobs where they faced questions about how Blockbuster had failed, and they were eager to set the record straight.

Blockbuster's corporate communications team declined to respond to several requests made over a number of months for an interview with Keyes. I had interviewed him several times in the course of covering Blockbuster for Reuters and am confident that I represented his thinking and strategy fairly as a result of those interactions.

On the Netflix side, as noted above, Hastings declined to participate in this book in any way, but the redoubtable Ken Ross and Steve Swasey were kind enough to fact-check parts of the manuscript I could not confirm from other sources. Of the key Netflix executives I tracked down and interviewed, most were generous enough to introduce me to colleagues, whose accounts enriched this story.

These executives humbled me with candid self-assessment, the likes of which I had rarely heard as a longtime journalist covering the financial, political, and legal realms. Simply being allowed to share their thoughts and emotional journey at such close range made this project highly satisfying.

BIBLIOGRAPHY

BOOKS

Bernays, Edward. *Propaganda*. New York: H. Liveright, 1928.

Conant, Jennet. *Tuxedo Park: A Wall Street Tycoon and the Secret Palace of Science that Changed the Course of World War II*. New York: Simon & Schuster, 2002.

Novak, David, and Boswell, John. *The Education of an Accidental CEO*. New York: Three Rivers Press, 2007.

PricewaterhouseCoopers. *Global Entertainment and Media Outlook: 2004-2010*. New York: PricewaterhouseCoopers, 2004.

Redstone, Sumner, and Knobler, Peter. *A Passion to Win*. New York: Simon & Schuster, 2001.

Tye, Larry. *The Father of Spin: Edward L Bernays and the Birth of Public Relations*. New York: Henry Holt and Company, 1998.

Wilkofsky Gruen Associates. *Global Entertainment and Media Outlook: 2010-2014*. New York: PricewaterhouseCoopers, 2010.

ARTICLES

"Blockbuster to accept online DVD returns at stores." Reuters, Nov. 1, 2006.

"Blockbuster names former 7-Eleven chief as its new CEO and chairman." Associated Press, July 3, 2007.

"Blockbuster Rollout and Sony Ad Campaign Boost DVD." *Video Week*, Sept. 14, 1998.

"Deaths: Randolph, Stephen B." *New York Times*, March 16, 2000.

"DIVX Says It's Poised for National Rollout." *Audio Week*, Sept. 28, 1998. *USA Today*, April 22, 1998.

"DIVX and DVD Jockey for Position." *Audio Week*, Aug. 17, 1998.

"DVD Online Service Stresses Rentals." *Consumer Multimedia Report*, May 4, 1998.

"DVD Rentals Ready for Mainstream with Blockbuster Announcement." Consumer Multimedia Report, Oct. 18, 1999.

"Exec Exits after Offer; Mark Wattles Leaves Hollywood Entertainment Corp. on Blockbuster Inc.'s Proposal of Takeover." *Daily Variety*, Feb. 4, 2005. "Factory Sales of DVD Players." *DVD News*, Sept. 1999.

"First Online DVD Rental Store Opens: Netflix Site Offers Unprecedented Title Selection, Availability and Convenience." Business Wire, April 14, 1998.

"Internet's Netflix Debuts DVD Rental Program." *DVD Report*, April 20, 1998.

"Janet Bissell Fiancee of William Loomis Jr." *New York Times*, Nov. 1, 1962.

"Joan Amory Loomis Becomes Affianced." *New York Times*, Dec. 23, 1957.

"Miss Violet Amory Engaged to Marry." *New York Times*, March 15, 1937.

"Miss Joan Loomis Becomes Engaged." *New York Times*, Dec. 22, 1957.

"Mrs. V.A. Loomis Married." *New York Times*, Sept. 3, 1946.

"Netflix Cancels $86 Million IPO." *DVD Report*, Aug. 14, 2000.

"Netflix Makes $86 Mil. IPO Bid." *DVD Report*, April 24, 2000.

"Netflix shares feel tailwind of good news." Associated Press, Dec. 7, 2011.

"New DVD Online Service Emphasizes Rentals." *Audio Week*, April 20, 1998.

"Online Renters Swamp Netflix." *DVD Report*, June 15, 1998.

"Online DVD Sales Grow." *Consumer Electronics*. Sept. 7, 1998.

"The Rental Revolution." *Inside Multimedia*, Oct. 26, 1998.

"$700 Million for Next Generation Nets." *CBS MarketWatch*, April 14, 1998.

"Tech Group Backs Charter Schools Step." *San Jose Mercury News*, Feb. 28, 1998.

"2 named to Board of Education." *San Diego Union Tribune*, Feb. 26, 2000.

"Unit Sales to Dealers—DVD Players." *DVD News*, Oct. 4, 1999.

"Video Biz in Slash Rash." *Daily Variety*, Dec. 23, 2004.

Video Software Dealers Association. "The Annual Report on the Home Video Market." *PRC News*, Sept. 13, 1999. "Washington: For the Record." *New York Times*, Sept. 8, 1970.

"We'll Support DIVX Only after DVD Is Established—Sony." *Audio Week*, Nov. 16, 1998.

"Wrong Disks Ship to Some Clinton DVD Customers." *DVD Report*, Oct. 12, 1998.

Abkowitz, Alyssa. "How Netflix Got Started." *Fortune*, Jan. 28, 2009.

Ali, Rafat. "Interview: Blockbuster CEO: Skeptics Aside, Confident of Physical's Digital Future." paidContent, Aug. 14, 2008.

Anderson, Nick. "A New Lesson Plan? Voter Initiative Proposed for Fall Ballot Could Spawn Hundreds More Charter Schools." *Los Angeles Times*, Feb. 25, 1998.

Antioco, John. "How I Did It: Blockbuster's Former CEO On Sparring with an Activist Shareholder." *Harvard Business Review*, April 2011.

Applefield Olson, Catherine. "Online Retailers Slash DVD Prices—Competition Over New Format Heats Up in Cyberspace." *Billboard*, May 16, 1998.

Arango, Tim. "Time Warner View Netflix as a Fading Star." *New York Times*, Dec. 12, 2010.

Arnold, Thomas. "Company Town: Virtual Video Chain Builds Its Presence on PCs." *Los Angeles Times*, Aug. 12, 1998.

Bathon, Mike. "Movie Gallery Files for Bankruptcy." Bloomberg, Feb. 3, 2010.

Bazeley, Michael. "Pair Attempt to Change Law Pushing for More Charter Schools." *San Jose Mercury News*, Feb. 2, 1998.

———. "Boost for Charter Schools Bill Advances: A Silicon Valley Group Helps Broker a Deal that Gov. Wilson May Sign by Friday." *San Jose Mercury News*, April 29 1998.

Bebitch Jeffe, Sherry. "The State: Hi-Tech Makes Its Political Mark." *Los Angeles Times*, Nov. 5, 2000.

Bell, Robert; Bennett, Jim; Koren, Yehuda; and Volinksy, Chris. "The Million Dollar Programming Prize." *IEEE Spectrum*, May 2009.

Bell, Robert; Koren, Yehuda; and Volinksy, Chris. "Matrix Factorization Techniques for Recommender Systems." *Computer*, August 2009.

———. "Statistics Can Find You a Movie, Part 2." AT&T Labs Research, May 19, 2010.

Bloom, David. "Digital LA: Shortage of Outlets Carrying DVD Movies Creates Niche." *Daily News* (Los Angeles), June 24, 1998.

Bond, Paul. "Netflix.com Subscribes to DVD Passions." *The Hollywood Reporter*, Oct. 14, 1999.

———. "Blockbuster to Drop Late Fees." *The Hollywood Reporter*, Dec. 15, 2004.

———. "Movie Gallery Gains Upper Hand in Bid for Hollywood Video." *The Hollywood Reporter*, Jan. 11, 2005.

Buck, Claudia. "Silicon Valley." *California Journal*, June 1, 1998.

Chasan, Emily, and Keating, Gina. "Blockbuster seeks debt overhaul, shares halted." Reuters, March 3, 2009.

Chmielewski, Dawn. "Hot Products: DVDs to Your Door." *Orange County Register*, July 12, 1998.

Cohen, William. "Seeing Red." *Vanity Fair*, Feb. 22, 2012.

Copeland, Mike. "Waco, Texas, Blockbuster Outlets Aren't Jumping on 'No Late Fees' Bandwagon." *Waco Tribune-Herald*, Dec. 22, 2004.

———. "Reed Hastings: Leader of the Pack." *Fortune*, Nov. 18, 2010.

Coplan, Judson. "Diagnosing the DVD Disappointment: A Life Cycle View." Leonard N. Stern School of Business, Glucksman Institute for Research in Securities Markets, April 3, 2006.

Coursey, David. "Harbingers of DVD." *Upside*, October 1998.

Cruz, Sherri. "Online Movie-Rental Service to Open Distribution Center in Minneapolis; Netflix Planning 9 Other Facilities." *Minneapolis Star Tribune*, June 19, 2002.

Dash, Eric, and Fabrikant, Geraldine. "Payout Is Set by Blockbuster to Viacom." *New York Times*, June 19, 2004.

Demerjian, Dave. "Rise of the Netflix Hackers." *Wired*, March 15, 2007.

Demery, Paul. "The New Walmart?" *Internet Retailer*, May 5, 2004.

Donahue, Ann. "Netflix: 300,000 Customers and $75 Million in Revenue, All in a Postage-Paid Envelope." *Video Business*, Dec. 17, 2001.

———. "Netflix Goes on Public Display; Online DVD Rental Service Files for IPO Again." *Video Business*, March 11, 2002.

Edwards, Cliff, and Grover, Ronald. "Can Netflix Regain Lost Ground?" *Bloomberg Businessweek*, Oct. 19, 2011.

Elkin, Tobi. "Toshiba, Netflix Put Friendlier Face on DVD." *Brandweek*, May 1998.

Espe, Eric. "Retailer's Plan: 'DVD' and Conquer." *San Jose Business Journal*, July 20, 1998.

———. "Educating Reed." *San Jose Business Journal*, Sept. 3, 1999.

Fabrikant, Geraldine. "So Far, Icahn's Midas Touch No Help to Blockbuster." *New York Times*, Jan. 16, 2006.

Fitzpatrick, Eileen. "Netflix Drops Per-Movie Rentals, Offers Monthly DVD Subscription." *Billboard*, Feb. 26, 2000.

Fonseca, Natalie. "TechNet's Reed Hastings on Shareholder Suits and Aggressive Accounting." *Upside*, Feb. 1999.

Franklin, Paul, and Gershberg, Michele. "CEO sees Blockbuster role in leading media devices." Reuters, Nov. 8, 2007.

Franklin, Paul, and Keating, Gina. "Blockbuster same-store stales rise, shares jump." Reuters, March 5, 2009.

Fritz, Ben. "Blockbuster Files for Chapter 11 Bankruptcy, Sets Plan to Reorganize." *Los Angeles Times*, Sept. 23, 2010.

Garrity, Brian. "Blockbuster Readies Itself for Digital Age." *Billboard*, Nov. 10, 2001.

Gelsi, Steve. "Netflix.com Refiles IPO Amid Cocooning Trend." *CBS MarketWatch*, March 7, 2002.

———. "Netflix Founder Touts Future Role in Digital Movies." *CBS MarketWatch*, June 19, 2002.

Gershberg, Michele, and Keating, Gina. "Blockbuster to test prices, store formats." Reuters, Nov. 8, 2007.

Gilpan, Kenneth N. "Online DVD Rental Service Performs the Best of 3 Initial Offerings." *New York Times*, May 24, 2002.

Glenn, David J. "Profits from Passion: Muriel Randolph from Front Porch to In Town Office." *Fairfield County Business Journal*, Sept. 9, 2002.

Goldman, Andrew. "Reed Hastings Knows He Messed Up." *New York Times*, Oct. 20, 2011.

Goldsmith, Jill. "H'wood Vid Bid Battle Heating Up." *Daily Variety*, Jan. 11, 2005.

———. "Vidtailers in Hostile Territory." *Daily Variety*, Feb. 3, 2005.

———. "Vid Bid Gets Rejected." *Daily Variety*, Feb. 18, 2005.

Goldsmith, Jill, and Sweeting, Paul. "Vid Fast-Forward: Icahn Pushes Merger of Top Rental Chains." *Daily Variety*, Dec. 15, 2004.

Goldstein, Seth. "DVD Rentals on Their Way From Warner." *Billboard*, April 25, 1998.

———. "DIVX Backers Upbeat Despite Hurdles as DVD Base Grows, Alternate Format Could Still Prompt Confusion." *Billboard*, Oct. 24, 1998.

———. "Picture This: British Research Report Underscores VHS' Decline, DVD and DVD-ROM Growth." *Billboard*, April 24, 1999.

———. "Circuit City Pulls Plug on DIVX—Home Entertainment War Won by 'Open' DVD." *Billboard*, June 26, 1999.

———. "Picture This: Blockbuster Finally Joins DVD Crowd." *Billboard*, Oct. 9, 1999.

Gomes, Lee. "Netflix Aims to Refine Art of Picking Films." *Wall Street Journal*, Nov. 29, 2007.

Gottfredson, Mark; Puryear, Rudy; and Phillips; Stephen. "Capability Sourcing at 7-Eleven." *Harvard Business Review*, March 28, 2005.

Graham, Jefferson. "DVD Rentals with No Late Fees Netflix, Others Are Challenging Video-Store Supremacy." *USA Today*, June 19, 2001.

Graser, Marc. "Netflix, Amazon Ink DVD Deal." *Daily Variety*, Dec. 7, 1998.

———. "Netflix Gets $30 Mil Influx." *Daily Variety*, July 8, 1999.

Grossman, Robert J. "Tough Love at Netflix." *HR Magazine* 55 no. 4 (April 1, 2010).

Gustin, Sam. "Netflix CEO Reed Hastings: No Armageddon Battle with Cable Giants." *Wired*, May 3, 2011.

Halkias, Maria. "DVD Rentals Slashed; Blockbuster Cuts Online Subscription Fee Again; Netflix Won't Follow." *Dallas Morning News*, Dec. 23, 2004.

————. "Blockbuster Meeting May Offer Latest Twist in Saga." *Dallas Morning News*, May 9, 2005.

————. "Blockbuster Chief Keeps Post: Antioco Re-elected to 3-Year Term; Icahn Absent from Meeting." *Dallas Morning News*, May 26, 2006.

————. "Blockbuster Is Trying to Turn It Around." *Dallas Morning News*, May 8, 2010.

Hargett, Joseph. "Puts Popular on Apple, Bank of America, Netflix, Amazon.com and Citigroup." *Forbes*, Nov. 27, 2011

Hawkins, Robert J. "Entertainment, television and culture." Copley News Service, April 20, 1998.

Hays, Kathleen, and Francis, Bruce. "Netflix on the Rise." CNNfn, June 24, 2002.

Helfand, Duke, and Rau, Jordan. "Education Official Is Targeted." *Los Angeles Times*, Jan. 11, 2005.

Helman, Christopher. "7-Eleven's Inconvenience." *Forbes*, April 11, 2005.

Hennessey, Raymond. "Dropping 'dot-com' does wonders for firm." Dow Jones Newswires, May 27, 2002.

Herhold, Scott. "The Honeymoon Goes On as Record $1.25 Billion Poured in during 2nd Quarter." *San Jose Mercury News*, Aug. 16, 1998.

Hettrick, Scott. "Netflix Puts DVD Rentals on the Web." *The Hollywood Reporter*, April 16, 1998.

Hettrick, Scott, and DiOrio, Carl. "Divx Clearance at Circuit City." *The Hollywood Reporter*, June 17, 1999.

Icahn, Carl. "Why Blockbuster Failed." *Harvard Business Review* (April 2011).

Isensee, Laura, and Keating, Gina. "Blockbuster loss grows as sales drop, shares fall." Reuters, Nov. 12, 2009.

James, Frank. "New Winner Emerges in the Game of Lobbying; Reluctant Tech Sector Proves a Quick Lesson." *Chicago Tribune*, Dec. 29, 1998.

Johnson, Greg. "Taco Bell Chief Leaving for Blockbuster." *New York Times*, June 4, 1997.

Kadlec, Daniel; Keith, Andrew; and Pascual, Alixa. "How Blockbuster Changed the Rules." *Time*, Aug. 3, 1998.

Kaltschnee, Michael. "Blockbuster Online Rental Service Beta Site Leaked to Hacking Netflix." HackingNetflix.com, July 16, 2004.

Keating, Gina. "Blockbuster cuts online price, challenges Netflix." Reuters, Oct. 15, 2004.

————. "Netflix move sparks market concern, shares tumble." Reuters, Oct. 15, 2004.

————. "Netflix sticks to guns in online DVD rental fight." Reuters, Oct. 18, 2004.

————. "Amazon CEO Bezos predicts record holiday season." Reuters, Nov. 9, 2004.

————. "Netflix, Warner partner to push movie 'Engagement.'" Reuters, Nov. 30, 2004.

————. "Netflix CEO rates Blockbuster, Amazon threats." Reuters, Dec. 10, 2004.

————. "DVD sales boom again in 2004—slower growth seen." Reuters, Jan. 13, 2005.

————. "Netflix profit up, sees '05 loss and 4 million renters." Reuters, Jan. 24, 2005.

————. "Netflix CEO vows to fight, win price war." Reuters, Feb. 22, 2005.

————. "Netflix downplays online movie delivery." Reuters, March 2, 2005.

————. "Netflix prepared to trade profits for growth—CEO." Reuters, March 2, 2005.

————. "Blockbuster in talks over late fee claims—sources." Reuters, March 7, 2005.

———. "Amazon eyeing DVD rental partnership in U.S.-source." Reuters, April 15, 2005.

———. "Netflix posts first-quarter loss." Reuters, April 21, 2005.

———. "Interview: Icahn says Blockbuster a long-term play." Reuters, April 29, 2005.

———. "Blockbuster board urges vote for incumbents." Reuters, May 2, 2005.

———. "Advisory firm urges vote against Blockbuster CEO." Reuters, May 9, 2005.

———. "Walmart ends Web DVD rentals, promotes Netflix." Reuters, May 19, 2005.

———. "Netflix posts surprise profit, shares jump." Reuters, July 25, 2005.

———. "Blockbuster CEO warns of weakness in rental sector." Reuters, Aug. 2, 2005.

———. "Netflix targets strong profit growth, shares jump." Reuters, Sept. 8, 2005.

———. "Blockbuster shares tumble on debt and growth fears." Reuters, Sept. 16, 2005.

———. "Netflix 3rd quarter earnings dip, subs top forecast." Reuters, Oct. 19, 2005.

———. "Blockbuster posts loss; sees more cost cutting." Reuters, Nov. 8, 2005.

———. "Blockbuster completes $150 million offering." Reuters, Nov. 15, 2005.

———. "Netflix shares rebound after four-day slide." Reuters, Dec. 15, 2005.

———. "Netflix wins first round in online DVD rental war." Reuters, Dec. 23, 2005.

———. "Blockbuster to push customers toward online—CEO." Reuters, Jan. 10, 2006.

———. "U.S. rental revenue down 3 pct in 2005—Rentrak." Reuters, Jan. 17, 2006.

———. "Netflix testing $5.99 subscription plan." Reuters, Feb. 15, 2006.

———. "Movie Gallery shares drop after meeting with banks." Reuters, March 8, 2006.

———. "Blockbuster profit up but revs miss Street target." March 9, 2006.

———. "Blockbuster CEO sees digital future." Reuters, March 9, 2006.

———. "Movie Gallery posts loss on weak box offices, closures." Reuters, March 23, 2006.

———. "Netflix hopes customers will fall for 'Cowboy.'" Reuters, April 2, 2006.

———. "Netflix sues Blockbuster to shut online service." Reuters, April 4, 2006.

———. "Blockbuster says Netflix suit without merit." April 6, 2006.

———. "Netflix turns to profit in 1st quarter, ups forecast." Reuters, April 24, 2006.

———. "Blockbuster loss narrow, U.S. rentals improve." Reuters, April 27, 2006.

———. "Tepid interest seen for next-generation DVDs in 2006." Reuters, May 3, 2006.

———. "Netflix has edge in Blockbuster lawsuits—attorneys." Reuters, June 28, 2006.

———. "Analysis: Web to TV still a long road for movie downloads." Reuters, July 19, 2006.

———. "Netflix qtly profit top views, outlook disappoints." Reuters, July 24, 2006.

———. "Blockbuster 2nd-quarter results miss view, shares fall." Reuters, July 27, 2006.

———. "Movie Gallery posts unexpected loss, shares plunge." Reuters, Aug. 10, 2006.

———. "Netflix profit beats Street, shares jump." Reuters, Oct. 23, 2006.

———. "Blockbuster posts narrower loss, stock up." Reuters, Nov. 2, 2006.

———. "Netflix sees struggle for movie download model." Reuters, Dec. 1, 2006.

———. "JP Morgan raises Movie Gallery earnings target." Reuters, Dec. 6, 2006.

———. "Netflix launches 1,000-title online movie feature." Reuters, Jan. 15, 2007.

———. "Netflix shares rise after online delivery unveiled." Reuters, Jan. 16, 2007.

———. "Movie Gallery faces risk of bankruptcy—analysts." Reuters, Jan. 24, 2007.

———. "Netflix 4th-qtr earns top estimates, shares up." Reuters, Jan. 24, 2007.

———. "Walmart entry to video downloads signals change." Reuters, Feb. 6, 2007.

———. "Movie Gallery to open online rental service." Reuters, March 19, 2007.

———. "Netflix warns on quarter and year; shares drop." Reuters, April 18, 2007.

———. "Blockbuster reports wider 1st-quarter loss, shares off." Reuters, May 2, 2007.

———. "Netflix stock up on Amazon takeover talk—analysts." Reuters, June 6, 2007.

———. "Blockbuster takes on Netflix with mail-only plans." Reuters, June 12, 2007.

———. "Blockbuster CEO promises 'pedal to metal' online." Reuters, June 14, 2007.

———. "Netflix turns on star power in U.S. DVD rental war." Reuters, June 27, 2007.

———. "Blockbuster names former 7-Eleven chief CEO." Reuters, July 2, 2007.

———. "Movie Gallery in talks with lenders, fails covenants." Reuters, July 2, 2007.

———. "Netflix cuts prices of two more rental plans." Reuters, July 23, 2007.

———. "Netflix shares drop after price cut, downgrade." Reuters, July 23, 2007.

———. "Netflix reports first drop in subscriptions." Reuters, July 23, 2007.

———. "Blockbuster flips to loss on higher spending." Reuters, July 26, 2007.

———. "Movie Gallery faces survival doubts, loss surges." Reuters, Aug. 10, 2007.

———. "Movie Gallery to close 520 underperforming stores." Reuters, Sept. 25, 2007.

———. "Blockbuster posts wider third-quarter loss." Reuters, Nov. 1, 2007.

———. "Blockbuster to raise subscription prices." Reuters, Dec. 20, 2007.

———. "Walmart cancels movie download service." Reuters, Dec. 27, 2007.

———. "Netflix surveys members on Microsoft Xbox." Reuters, March 24, 2008.

———. "Court upholds Netflix 'throttling' settlement." Reuters, April 22, 2008.

———. "Netflix to beat 4th quarter subscriber target—CFO." Reuters, Dec. 11, 2008.

———. "Netflix profit up surprising 45 pct, shares rise." Reuters, Jan. 26, 2009.

———. "No pay raise for Netflix execs in 2009." Reuters, April 6, 2009.

Keating, Gina, and Adegoke, Yinka. "Blockbuster CEO to leave with lower pay package." Reuters, March 20, 2007.

Keating, Gina, and Dorfman, Brad. "Blockbuster posts loss, drops forecast, stock hit." Reuters, Aug. 9, 2005.

———. "Blockbuster won't pay Q3 dividend." Reuters, Sept. 2, 2005.

Keating, Gina, and Henderson, Peter. "Netflix seeks growth, not profit, shares plunge." Reuters, Oct. 14, 2004.

Kee, Tameka. "Warner Bros Throws DVD Rental Gauntlet Down at Redbox—and Netflix." paidContent, Aug. 14, 2009.

Kerstetter, Jim. "Blockbuster/Circuit City: OK, I Don't Get It Either." CNET News, April 14, 2008.

Kilgore, Leslie. "Netflix Clicks." *The Hub,* January/February 2006.

Knapp, Shelley. "DVD Get Net Boost." *Calgary Herald,* April 16, 1998.

Koenig, David. "Blockbuster Raises Takeover Bid Pressure: Hollywood Entertainment Chain Is Target." *Washington Post,* Dec. 29, 2004.

———. "Blockbuster 3Q Loss Narrows: Shares Soar." Associated Press Online, Nov. 2, 2006.

LaGanga, Maria, and Anderson, Nick. "Lungren Joins Call for More Charter Schools." *Los Angeles Times,* Feb. 13, 1998.

Landy, Heather, and Shlachter, Barry. "Icahn Blasts Board, Aims to Take Over." *Fort Worth Star-Telegram,* April 8, 2005.

Lewis, Peter. "Clinton Testimony for Sale (Real Cheap) on DVD." *New York Times*, Sept. 24, 1998.

Lieber, Ed. "Netflix vs. DIVX: Round One Under Way." HFN, the Weekly Newspaper for the Home Furnishing Network, April 27, 1998.

——. "Sony Ready to Flex DVD Muscle in Fourth Quarter." HFN, Sept. 14, 1998.

——. "Blockbuster Rollout and Sony Ad Campaign Boost DVD." *Video Week*, Sept. 14, 1998.

——. "DVD's Success Helps Limit DIVX's Launch." HFN, Oct. 19, 1998.

Lieberman, David. "Blockbuster Sweetens Hollywood Bid." *USA Today*, Feb. 3, 2005.

Liedtke, Michael. "Online DVD rental service Netflix emerging as Internet star." Associated Press, Sept. 10, 2001.

——. "Online DVD service Netflix prices IPO at $15 per share." Associated Press, May 22, 2002.

——. "Humbled Netflix CEO still thinking, talking big." Associated Press, Dec. 6, 2011.

Lindow, Megan. "Fee Changes Helped Propel DVD Rental Company to Fast Growth." *San Jose Business Journal*, Nov. 23, 2001.

McAleer Vizard, Mary. "If You're Thinking of Living in Westchester." *New York Times*, Oct. 21, 1990.

McGinn, Daniel, with Setoodeh, Ramin. "Rewinding a Video Giant." *Newsweek*, June 27, 2005.

MacMillan, Robert, and Keating, Gina. "MovieBeam Offers 1st High-Definition Movie Rentals." Feb. 14, 2006.

Marshall, Matt. "Number of Internet Start-Up Companies Begins to Slow." *San Jose Mercury News*, Aug. 21, 2000.

——. "Silicon Valley IPOs Maintain a Holding Pattern for the New Year." *San Jose Mercury News*, Dec. 17, 2000.

Meek, Andy. "Blockbuster Suit Meets with Failed Injunction Request." *Memphis Daily News*, Sept. 8, 2009.

——. "Blocked and Tackled; Lawsuit Dies between Blockbuster, Local Franchise Group." *Memphis Daily News*, Jan. 27, 2010.

Mendel, Ed. "Entrepreneur Aids Charter School Growth." *San Diego Union Tribune*, Feb. 1, 1998.

——. "Legislators Compromise, May Keep School Initiative Off Ballot." Copley News Service, April 29, 1998.

Menefee, Sami. "DVD Movie Rentals Come Online." *Newsbytes*, April 15, 1998.

Mitchell, James J. "James J. Mitchell Column." *San Jose Mercury News*, March 29, 1998.

Mnyandu, Ellis. "Blockbuster profit up, fueling battle with Netflix." Reuters, March 9, 2005.

Mollison, Andrew. "Political Giving Begins to Compute; Tech Companies Seeking More Pull." *Austin American-Statesman*, Aug. 24, 1998.

Morain, Dan. "Making of a Ballot Initiative." *Los Angeles Times*, April 16, 1998.

——. "Wilson Expected to OK Bill on Charter Schools." *Los Angeles Times*, April 29, 1998.

Morris, Valerie. "The Leading Edge: Netflix, the Virtual DVD Rental Store, Coming Soon to a Browser Near You." CNNfn, Jan. 23, 2001.

Munoz, Lorenza. "Blockbuster to Halt Late Fees, but There's a Catch." *Los Angeles Times*, Dec. 15, 2004.

Netherby, Jennifer, and Sweeting, Paul. "Some Predicting Rental Resurgence; but Hard Evidence Is Tough to Identify." *Video Business*, Dec. 20, 2004.

Nichols, Peter. "Amazon Joins the Film Fray." *New York Times*, Nov. 20, 1998.

Osbourne, Jeffrey M. "The Netflix Effect." *Wired* (December 2002).

Ostrom, Mary Anne. "With .com Dropped from Name, Netflix Shares Up 12% in IPO: Market Warms to DVD-Rental Firm." *San Jose Mercury News*, May 24, 2002.

———. "With newer releases, Netflix users can anticipate a 'very long wait.'" *San Jose Mercury News*, July 7, 2002.

Patsuris, Penelope. "Blockbuster Takes On New Strategy vs. Netflix." *Forbes*, April 24, 2003.

Peers, Martin. "Will Starz Turn into a Black Hole for Netflix?" *Wall Street Journal*, Sept. 16, 2010.

Pogue, David. "Where Are the Netflix Profiles?" *New York Times*, June 23, 2008.

Puzzanghera, Jim. "Immigration Bill Stalls: Labor Ally in Senate Stymies Measure to Raise Cap on Tech Visas." *San Jose Mercury News*, Oct. 10, 1998.

———. "Foreign Worker Visas Revived: Bill to Close Loophole on Lawsuits Also Alive." *San Jose Mercury News*, Oct. 14, 1998.

———. "Behind High-Tech Successes as Congressional Victories Show, Silicon Valley Now Has Some Clout." *San Jose Mercury News*, Oct. 17, 1998.

Quintos Danyliw, Norie. "Disks for Rent." *U.S. News & World Report*, May 4, 1998.

Rabinovitz, Jonathan. "High-Tech Lobby Picks New President." *San Jose Mercury News*, May 6, 1999.

Ralli, Tania. "Brand Blogs Capture the Attention of Some Companies." *New York Times*, Oct. 24, 2005.

Rau, Jordan. "Democrats Reject Gov.'s Nominee." *Los Angeles Times*, Jan. 13, 2005.

Ray, Tiernan. "Down 79% from Their July High, Netflix Shares May Be a Buy." *Technology Trader*, Nov. 26, 2011.

Redburn, Tom. "Forget Plastics. Go Find Subscribers." *New York Times*, Dec. 9, 2001.

Roberts, Jeff. "Time Warner's Bewkes: 'Netflix Is Our Friend.'" paidContent.org, Dec. 6, 2011.

Rose, Derek. "W'chester Granny Dies on Viet Trip." *New York Daily News*, March 16, 2004.

Roth, Daniel. "Netflix Everywhere: Sorry Cable, You're History." *Wired*, Sept. 21, 2009.

Sandoval, Greg. "Redbox, Kiosk Rentals Now Outpace Video Stores." CNET News, Jan. 17, 2011.

———. "Who Stole Netflix's Mojo?" CNET News, Sept. 19, 2011.

Savitz, Eric. "Netflix: Obvious Takeover Bait, or Risky Value Trap?" *Forbes*, Nov. 27, 2011.

Schlachter, Barry. "Icahn Sweeps Blockbuster Vote." *Fort Worth Star-Telegram*, May 12, 2005.

Seitz, Patrick. "Consumer Web Services DVD Movie Rental Plot Pits Tiny Netflix vs. Blockbuster." *Investors' Business Daily*, March 21, 2001.

Seitz, Patrick. "Netflix Could Challenge Blockbuster in DVD Field." *Investors Business Daily*, Dec. 20, 2001.

——. "Netflix Is Moving to Get Big Fast; Overnight Service Firm's Aiming for Profit and a Million Subscribers in Second Quarter of '03." *Investor's Business Daily*, July 2, 2002.

Simon, Mark. "Widespread Success for TechNet: Silicon Valley Political Action Group Is a Big Hit." *San Francisco Chronicle*, July 16, 1998.

——. "Political Action Chief Steps Down: Reed Hastings Will Stay Active in Silicon Valley Group." *San Francisco Chronicle*, Jan. 12, 1999.

Sinton, Peter. "Start-ups Fetch Record Financing." *San Francisco Chronicle*, Aug. 11, 1999.

Spector, Mike. "Icahn Takes Blockbuster Debt Holding." *Wall Street Journal*, Sept. 17, 2010.

Sporich, Brett. "Vid Firm Quick to Market Clinton Tape." *Daily Variety*, Sept. 22, 1998.

Stack, Peter. "DVD Puts a New Spin on Old Movies." *San Francisco Chronicle*, July 26, 1998.

Summers, Nick. "Netflix: The Sequel." *Newsweek*, July 13, 2010.

Swartz, Jon. "New Web Site Sells, Rents DVD Movies." *San Francisco Chronicle*, April 18, 1998.

Swanson, Tim. "Netflix Clicks Pix with New Studio Mix." *Daily Variety*, June 13, 2001.

Sweeting, Paul. "Blue Turns to Distribs for Online Product; Chain Aims to Sync Store, Online Eventually." *Video Business*, Feb. 28. 2005.

——. "Big Retailers Socked by Stock Woes: Marketing Softening Undermines Blockbuster, Gallery." *Video Business*, Sept. 19, 2005.

Tan, Shannon. "Blockbuster Goes DVD." *Miami Herald*, Sept. 11, 2001.

Tedeschi, Bob. "E-Commerce Report: As Blockbuster Moseys Online, Two Competitors Are Already Running Hard. But Will That Matter?" *New York Times*, April 28, 2003.

Thompson, Clive. "If You Liked This, You're Sure to Love That." *New York Times*, Nov. 23, 2008.

Thompson, Wayne. "DIVX, DVD's Poorer Cousin, Looks for a Place in Your Home but Is More Trouble Than It Is Worth." *The Oregonian*, Sept. 25, 1998.

Traiman, Steve. "DVD's Steady Climb Mapped Out at Industry Conference." *Billboard*, Sept. 5, 1998.

Tsering, Lisa. "Can Netflix Deliver On Its Promise to Bollywood Fans?" *India-West*, Dec. 28, 2001.

Turner, Megan. "The Death of Video? Booming DVDs Hit Fast Forward." *New York Post*, Jan. 6, 2000.

Volinsky, Chris. "Statistics Can Find You a Movie, Part 1." AT&T Labs Research, Feb. 16, 2010.

Williams, Leticia. "Can Netflix Become an Internet Success Story?" *CBS MarketWatch*, Sept. 1, 2001.

Wilmouth, Adam. "Kerr-McGee Agreement Keeps the Peace." *The Oklahoman*, May 11, 2005.

Zajac, Andrew. "Bill to Add Tech Visas Moves Ahead: House Approves Plan to Admit More Workers." *Chicago Tribune*, Sept. 25, 1998.

Zaragosa, Sandra. "Jim Keyes, 7-Eleven Both Poised for Change." *Dallas Business Journal*, Jan. 1, 2006.

Zeidler, Sue. "Blockbuster buys movie download service Movielink." Reuters, Aug. 8, 2007.

———. "Netflix scrambles future of TV and films." Reuters, Dec. 1, 2010.

Zeidler, Sue, and Keating, Gina. "Blockbuster takes on Netflix with new set-top box." Reuters, Nov. 25, 2008.

Zipkin, Amy. "The Boss: Out of Africa, Onto the Web." *New York Times*, Dec. 17, 2006.

INDEX